TRANSITIONS AND TRANSFORMATIONS
Literature, Politics, and Culture

I0641522

STEVEN EDMUND WINDUO

TRANSITIONS AND TRANSFORMATIONS
Literature, Politics, and Culture

STEVEN EDMUND WINDUO

2012

Copublished by:

UPNG Press and Bookshop

and

Manui Publishers

ISBN: 978-9980-9920-2-4 (Manui Publishers)

University of Papua New Guinea Press and Bookshop
Post Office Box 413
University Post Office
National Capital District
Papua New Guinea

MANUI PUBLISHERS
Post Office Box 47
University Post Office
National Capital District
Papua New Guinea
Email: sewinduo@gmail.com
Blog: www.stevenswindow.blogspot.com

Dedicated to
Howard MacNaughton
who never doubted.

Table of Contents

Illustrations

INTRODUCTION

MAPPING UNCHARTED PASSAGES

The book encapsulates emerging issues on literature, culture, and politics in Papua New Guinea. The essays capture my reflections on the literature and culture of Papua New Guinea. Literature is a window into a society. Through novels, poetry, plays, and short stories writers present an imagined community to readers. The discussions here are by no means the only way of reading Papua New Guinea literature. I do make one statement at the outset, though: this book is a reflection of the transitions and transformations I made in my life as a writer scholar in Papua New Guinea. In the process I met many friends, students, readers, and mentors, whose creative and intellectual influences rubbed off on me as well. It is a process that helped me understand literature and the kinds of scholarship on cultural knowledge productions that I deal with in Papua New Guinea. This book is an attempt to map such uncharted passages I had travelled through since I was first introduced to literature.

Literary works of Papua New Guineans considered in this book have interested me long enough to warrant the discussions I have on them as representative works of literature published before 2000. These works helped me to position myself within a structure of viewing known as the literature and culture of Papua New Guinea. In that structure I operate as a reader, a writer, and a scholar, who is left with the responsibility of mediating, as it were, with the diverse social and cultural exigencies of contemporary Papua New Guinea.

Papua New Guinea as a postcolonial nation struggles to free itself from a colonized history, more particularly from the neocolonial practices and influences of its former colonizer. Achieving political Independence has never freed Papua New Guinea from Australia and its neocolonial influences.[1] Early Papua New Guinea writings tackled Australian colonialism with ferment and nationalist fury to the extent of achieving Independence without bloodshed. After Independence Papua New Guinean writers disappeared, except for a few committed ones, who continue to write. Russell Soaba and Paulias Matane continue to write literary and non literary works beyond the 2000s. Soaba returned to the University of Papua New Guinea after an absence from the literary scene in the 1980s. He continues to write and teach literature at the University of Papua New Guinea. Soaba is the most influential writer of the first generation.

Paulias Matane continues to write non fiction works after he moved away from the *Aimbe* fiction series. His interests in writing led him to publish many non fiction works throughout the years, even after becoming the then Governor General of Papua New Guinea. Grand Chief Sir Paulias Matane also assisted many Papua New Guineans to publish their books. Writing was used and is still used as a tool for resisting the continued neocolonial, patronizing, and hegemonic influences of the former colonizer, its agents, and the various programs established to maintain its interests in Papua New Guinea after Independence.

Australian influence in Papua New Guinea is deeper than perceived at the political level. Australia continues to play a major part in the economic, social, and political development of Papua New Guinea. The relationship between Australia and Papua New Guinea is often tested, but always maintained through diplomatic dialogues and other political processes.

The writings of the 1980s to the present are about this neocolonial presence, dependent relationship, as well as about the lack of critical reassessment of the changing experiences in postcolonial Papua New Guinea.[2] Papua New Guinean writers are concerned with diverse issues of identity, social change, economic change, cultural change, the movement between village and urban areas, experiences of growing up, adolescence, education, unemployment, wantok systems, and conflicting cultural situations. Their writings are about the contemporary experiences, the traditional cultures and customs, and immediate past they seemed to have lost in the transition from a stone-age culture to one of electronic media networking. The experience of Papua New Guineans in using literature to represent themselves and their experiences is similar to other Pacific Islanders.[3] The mundane to important events in the lives of Papua New Guineans are concerns of contemporary writers. Literary expressions are inspired from the personal experiences of writers and anecdotes of other Papua New Guineans.[4]

Papua New Guinea is a hybridized postcolonial society with a fusion of diverse cultures, modern global influences, and the result of a synthesis of multicultural experiences. Questions of nationalism after Independence are raised every so often, suggesting that, perhaps it has served its purpose at the time of its emergence. Constant internal conflicts, uncontrolled social disorder, cultural conflicts, violence, ethnic differences, stagnant views, and rampant corruptions, poor governance, and massive squandering of royalties from its mineral and natural resources often stun the growth of nationalism. Nationalism, in most cases, is evoked by elites as the self-appointed guardians of their people's interests. Nationalism is not what it claims to represent in Papua New Guinea as it fails to eliminate the ethnocentrism fueling regionalism within a national boundary.[5]

Literary culture developed in different phases in Papua New Guinea. The first phase characterizes dissent, protest, and anticolonial resistance. The period between 1968 and 1975 marks this phase. The second phase, between 1980 and 1999, covers the village pastoral and sociological literature. In this phase Papua New Guineans wrote out of the need to assess their conditions of living, of existence, to make sense of the world around them, and to revive the experiences of an earlier era.

Writing struggled to survive against polarized national developmental priorities and civil conformity since Independence. The third phase is a combination of the previous phases and the independent emergence of new voices of a new generation. The third phase, between 1990 and 2000 came about as a result of Papua New Guineans reading the works of earlier writers and seeking out avenues to speak for themselves, about their experiences, and their visions for a democratic society. The later category makes use of new literary structures, both appropriated and experimental in style, to represent their experiences as Papua New Guineans.[6]

Papua New Guineans re-imagined themselves in their writings. They create various discourses about themselves. Papua New Guineans realize the process of rethinking and re-evaluation of some of the inherited values or those created by Papua New Guineans need urgent critical attention. The methods and procedures used for investigating and conducting research of Papua New Guinea cultures need to be reframed so as to produce a balanced critical reading of Papua New Guinea literature.[7] Papua New Guineans need distinctive signposts to navigate through the many inroads created in their lives. All these are politically invested. The localized struggles and their responses to the globalized economy make them more vulnerable than is imagined. Accepting the passive, non active, unquestioning life is a form of conformity and cultural paralysis. Papua New Guineans can articulate their experiences in a radical and progressive ways.

The notions of text, discourse, and discursive practices are central to the discussions in various chapters of the book. Various discourses come together in a dialogic manner to interact in divergent ways thereby reproducing themselves and new discourses in Papua New Guinea. New discourses work at transforming Papua New Guinean identities as well as formulating new ideas from existing works of literature. The process is considered a discursive practice. Discursive, according to Laclau, refers "to the ensemble of phenomena in and through which the social production of meaning take place, an ensemble which constitutes society as such."[8] The discursive activity brings about meaning that is socially produced with political energy in as far as history and society are concerned.

This line of argument bears testimony to Foucault's original formulation of discourse where it "is made consubstantial with sociality as such" and therefore is "conceived as relations insofar as they are mediated by and through discourse."[9] The use of terms 'discourse' and 'discursivity' lands us in the middle of a cultural criticism that is post-Marxist and postmodernist. Discourse has become for us the mediating process in which we seek to disclose our various social and political relations. Literary texts are therefore constitutive of the various social relationships enabled by the society (superstructure) and history (base). In this kind of formulation a society is seen as a discourse that can be interpreted. Discourse is "a general name for the class of practices (what, in an older vocabulary, might have been called behaviours and institutions) that define the perceptible surface of society."[10] To make sense of these ideas I employ different approaches to dissect, distinguish, and expose the different writings of Papua New Guineans. The attention here is to the links such theoretical formulations make to various discourses that emanate in the literature of Papua New Guinea.

Our discussions operate within the structure of experience unique to Papua New Guinea.[11] This book deals with issues of political consciousness, social change, history, folklore, culture, language, and ideologies. The book highlights the influence of folklore in the development of nationalism, the construction of double consciousness, the emergence of a novelistic discourse in Papua New Guinea, the fictionalizing of history, and the participation of women in the literature of Papua New Guinea.

Literature and politics have a unique relationship to each other. So long as literature continues to be useful to people it maintains its political function.[12] It is difficult to resist viewing the political and ideological overtones present in Papua New Guinea writing. No writers are free of the social, political, economic, and cultural influences of their societies. Writers are creatures of their societies. Hence, a writer's work carries with it the social and political responsibility of his or her society.

In this book we are also investigating concurrent social issues and political themes in a postcolonial nation. The act of writing and reading is linked to the issue of voice. Having my own voice to speak about my experiences is significant to me.[13] Voice includes utterances, writings, texts, languages, and ways of viewing the world. I explore some of these issues affecting me as a postcolonial writer scholar. I use my own voice and it is answerable to others cohabiting the same space and time in society. In the process of recognizing my own voice I reproduce other voices in dialogue with each other.

A number of factors led me to write this book. First, I am often asked in conferences, workshops, and meetings around the world, about Papua New Guinean literature. Many people in the world have little knowledge of what is happening in Papua New Guinea. Students of postcolonial literature, South Pacific literary and cultural studies, and researchers with interests in Papua New Guinea are in constant search for writing by Papua New Guineans. Many Papua New Guinean novels and other forms of writings are no longer in print.

New books written by Papua New Guineans are limited in circulation within the national borders and have limited print runs.

This study, insofar as it seeks to ground the study of Papua New Guinea literature within the academy, it also works at registering the emergence and continuity of a literary culture in Oceania. It also enables me to participate in the social, political, and economic struggles of the present. Scholarship on writings of Papua New Guinea is undeveloped. Lost grounds in the study of Papua New Guinea literature is recovered in a critical study such as our present project. Our intention here is to widen the interests in the emergence and existence of Papua New Guinea literature. This book will at least soothe some of these nagging issues in Papua New Guinea literature.

Second, the need for a critical analysis of Papua New Guinea literature is long overdue. Apart from a recent study of Papua New Guinea literature by Regis Stella, no other books are out there to guide students studying Papua New Guinea literature. Literature is poorly taught in Papua New Guinea schools. No published books on Papua New Guinea literature are available to students and teachers in the country. Papua New Guineans themselves have never read the books and literary pieces published by their own writers. The consequence therefore is the poor understanding of literature and with it the difficulties writers face in Papua New Guinea. Many of the difficulties are linked to lack of government support, no access to publishing outlets, and less supporting environments for the development of a literary culture.

I have traveled the literary and intellectual road without a road map. There are no guides to direct me to specific destinations. In the poem "From Sepik to Mississippi" I capture this journey, this sojourn, this going and coming, and the now the-too-frequent a road traveled.[14] I moved from the position of a reluctant student introduced to literary studies to someone professing human values in literature, English, and cultural studies. The essays in *Transitions and Transformations* reflect part of this experience.

The interest in the influence of oral traditions in contemporary Papua New Guinea launched the research for this book.[15] The next phase of research looked at the construction of prose narratives in Papua New Guinea since 1968.[16] The emergence of postcolonial theory in the 1980s reinforced the critical study of Papua New Guinea literature. I had the good fortune of learning postcolonial theory under Bill Ashcroft, one of the leading theorists in the forefront of this theoretical whirlwind sweeping through the world academia and political discussions. Postcolonial theories and cultural studies provided me the relevant tools for analyzing Papua New Guinea literature.

Transitions and Transformations is about Papua New Guinean writing in as much as it is about my own reflections as an indigenous writer and scholar of literature in Papua New Guinea. Intuitive transitions and transformations took place in my life as a student of literature and as a young writer. The creative

5

and intellectual growths in me are also based on my life as a writer and scholar of Indigenous literary and cultural knowledge systems. I continue to study and publish my own writings without diminished interests in the development of Papua New Guinean literature.

Papua New Guineans published several books in the late 1990s and the early part of 2000s. I have not, at this time, advanced far afield in my analysis of such works under the scope of this book. I leave that to future considerations or better still to others in the field to consider the literary values in these Papua New Guinean works of literature. What I have considered here is only a selection of the works that I have read, liked, and used as teaching materials in various courses taught at the University of Papua New Guinea.

Shortcomings in the book are part of my transitions and transformations in my intellectual and creative growth. I hope, however, such spaces will serve as sites for new investigations and interesting dialogues to begin.

To be sure, the emergence of Papua New Guinean literature has made it possible to see the emergence of a nation and what we risk losing if discussions on the literature of the nation is left unattended. As is already observed of the literary development in the country, a literary silence occurred, when no one wrote, published, or discussed Papua New Guinea literature. To avoid this trap, my efforts in bringing the discussions together, in this book resist such pretensions. Before anyone drifts off in the direction of ignorance and simple avoidance of what maybe considered too distant from 'our interests' kind of culture, sweeping academy, and publishing programs I am applying the brakes to the trend with the publication of this book. This, more than anything, constitutes the current discussions that emerge in classrooms and spaces where Papua New Guinea literature is studied.

Transitions and Transformations maps the study of Papua New Guinean writers and their writings. It is also a book demonstrating the development of personal scholarship in the field of literary and cultural studies in Papua New Guinea.

1

UNWRITING THE PAPUAN VILLAGER

"The sea was open to anyone who could navigate a way through."
Epeli Hau'ofa "Our Sea of Islands".[1]

"The print media thus acted as a major agent in the colonizing activities, especially of the Protestant mission, but also acted to cohere the "imagined community" that was the nation, which was coming into being at the same time."
Noenoe K. Silva, *Aloha Betrayed*.[2]

The connection between the colonizing project in getting Papuan New Guineans to write in the 1920s and the literary activities of 1960s and 1970s is an important link to our research and discussions on Pacific literatures. The emergence of a literary culture in Papua New Guinea in the late 1960s and 1970s was a response to an earlier colonial experiment on the Papuan New Guinean subject and the pressing desire for self-assertion. Making that connection allows us to understand the genealogies of writing and literature in postcolonial sites of knowledge production. The emergence of indigenous literary traditions across Oceania goes far back to the early introduction of European technologies, ideas, writing instruments, literacy, and print media.[3] Keown's insights into the origins of the Pacific literature as a 'textual' corpus is relevant here: "Although 'postcolonial' Pacific literatures emerged during and beyond the decolonizing period of the 1960s and 1970s, these texts can be situated within a Pacific *literary* (as opposed to oral) tradition that dates back to the early nineteenth century, when European missionaries first developed orthographies for Indigenous Pacific languages."[4] From there the missionaries translated the Bible and other Christian literature into local languages and "taught Pacific Island peoples to read and write, first in their own vernaculars and then in English, primarily in order to disseminate the Bible and other Christian tracts."[5] Pacific Islanders "began to produce written texts of their own: along with mission-inspired publications; other forms of Indigenous writing that emerged during the nineteenth and early twentieth centuries included biographies, autobiographies, family histories, and genealogies."[6] The writing of fiction was discouraged by missionaries until "1960 that the first Indigenous Pacific novel — *Makutu*, by Cook Islander Tom Davies and his wife Lydia — was published."[7] By the 1960s signs of Indigenous literary production was evident with the publication of the Maori poet Hone Tuwhare's *No Ordinary Sun* (1964), Papua New Guinean Albert Maori Kiki's *Ten Thousand Years in a Lifetime* (1968), and individual pieces by Albert Wendt, which were published in metropolitan literary journals, magazines, and newspapers: "However, the first major phase of Indigenous literary efflorescence was to begin in Papua New Guinea, where the establishment of a national university in 1966 [sic] brought substantial numbers of Indigenous Pacific writers together for the first time."[8] We need to go beyond the present to investigate how and what some of the discourses were, their formations and deployment, and how these helped the emergence or absence or deferment of a literary culture in Oceania.

The colonial project in the 1920s to encourage Papua New Guineans to write failed its objectives. The failure is attributed to the negative views held by the colonial administration on the education of indigenous subjects. Such views remained up until the introduction of higher education in the 1960s. In this paper I investigate some of those views promoted through what I describe as the 'Papuan Experiment' in literacy and literary development. This colonial project was 'unwritten' by Papua New Guineans in the years before Independence. The effort here is to narrow down to a specific national project of 'Unwriting Oceania' as articulated elsewhere.[9]

THE PAPUAN EXPERIMENT

Reverend W. G. Lawes, who settled with his family in Hanuabada in 1874, began to translate the four gospels in Motu. The translation of the gospels was completed in 1885. Lawes held the view that to establish the Christian church it was important to develop the abilities of people to read Christian literature.[10] By 1920s a reasonable number of Motu Koitabuans knew enough English to communicate with the missionaries and the administration officials.

Many Papuans, however, were uninterested in using English to capture their experiences or to express themselves in writing. The English language was viewed as an uncultured language with the power to corrupt the cultural and social fabric of the Papuan society: "the Hanuabada Council deplored the education of women because it enabled them to arrange their own marriages through correspondence and it also enabled married women, to write to men not their husbands."[11] The Papuans were suspicious of the power of the Western language and cultural tool as an instrument of cultural obliteration. Learning to read and write in English or vernacular was considered dangerous to society.

The Hanuabada Council held the view that women with the knowledge of writing were dangerous to the continuity of the Koita traditions. The fear was that the new tool and language would undermine tradition, traditional authority, family values, social cultural morals, and time tested indigenous values of their societies.

Against this backdrop, Ahuia Ova, a Koita man wrote his memoirs in Motu.[12] A Hanuabada clerk, Igo Erua, translated the memoirs into English. The memoirs were published in the *Journal of the Royal Anthropological Institute* in 1939 as "The Reminiscence of Ahuia Ova."[13] The Ahuia Ova episode set in motion a series of interesting relationships between the Papuans and the colonial administration. Ahuia Ova had acquired quite a reputation as the friend of Lieutenant Governor Murray and a host of other Europeans. Among the Motu and Koitabuans, he was feared, revered, and disliked because of his negative actions and attitudes to other Papuans.

Ahuia Ova maintained a close relationship with the Europeans. He spoke in their language with ease and comfort. In return the administration appointed him as the village constable, court interpreter, and village councilor. "His early knowledge of the *taubada*s [European's] language was due largely to his daily association with the Catholic mission that set up base next door to Hohodae. In his early years, his errand running for the fathers and nuns, and the odd jobs here and there with the mission enabled him to get a head start in learning English from the Catholic *taubadas* [Europeans]"[14] Fellow Papuans saw Ahuia as a spoilt 'native', a betrayer, untrusted, double-tongued, and as someone who did not belong to the Motu Koitabuan societies.

Whether Papuans read what Ahuia wrote remains to be seen. Following the publication of Ahuia Ova's memoirs: "a great deal of biographical material [was] published about him."[15] Ahuia's story is one that is a reflection of the kind of Papuan, the colonizers wanted to churn out from instituting the learning of English to absorb the cultures of the Europeans at the expanse of forsaking the indigenous cultures and political structures.

PAPUA UNDER MURRAY

A number of writers, anthropologists, and government officials saw the need to bridge the gap between the pre-European Indigenous cultures and the modern Western cultures. The colonial administration was aware of the changes, both positive and negative changes, to the extent that a government anthropologist was recruited to document the changes and all aspects of social, cultural, and religious practices of the Papuans. John Hubert Plunkett Murray, the lieutenant-governor of Papua, recruited F. E. Williams as the government anthropologist on 8 March 1922. Murray believed that anthropology was an important part in his administration. "At the beginning of his administration, he saw that anthropology would be critical in assisting the process of replacing bad and barbarous customs with others more compatible with good government and humane principles."[16]

Murray's Papua was divided between the races, essentially between the Europeans and the Papuan natives. Murray had no interest in erasing this racial divide as reflected in his position on education of the Papuans. Murray wrote in late 1925 that education was "'not absolutely essential to a Papuan', and he was 'opposed to the creation of a Papuan intelligentsia' until opportunities for advancement were open to them. That could not happen, of course, until the colour bar had disappeared."[17] The thirty or so years Murray spent in the territory, his view of the Papuans was "that the best Papuans were superior in ability to the worst Europeans, 'but I cannot think that they are equal'. Education was not central to Murray's native policy, therefore, and with the limited resources at his disposal he was content to leave it to the missions.'"[18] Murray's eurocentrism was at best a reflection of his inability to reason beyond his own shortcomings as the person entrusted with the power to change the course of history.

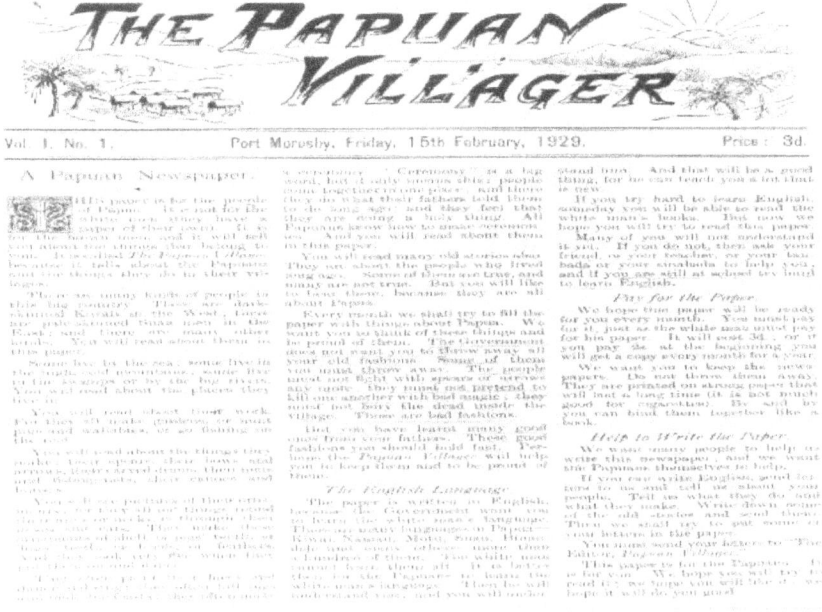

The first issue of *The Papuan Villager*, F. E. Williams.

THE PAPUAN VILLAGER

In 1929, F. (Francis) E. (Edgar) Williams founded *The Papuan Villager* (1929-1942) a monthly newspaper in simple English: "The idea was to publish reading matter for adult Papuans that was interesting and informative. He envisaged that eventually it would be written entirely by Papuans, but to his continual frustration he and a small group of regular contributors, mainly government clerks and mission teachers, had to write it. The [Papuan] *Villager* was distributed free to schools, but the majority of subscribers were Europeans (230 of a total of 307 in 1931, for instance)."[19] Williams felt *The Papuan Villager* would help increase the knowledge and understanding of the English language, a process that would eventually bring the Papuans to participate in a meaningful way in the colonial environment.

CULTURE COLLECTORS

Through writing and reading about their own cultures, the Papuans, as Williams envisaged, would teach their own kind about themselves: "But their contributions (most frequently folktales) rarely exceeded one quarter of the magazine's content, and one must suspect that their imperfect English provided smug amusement for white readers. Photographs were an important feature of the newspaper, and Williams presented a few of his own in each issue, sometimes in startling juxtaposition to pictures of the royal family, aeroplanes, sporting events and solemn European ceremonies." [20] Williams, much like his contemporaries such as Bronislaw Malinowski, Margaret Mead, and Reo Fortune — were active 'culture collectors' in Papua New Guinea as James Clifford would say. They saw "ethnography as a form of culture collecting (not, of course, the only way to see it)" — an enterprise that "highlights the ways that diverse experiences and facts are selected, gathered, and given enduring value in a new arrangement. Collecting — at least in the West, where time is generally thought to be linear and irreversible — implies a rescue of phenomena from inevitable historical decay or loss. The collection contains what 'deserves' to be kept, remembered, and treasured."[21] The photographs, in addition to Williams' ethnographic field work in Papua, were within this scheme of things. Williams, if you like, was aligning himself "with the functionalist camp in declaring that the kind of anthropology he was called (and paid) to do was "the study of cultures and societies as they exist at present, whether virtually unchanged or in a process of changing" and the "most productive method consists in the intense study, lasting over long periods, of certain specimen societies."[22] The fieldwork involves thorough and meticulous documentation.

The illustrations in *The Papuan Villager* reinforced the racial divide through vivid imageries. The Papuans were never going to become Europeans or come anywhere closer to achieving the intelligence of the Europeans, their masters, at anytime. *The Papuan Villager* served the purpose of "explicitly stating what European practices Papuans could and could not emulate."[23]

Williams "assumed the role of judgmental spokesman and arbiter of taste for his white casts. No matter how he tried to bolster Papuan self-esteem ('there are things you can do that the white man cannot do'), there was always the implicit command: 'Know thy place.' Often enough, indeed, this was conveyed in direct, unambiguous English."[24] In the end the objective of psychological rearrangement of the colonized to differentiate between what is European and what is native is reinforced through the persistent voice of the government anthropologist.

The Papuan Villager had its own failure. Instead of liberating and promoting Papuan cultures it became an instrument of racial differentiation, imperialist paternalism, and cultural denigration. "*The Papuan Villager* was not the most edifying of Williams' achievements... The editor's patronizing homilies and condescending tone made of it an unsubtle vehicle for colonial attitudes" that it is easy to see the disinterestedness in this journal among the Papuans.[25] Williams, however, remained convinced that *The Papuan Villager* was the appropriate vehicle to educate Papuans on European manners, customs, and civilization: "The paper was a mixture of news (much of it European) and moral exhortations — aeronautical exploits and sport, coupled with reminders not to fight at cricket matches or eat your neighbour's cat. Health and hygiene, the rewards of learning English ('so that you can talk to the white man and get a good job') and the joys of large families always featured."[26] In the tone of a public school prefect, Williams offered "'Friendly Words of Warning — we don't want any more killing. The men who go around killing people are a beastly nuisance and we put them in gaol.'" [27]

CULTURAL ASSIMILATION

The tactical approach staged by Williams and supported by Murray drives the point that we now understand as cultural assimilation. In British India, as was elsewhere, such cultural assimilation was used to strengthen the political action of the imperialists. Gauri Visnawathan cites the chilling perspectives held by J. Farish in a minute issued to the Bombay Presidency: "The Natives must either be kept down by a sense of our power, or they must willingly submit from a conviction that we are more wise, more just, more humane, and more anxious to improve their condition than any other rulers they could possibly have."[28] The mission of Williams and other Europeans in colonial Papua was really about "educating and civilizing colonial subject in the literature and thought of England, a mission that in the long run served to strengthen Western cultural hegemony in enormously complex ways."[29] European cultures, images, and narratives published in *The Papuan Villager* were as powerful as the study of English was in British India. The juxtaposition of western cultural and technological structures against those of the Papuans deliberately heightened the political project of European domination and subjugation of native cultures. *The Papuan Villager* project became a vehicle to institute a process of voluntary cultural assimilation that required consistent education of the Papuan minds. Ironically, the Papua New Guinean contributors to *The Papuan Villager* could only write folklore, legends, and traditional stories — no longer than a paragraph of five lines or so. Irrespective of this lack of contributions from the Papuans, Williams held the belief that as long as *The Papuan Villager* continued, he was duty bound to maintain the voice of reason, civilized cultures, and colonial authority in colonial Papua.

Williams used *The Papuan Villager* to explain the expectations of the administration. The "native regulations" Williams explained "forbade them alcohol and playing cards, he told his readers that the white men were allowed to drink and gamble because, unlike Papuans, 'they usually know when to stop'. On Europeanisation in general, he warned: 'You can never be quite the same as a white man; and you will only look silly if you try to be. Another offence against white aesthetics was the Papuan's appropriation of European building materials: 'If you build [your house] like a European copra shed it will not look very pretty.' Such condescending judgments would have done nothing to boost the Papuan reader's confidence and everything to remind him of the insurmountable barrier of race."[30]

Williams, we could say, is working within the context of eurocentrism: "the bifurcated fear/friendship fantasies that pervade" the colonial Europeans.[31] The result is often marred by ideological and epistemic violence that are implicit in such colonial preoccupations. Williams is reinforcing the colonial and Eurocentric discourses that rank and profile cultures outside of European civilization. "'These rankings," writes Regis Stella, "were influenced at least in part by European responses to the varying physical characteristics of indigenous people, in accordance with European ideals of beauty."[32]

Williams succeeded in achieving two important objectives. First, he succeeded in reinforcing the Europeans false believe in the inferiority of native cultures and lack of intelligent decisions. "In short, Williams' respect for Papuan cultures did not extend to their innovative responses to European contact. He admired them for what they were, not for what they might become. As did the majority of Europeans, Williams abhorred the kind of crude and ostentatious 'aping of the white man' signified by shirts and collars, playing cards and iron roofing."[33] Second, Williams succeeded in making *The Papuan Villager* become the voice of the colonial government and the Europeans in Papua, rather than the voice of the Papuan villagers who were the subject of the colonial project. The Papuan experiment, however, failed to interest the Papuans to take up writing in a serious way to counter European discourses promoted in *The Papuan Villager*.

We can draw the parallel here to the experience of Hawai'ians in the 1880s where print media was the main instrument in the promotion of Western discourse. "For forty years the mission controlled the power of the printed words in Hawaii," writes Noenoe Silva. "The missionaries used this power not just to save souls but to assist in the progress of plantation/colonial capitalism, to control public education, to mold government into Western form and to control it, and to domesticate Kanaka women."[34] Ironically, the missionaries and the planters did not expect "a group of Kanaka Maoli, maka`ainana, and the ali'i" to "transform themselves into speaking subjects proud of their Kanaka ways of life and traditions and unafraid to rebel. Their medium was a Hawai'ian-language newspaper called *Ka Hoku o ka Pakipaki* (The star of the Pacific). This paper began a long tradition of nationalist, anticolonial resistance through the print media."[35] The colonizers used the printed media to impose their cultures and European ideals onto the Pacific Islanders indiscriminately until a challenge was issued from the voiceless Indigenous peoples.

PAPUAN SCHOOL READERS

The Australian colonial administration imposed on Papua New Guinean students to read Rev. W. J. Saville's first *Papua School Reader* (1927) and later the *Papuan Villager* (1927-1942).[36] These materials were, however, too difficult and hard for Papua New Guinean students. In 1932 a series of *Papua Junior Readers*, written by visiting Queensland inspectors of Education and local teachers were issued to students. The *Papua Junior Readers* remained as the main text of education up to 1945. Even the *Papua Junior Readers* "were blatantly paternalistic in tone… [and] praised the work of the civilizing mission and condemned the traditional life of the people."[37] Change to the system began with W. C. Groves, the first Director of Education in June 17th, 1946.[38] Groves had the good intentions of changing the education system to suit the needs of the Papuan New Guineans: "However Groves' policy was undermined by the paradox of colonial education itself. There was still the average European teacher who maintained the patriotic feeling as reflected in his/her negative attitude to teach Papua New Guineans to speak English."[39] Conflicting attitudes and feelings permeated the education of the Papua New Guineans. In 1955 Paul Hasluck, the Administrator of the Trust Territory of Papua and New Guinea made it mandatory that English became the language of education.[40] Between 1963 and 1965 some attempts were made to develop a local syllabus in English. These efforts were unsuccessful as they lacked a local culture and creative consistency at its core: "The [Papua and New Guinea] syllabus included a list of common errors in language and a few literature texts set for detailed study. Literature was still a trivial aspect of the Papua New Guinea English syllabus."[41]

The reluctance to introduce higher education was based on the assumption that Papua New Guineans have low intelligence and were slow in absorbing the European knowledge: "Higher education in Papua New Guinea was not considered until 1962, when the United Nations Visiting Mission expressed

Stamp based on F.E.Williams photograph below.

Man Fishing from Original F.E.Williams's photograph.

criticism "of the rate of development in the country in such areas as education and demanded the introduction of crash programs with the objective of training an indigenous elite."[42] Higher education began in 1963 following a report by the Australian government appointed Commission of Higher Education. The first students to attend the University of Papua New Guinea, the Administrative College, and other colleges in the 1960s took up the responsibility to unwrite

The Papuan Villager's racial, paternalistic, and Eurocentric discourses. To un-write was to prove the views and positions of Murray and Williams as poorly conceived and founded on the basis of false ideology.[43]

UNWRITING THE *PAPUAN VILLAGER*

The process of 'unwriting' *The Papua Villager* began with the introduction of higher education in Papua New Guinea in the 1960s. Institutions such as the University of Papua New Guinea and the Administrative College were already going through a transformation as a result of the creative and political energy that saturated these institutions. Similar effects took place in the University of Technology in Lae. Four years after the establishment of higher education in Papua New Guinea resulted in the first published writings by Papua New Guineans: "The first wave of indigenous creative writing in Papua New Guinea began in 1967 when Ulli Beier — who had already been a catalyst in the de-velopment of contemporary Indigenous literature and art in Nigeria during the 1950s and 1960s — began teaching a creative writing course at the University of Papua New Guinea (UPNG)."[44] Beier cultivated the creative spirit in young Papua New Guineans without haste. As it is now common knowledge, Beier exposed the writings of Papua New Guineans to 'Western' readers in Australia and the US, through his own local literary imprints, *Papua Pocket Poets, Kovave* (1969-74) and major international anthologies: "In his teaching, Beier exposed students to a wide variety of African literatures, and a range of Papua New Guinean literature published during the 1960s and 1970s" directing his students to emulate "the pseudo-ethnographic realism evident in texts such as Chinua Achebe's *Things Fall Apart* (1958). As Beier reveals, many Papua New Guinean writers of this period identified closely with the 'cultural anxieties and political issues explored in African writing, and various African writers, including Taban Lo Liyong (from Uganda) and Wole Soyinka (from Nigeria), [who] visited the UPNG campus in these early years."[45]

In the 1970s the University of Papua New Guinea made the decision to use literary studies to instill national consciousness and awareness in students through an emphasis on oral traditions and on the "emerging New Guinea Literature."[46] The Department of Language and Literature created four ma-jor sequences: Language, Literature, Language and Literature, and Creative writing. Greicus writes that "each of the major sequence is directly related to specific challenges in education within Papua New Guinea."[47] Furthermore it was envisioned that a major in literature "will continue to place considerable emphasis on oral traditions and the literature of new nations, as well as on de-velopments in contemporary literary forms around the world."[48]

The principles underlying the setting up of the literature program at UPNG allowed students to: (1) Read literature and secure as complete as possible a response to it, at the same time develop a critical literary appetite and taste which would generate a desire for further reading of literature; (2) Study literature as a creative art form and this develops an appreciation of and a response to creativity in all communication arts leading to ultimately self-creativity; (3) Discover, maintain, propagate and develop the traditions of oral literature of Papua New Guinea. The result was a politically conscious and vibrant population of young Papua New Guineans in institutions of higher education. The sudden unleashing of the creative and political energy in literary forms unexpectedly fuelled the political activities that led to political nationhood.[49]

Papua New Guinean students seized the opportunity by expressing themselves in creative ways. The inspiration came from the students' own experiences as colonized subjects and from their rich oral traditions.[50] Papua New Guinean students approached written literature in two ways: "One was the direct translation of traditional legends, poems, etc. so as to carry over into English as much of original significance and feeling as possible. The other is the free interpretation and adaptation of traditional literature by writers wishing to suit their own artistic purposes."[51] Their conscious efforts to transfer oral literature to written forms were twofold. First, it was to create a literary culture that was influenced by the oral traditions.[52] Second, it was to use their own oral traditions to view the world or to express their cultural identity using their own cultural symbols. Papua New Guinean literature was "neither traditional nor popular like oral literature was and still is in the villages," rather what was happening was that the writers were "replacing the more elaborate and ritualistic literature and art with a kind of literature which is idealistic and artificial."[53] The early writings were published in journals such as *New Guinea Writing* (1970-1978), *Kovave* (1968-1976), *Gigibori*, and *Oral History*. Ulli Beier started the *Papua Pocket Poets* series that expanded their literary horizons. Several translated folklore and individual collections of poetry were published in this series.[54]

WRITTEN CULTURAL MEMORY

Students used cultural stories to define their sense of cultural consciousness in the last moments of colonialism in Papua New Guinea. The students "were fully conscious of their status as role models and as possible future leaders of the nation. They experienced life between two worlds, coping with the new, while remaining intent upon maintaining their ties to their traditional heritage. As well as knowing several languages besides their own *tokples*, they had internalized the oral literature that had, for generations, defined their physical and social environments" (*italics mine*).[55] The urgency to maintain their cultures, provide self-definitions of who they are, and about their societies provided the impetus to write: "As role models and future leaders these students realized

17

the importance of cultural maintenance, self-explanations, and collective consciousness drawn from different cultural and language backgrounds."[56] To live together as a society they need to teach each other their own cultures.

The opportunity to wrestle the bull by its horn was before these students: "Papua New Guinean students recognized the need to provide their own cultural explanations of the world, their social relationships with each other, and to the natural and spiritual environment inherited from their ancestors."[57] The most powerful expressions of cultural nationalism were captured in the novels produced in the 1970s. "Perhaps the literary form most associated with the nation and subject formation remains the novel. It has been connected in a variety of ways to questions of citizenship and the imagined community of the nation as well as to forms of knowledge production: psychoanalysis, history, ethnography, and travel narrative."[58]

CONCLUSION

We know now that the formation, consolidation, and transformations of consciousness are also linked to the early efforts of Europeans to introduce print literacy and print media in Oceania.[59] Our task now is to re-vise the old perceptions by providing new perspectives of Oceania as promoted in recent times across various institutional spaces and through various publications.[60] The print media acted as the main agent for colonization but later as an instrument of imagining a community in Oceania. Papua New Guineans began to write about their own experiences as a way of unwriting *The Papuan Villager* experiment to form an imagined community known as the Independent State of Papua New Guinea.

2

LITERARY CULTURE AS INTELLECTUAL CAPITAL[1]

> *"Nation builders use a patchwork of scholarly materials, old songs, obscure dances, and historical legends, all apparently quaint and local, but in reality selected and reinterpreted by intellectuals to create a culture upon which the life of the nation can rest."*[2]
> Ernest Gellner, *Nations and Nationalism*

Cultural literacy works at establishing nations and nationalism by insisting that a nation defines itself through a parchment of shared cultural experiences. These shared cultural experiences are known as cultural knowledge. Cultural knowledge is constantly reinvented so that it accommodates the changing times. The danger of course is that cultural knowledge, traditions, and languages are often taken for granted that nations go through a process of forgetfulness, resulting in undermining their integrity: "It is all too easy for us to make this mistake, because of our history."[3] During the Independence celebration in 1998 I was in Dona village on the banks of Waria River in Morobe Province. I was always in school when the Independence celebration was celebrated. I have never celebrated a single Independence Day in my village. I was in Dona village to participate in the first conference organized by the Zia speakers on their culture, language, and knowledge systems. I was there as a guest of the Zia villagers. I was there to learn their culture.

I was more aware of how various discourses of cultures converge, intersect, and interact with each other. I learnt from the Zia villagers their traditional knowledge systems. In exchange they learnt from me what I know of the Western knowledge system. Most often we witness this happening in classrooms all over the country, without realizing the formation of a culture that reflects the diversity of this nation.[4] We come to reassure ourselves as a nation of different cultures through this process. In the discussions that follow I focus more specifically on literary culture and how it contributes to nation and national identity.

LITERARY CULTURE AND THE NATION

Culture is a composite of various recognizable traits that reflect a society. I discuss culture as constructed from the writings of Papua New Guineans. Let us cogitate on the word "culture" before attaching it to other words. Raymond Williams explains three proper uses of the word. First, culture is an "independent and abstract noun which describes a general process of intellectual, spiritual and aesthetic development," beginning in the Eighteenth Century. Second, the definition of culture has come to mean a "particular way of life, whether of a people, a period, a group, or humanity in general." Third, culture "describes the works and practices of intellectual, and especially artistic activity. The last definition seems the most widespread in use: culture is music, literature, painting and sculpture, theatre and film."[5] Of these definitions we settle with second and third uses of the word culture. Our discussions are on the literary culture of Papua New Guinea. A literary culture is linked to the cultural matrix from which it emerged. Literary culture is part of the introduced system of knowledge. Written by Papua New Guineans, the literary culture reflects the experiences of Papua New Guineans, with attachments to the traditional and modern knowledge systems. What Papua New Guinean literary culture reflects is a collective experience of a postcolonial Pacific nation. Through the study of the literary culture we trace the development of a distinct consciousness embraced by many of our people.

Early writing in the western world owes its existence to the oral traditions from which it emerged: "the first script, or true writing, that we know, was developed among Sumerians in Mesopotamia only around the year 3500 BC."[6] Since its development writing has impressed itself as an instrument enabling cultural literacy to emerge consistently. Goody speaking of literacy in Ghana says: "writing is often regarded at first as an instrument of secret and magic power."[7] Before writing emerged all societies depended on their folk cultures and ancient methods of knowledge transfer. All learning and knowledge transfer systems used one form or another of an accepted system of decoding signs in a society.

Without culture a nation cannot claim a political identity. Nationalism is a defense of a nation's cultural inventions. Nationalism vindicates "its own inventions" by politicizing its culture.[8] A nation is denied of its identity once culture is separated from it. For a nation to differentiate itself from others it often relies on its cultural foundations to do so. Thus in the education of its youth, a nation requires that culture is included as an important component of its curriculum. We know that a "culture is, concretely, an open-ended, creative dialogue of subcultures, of insiders and outsiders, of diverse factions" that enables continuous reinvention of itself against that which challenges its form.[9] Through education cultural knowledge is presented to the learners as important defining characteristics of their lives. Learning to read, write, and do arithmetic without the input of cultural literacy is to ask for less. Cultural literacy consists of both traditional and modern knowledge systems.

TEACHING PNG LITERATURE

Over the years an assortment of students studied literature at the University of Papua New Guinea: Students with no understanding of literature to those who have some knowledge of literary studies, made up the list of students studying literature. Among them are teachers who have been teaching literature in secondary schools. Though they teach literature in schools they struggle to teach the subject effectively. The question then is how are teachers taught literature in their formative college years or at the university? The training at the college level should at least train teachers in literary analysis and criticism. Tools of unpacking meanings of texts would have helped teachers.

Education is a catalyst of positive change in most cases. In other cases it also introduced a negative development in the minds of its receivers. A negative knowledge developed out of the colonial education system. Students were taught to fulfill the goals of colonialism rather than to think for themselves. Educational practices were in line with the administrative policies of the time. The education of Papua New Guineans was seen as a waste of time and effort. Intellectual capacity building of students was discouraged. Passive and mechanical responses were instilled into the mindset of the learners. The orders and directions of the missionaries and the colonial government were enforced with strict disciplines and observations. English was the language of instruction in all administration schools forcing students to abandon their own languages. In Papua, the colonial administration, insisted on students reading Rev. W. J. Saville's first *Papuan School Reader* (1927) and later the *Papuan Villager* (1927-1941) produced by F. E. Williams, the government anthropologist.[10] These materials were, however, too difficult and hard for Papua New Guinean students. Graduates from this system were expected to understand the European language and participate in the colonial project in Papua New Guinea.

The depressing historical practice continued into the 1960s. Change to this attitude began with W. C. Groves, the first Director of Education in June 17th, 1946. Groves had the good intentions of changing the education system to suit the needs of the Papua New Guineans: "However Groves' policy was undermined by the paradox of colonial education itself. There was still the average

European teacher who maintained the patriotic feeling as reflected in his/her negative attitude to teach Papua New Guineans to speak English."[11] Conflicting attitudes and feelings influenced the education policy even early in Murray's administration. Between 1963 and 1965 some attempts were made to develop a local syllabus in English. These efforts were unsuccessful as they lacked a local culture at its core. This syllabus included a list of common errors in language use and a few literature texts, most foreign to Papua New Guineans.

With the establishment of the University of Papua New Guinea in mid 1960s literature was also introduced to Papua New Guinean students. The Department of Education, however, was unable to come up with a literature syllabus. A full literature syllabus was only tested in 1967, which inevitably proved unsuitable. The inappropriate methods of teaching and lack of materials for teaching were some of the problems with this new syllabus. Most teachers had no formal training in teaching or even in the methods of interpreting literature.[12] The colonial education was a product of an oppressive reality instigating dominance rather than intellectual development of the colonized. The fear was that the equipping of the colonized with intellectual knowledge would enable them to resist dominance and to challenge the white superior mythology: "The nature of education in any political society tends to reflect the requirements of those who provide it rather than those who receive it. The knowledge, skills, attitudes, and beliefs deemed suitable for transmission, the organization and methods by which they are transmitted and finally the extent to which they are made available, tend to reflect the views of those who provide the formal education."[13] The political and economic interests of those provide this type of education influences the leaner's view of nature.

Those were educated in the colonial system were denied sufficient intellectual training in the formal education system. Though not inadequate in intellectual capacity, Papuans and New Guineans struggled to liberate themselves from the mental colonization that was instituted by the early Western education system. What evolved in the 1970s, 1980s, and 1990s is a syllabus emphasizing vocationalism, rather than a liberalized education. Students enter the university with a vocational mentality without considering the interdisciplinary value of education. Economic security after graduation from the university is more important than an educated individual with the tools and knowledge of negotiating one's way around life in a postcolonial society.

LITERATURE CURRICULUM

In the same way the status of Literature as a department was reduced. Literature courses were restructured over the years to reflect the changing interests and challenges. It changed from a strong emphasis in creative writing in the Ulli Beier era to folklore studies in the Chakravarti era in the 1980s. Since then literary studies concentrate on postcolonial studies, Papua New Guinea, and South Pacific literatures. In recent times the program has identified three significant areas of specialization based on the staff strength in the program: creative writing, postcolonial and cultural studies, and folklore. This emphasis makes literary studies more relevant to our present condition as a postcolonial, cultural, and linguistically heterogeneous society. The emphasis of the literature program is more consistent with current literary programs elsewhere in the world.

The difficulties of teaching literature effectively have to do with the unavailability of literary materials such as textbooks and literary journals. This is the single most difficult problem. There are, of course, problems that exist as challenges for literary scholars: How do we attract students into literary programs? Do we operate as a service division in the overall university academic structure, or do we groom students to be literary scholars? Should we answer why literary studies is important to students in other disciplines? Working as writer scholars at the University of Papua New Guinea, we are pressured to produce our own works, while commenting and critiquing works by our own writers.

Critical scholarships produced by Papua New Guineans are absent. We could, as Graff suggests, make literary studies transmit humanism and cultural studies, but we are also aware of the trend in current scholarship to critique literary works to produce "texts" that illuminate some of the more repressed consciousness with which we carry around with us without questioning them.[14] Literary studies, it must be stressed, in its marginal position within the University of Papua New Guinea's academic preoccupation, struggles to gain a foothold in educating professionals with commercial and corporate interests. The struggle to define itself has caused so much confusion in the study of literature.

The challenge therefore is to salvage literary studies out of the "service" oriented direction. In a small institution such as the University of Papua New Guinea the success of literary studies is measured by: (a) producing graduates who are employed, and (b) by increasing the number of students completing their postgraduate degrees here and in overseas universities. This indicates that doing literary studies is a universal program where our students can pursue further studies at international universities without difficulties. Thus, in terms of teaching literary studies, we emphasize on cultural studies that crosses disciplinary boundaries of the traditional literature curriculum. In that way we produce a cadre of students with skills that enable them to succeed in various fields of their interests. In other words literature graduates are equipped with critical and cultural studies tools for use in various works of life and in research of Papua New Guinean cultures.

Paula Gunn Allen reminds us to see literature as a field that is not necessarily Western. She argues that the novel, for instance, emerged in the Eastern societies well before the Western novel: "The novel itself saw its earliest development in Japan of eleventh century in *The Tale of Genji* by Lady Murasaki Shikibu." Europeans developed the novel "a few centuries later." Poetry is a genre that is part of every culture "though a certain shape has unfolded in recent times, which marks it as a modern vehicle." The modern form of poetry, as is argued, was derived "from preexisting poetic forms in those nations that go back hundreds, even thousands, of years."[15] In Pacific societies the poetic forms and structures of experience found in their folk traditions have reemerged in the written literature. Scholars and literary specialists in Pacific literature see these elements as irreducible parts of the total literary culture of the Pacific.

Ironically, literature is poorly understood even by Pacific Islanders. The study of literature means literacy to some, for others it is about writing and reading of books. Many people see it as the study of writings by Westerners like Shakespeare, Dickens, and the best sellers on spies, terrorism, and romances. Studying literature is by no means a trivial pursuit, but an active participation in discursive exercises that enables citizens to critically undertake an active program in the issues of identity and nation formation. Programme financiers and scholarships awarding agencies consistently trivialize courses such as literature by ignoring the importance of the field in the development of culture, society, and nations. The ill informed and ignorant decisions of the government agencies responsible for developing the human resources necessary for the total development of a nation are as damaging as the ignorant attitudes exhibited and exercised by disciplinary biases that limit the understanding of the various processes that enable knowledge formations.

More than a gap exists when we allow the perpetuation of conservative attitudes and outdated views of learning to influence our decisions. Consequently, what we are creating is a society poorly educated on its values, traditions, and ways of knowing that form the foundations of an imagined community. In Papua New Guinea the desire to fulfill a national expectation is often the basis of half-baked educated bureaucrats and technocrats, reluctantly writing off their cultures and dynamiting the earth, which holds the life of a people together. In the policy and planning oriented air conditioned offices countless hours are spent conferencing and generating discourses in every utterance in the most stoic and noncreative manner, only to find the implementation much more troublesome. The captains of the industry ignore reactions and protests against the artificial and insensitive policies and decisions made by politicians and approved by the National Executive Council. In most cases the National Executive Council is likely to approve it as it too has a membership that is drawn from the elite who could no longer be useful in the trade they have chosen prior to entering parliament. This group we must think of as apprentices in a career that is marked with hazards that they are poorly prepared to avoid. The consequence is a nation struggling to stand on its own feet, albeit as an independent nation with liberated peoples from the shackles of colonialism manifests in whatever form and space.

In my career as a lecturer in literature at the University of Papua New Guinea I have had to listen to students express the pressure to change their studies in the Humanities to the fields of Law and Business studies or in the Social Sciences. The main argument has to do with career expectations and job opportunities. Most students want to have a high job upon graduation. An argument that is easily defeated when I explain the importance of studying a discipline that is not overcrowded. Nearly all graduates in Literature end up with jobs and have contributed immensely to the development of the nation.

In the literature program we hope students would become critically aware of their position as educated Papua New Guineans with the necessary skills to deconstruct the colonized mentality that we have inherited. The graduates of our new literary programs are taught to critique the foundations that structured an oppressive reality: "Literature is clearly not an ideologically neutral field" as Pam Gilbert argues: "It is obviously naive to imagine that any constructed text- -professional literature, school textbook, teenage comic, or a child's story — does not carry ideological messages, and a number of important studies have emphasized exactly this."[16] Students without literary studies experience are those who remain ignorant of the ideological constructs that the classroom culture has impressed on their conscience. Literary studies enable students to respond critically to problems encountered in their lives. These problems can either be cultural, spiritual, economic, or political. The everyday struggles of people within their own societies are problems that require a well-developed intellectual mind able to make reasonable evaluation and seek appropriate courses of action.

AN IDEOLOGICAL CHALLENGE

Zizek challenges us to be critical of the discourses that constructed us in his introduction to *Mapping Ideology*. We are left to accept the "unrelenting per- tinence of the notions of ideology" with which we perceive the "system of production with social organizations in different forms."[17] To understand the system of production one must have the knowledge about the production. Such knowledge is derived from the reservoir of cultural knowledge present in every society. Having the knowledge of culture enables a literate person to relate and make educated judgments on the world.[17]

The implication here can be applied to learning about South Pacific cul- tures from authors like Russell Soaba, Epeli Hau'ofa, Sia Figiel, Regis Stella, or Albert Wendt. Literature students are taught to separate the biographical reading from contextual reading of the texts. Literature is seen as a window into the world. It is difficult for most students to do so immediately. They tend to linger on in the comfort zones of the information they already know about the author. A limitation of knowledge is created out of this inability to read beyond the text. Needless to say, even if students know nothing about Anuki or Western Samoa, they need to make informed judgments about the cultural contexts from which a work of literature is produced. Students of literature are often expected to seek knowledge beyond the lines they read. Making a judgment based on surface reality is discouraged. The learning process must have critical attributes, as suggested in Freire's work that work at creating "of structural conditions that make a more democratic society possible."[19] In other words learners must think beyond the immediate experience. Learners must acquire knowledge that enables them to participate in the democratic process around the world.

Cultural literacy is about changing illiteracy itself. It is also about mechanisms that drive change in a society. These mechanisms are structured in a form that refuses to be changed. Through critical questioning by those who struggle against it; the structure can change to accommodate the conditions of a democratic society.

To achieve cultural literacy the education of our people must include the cultures of the learners. Cultural education should never be something that educational institutions preserve only for cultural and festival days in educational institutions. Such a practice is restrictive in intention. It reinforces the idea that culture is only visible outside of the classroom. Students' cultures are ignored in this practice. In *Pedagogy of the Oppressed*, Freire explains that the danger in a teacher who adapts an authoritative approach to learning without taking the needs of the students into account may indeed be a contradiction in the teacher's own pedagogical practice as an individual: "The educator places himself or herself before he or she recognizes the absoluteness of their ignorance as the reason for his or her existence. The unaware learners, very much in the manner of slaves in Hegelian dialectics, recognize their ignorance as the educator's reason for existing, but unlike the slaves in Hegelian dialectics, they don't get to discover themselves as the educator's educators." [20]

The most effective learning strategy in formal classroom is to erase the boundary between authoritarian set up and an interactive learning situation. In authoritarian learning there is a one-way process in which knowledge is processed.

A dialogical learning process takes place in an interactive educational environment. Learners' cultural background is included so that learners learn about themselves. There should never be any arguments about it. It is like learning Tok Pisin writing even when the learner is a fluent Tok Pisin speaker. Obviously, written Tok Pisin is very different to spoken Tok Pisin, but the rules that construct their practices often delude us. In any case, learning Tok Pisin is also a process in which the cultural knowledge is transmitted, reaffirmed, and recreated in the spoken and written medium.

We can learn from what Hirsch says of Americans: "Americans in their teens and twenties who were brought up under their individualistic theories are not less conventional than their predecessors, only less literate, less able to express their individuality."[21] The false emphasis on individualism is a pragmatist's view. Indeed the emphasis should be on the individual differences in the experience of the learners, whereby "the best teaching does accommodate itself to individual differences in temperament, but a child's temperament does not come freighted with content." Culture provides the environment for learning in children. Their individuality is defined by their cultures: "The greatest human individuality is developed in response to a tradition, not in response to disorderly, uncertain and fragmented education."[22]

It is important to recognize the individual differences that students bring to classrooms. These individual differences are precisely the places where interactive learning takes place. Knowledge is processed much more effectively in a heterogeneous environment where discourses intersect one another. It is often assumed that where heterogeneous cultures encounter each other an entirely new hybridized culture emerges. This, we are all too aware, is represented, in the novelistic discourses we study in Bakhtin's theory of dialogical imagination.[23]

In language as well as in literary cultures we witness this very process-taking place. Cultural literacy is well received if we can recognize the acquisition of certain kinds of knowledge as specific cultural capital. Pierre Bourdieu and Pam Gilbert argue that specific cultural capital "proposes that there are certain kinds of knowledge that are culturally valued and privileged. It is in this sense that knowledge becomes 'capital' which one can use."[24]

Two experiences highlighted the experiences expressed above: (1) the "negotiated classroom" in which "the students take a significant role in shaping the course their learning takes-and the kinds of cultures that emerge" from this strategy. Christie and Rothery share their view of the Australian education systems, especially in curriculum planning and assessment on literacy matters. Negotiation is the gist of good curriculum planning and assessment "so that through skilled teaching the students are involved both in exploring the topics appropriate to the various subjects they study, and in examining and discussing the genres in which such topics are built up to form the "content of the subjects."[25] It seems cultural literacy in our system needs to absorb the educator's responsibility, the student's background, and the classroom conditions. The pedagogical exercise works only if the above conditions are observed. Power relations within the classroom culture can be explained to students once they are made aware of the structures within the classroom culture that constitute such a relation.

Becoming aware of such a structure of authoritarian pedagogical exercise is not enough, as students should be motivated to erase negative knowledge in their learning process. Many students at the University of Papua New Guinea, for example, struggle to recognize that the greatest barrier to learning is the instilled notion that what the teacher says is always the gospel truth. To question it would lead them to their downfall. What downfall? Indeed this attitude to learning affects developing a nation of critical learners. Instead a nation is made up of "bureaucratized intellectuals". By bureaucratized intellectuals I mean a public service filled with educated Papua New Guineans unable to critique their own actions and decisions. Others like to categorize the bureaucratized individuals as the elite, who are completely alienated from their own cultures and societies.[26] This is a small powerful group. If a nation, however, desires a collective purpose it will have to redirect its emphasis away from producing a nation that is unable to liberate itself from the double consciousness syndrome inherited from the former colonizers. One way in which a nation can develop cultural consciousness is to read the writings produced by its own writers.

WRITING AND READING OURSELVES[27]

Within the space of competing discourses a dialogic encounter takes place. It is from such encounters a sense of consciousness emerges. This necessarily differentiates what one is to another person depending on the kind of discourses that one is exposed to. A dominant discourse can completely erase those aspects, which give Papua New Guineans their identity. The practice of writing books is a way of reading ourselves. Our society can be fully literate if we write and read ourselves. We cannot allow discourses of dominant societies to disempower our will to free ourselves from the prison of illiteracy.

We have a defined, structured, and textualised space of existence. This means that our societies, as we understand or pretend to understand, were previously inscribed by colonial discourses that produced typologies and hierarchies of difference. In such a defined space we confront the differences, acknowledge the typologies that describe us, and critique the texts, which were written about our conditions of survival, our environment, and our belief systems.

I address a perspective that is more significant to me. I speak as a Papua New Guinean writer and as a critic of Papua New Guinean literature. It is from these two vantage points that I feel I can contribute meaningfully to issues implied by the term "critical developmental literacy". We cannot understand ourselves better and develop as Papua New Guineans if we are unable to read ourselves in the literature produced by our own writers. Our ideas are developed from what we see of ourselves through works of literature. It is unfair if we allow over-politicized theories, practices, ideologies, dogmas, and dominant discourses to infiltrate our minds. We don't have to write for the disciples of the great western literary traditions, but for ourselves.

What is the point of writing our own books if we are unable to read what we write? Although it seems a cliché to assume that writing our own books means reading ourselves, it does, however, contribute greatly to the fuller understanding of ourselves, expands the knowledge of our societies, and promotes a sense of identity among Papua New Guineans. Reading ourselves from our own writings makes us fully understand ourselves better.

Papua New Guineans have to be their own critics. There are two concerns here. First, we must make our writings accessible so that many people will have access to Papua New Guinean literature. Papua New Guinean literature must not carry the tag "*elites*" and be left for the classrooms and libraries. It must be produced for everybody, for the national parliamentarians to the villagers, from the desk scholars to the domestic housewives.

Second, we must produce our writings in the languages that we understand well. This means that Papua New Guinean writing must be produced in all languages: English, Tok Pisin, Hiri Motu and the indigenous language of the writer. No one should be apologetic or ashamed of expressing himself or herself in his or her language or even in studying works of literature in his or her language.

We must accept our writings as the process in which we speak for ourselves. Until we speak for ourselves we cannot claim to be living the way we believe we are living. It is from the voices we hear from the books, stories, plays, and poetry of our writers that we come to some conclusions that we live in a responsible society. It is from these voices that we learn about our sufferings, we acknowledge the contradictions in it, and we seek ways to solve the conflicts in our societies. Papua New Guinean writing is characterized by its social consciousness and nationalism "that recognizes the multicultural, polylingual and diverse inheritance."[28] Critics of Papua New Guinean literature may disagree with this view. These are people who maintain that Papua New Guinean writing is inconsistent and poorly developed without any standard models of writing. It is rather too early for critics to make such premature comments. The relevance of this discussion is the confrontation Papua New Guineans experience as they encounter the world of writing. Writing is new and hosts a multitude of discourses. Using writing to describe their experiences is the most difficult thing to do. Writing in the western sense is still the dominant discourse. Papua New Guineans are sometimes hesitant in the use of English as they attempt to express themselves. To articulate one's experiences may seem futile, when one lacks the understanding of the powerful processes of dominant discourses.

Papua New Guinean literature is a representation of the people's culture, values, beliefs, and oral traditions. At the core of a Papua New Guinean writer's mind is the "preservation and keeping" of cultural, social and political systems of the people. A writer persists and intervenes in moments of crisis to represent his or her people.[29] The American critic, Charles Johnson argues: that "writing is a product of man's intervention," a comment attributed to the American writer Malraux who once said that "artists do not stem from their childhood, but from their conflicts with the achievement of their predecessors."[30] Writing becomes our vehicle of dialogic imagination.

We can represent our society better if we write for ourselves. In Soaba's *Wanpis* (1978) we realize that even our contemporary society is one that is poorly structured, educated, and forced to "worshipping old mistakes and the establishments of colonial institutions and this alienates them [us] from their [our] own social or cultural institutions."[31] In such an alienating environment we come to realize our own hopelessness, desolation, and subverted conditions. The irony is that Soaba wants us to see that we become self-conscious. We must become critically aware of our situation so has to intervene on behalf of ourselves. We become conscious of our identity as individuals, who make up a people, and as a people we make up a society, and as a society we assert ourselves as a nation. It is "within this liminality" that individuals realize "the dichotomy of their existence and declare their allegiances, their sense of belonging, cohesion and unity in a new social, cultural and religious order."[32] Papua New Guinean writers must construct their societies in a more critical way.

There is no denial that Papua New Guinean writers are at the centre of the described imaginative world, the social world beyond literature, actualized world, and the imagined world of an author. If these worlds are presented in an honest way these can reveal a society full of conflicts, contradictions, and confusion, often tainted with violence, terror, and fear. Even the pre-contact society boasted by early Papua New Guinean writers as the idyllic society is one that is full of conflicts (e.g., conflicts between warring tribes, chiefs against commoners, land disputes between two families), contradictions (e.g., sorcery, medical treatments, cosmological explanations) and confusion (e.g., men's sacred world and initiation processes). Such nature of pre-contact societies was evident during periods of contact and sustained European presence. The negative, often violent, reactions to first European encounters or between the first coastlanders encountered by Highlanders, was expected. People were living within their enclosed society. Whatever exists outside of it belongs to the realm of the supernatural, the dream world, or moreover in the mythological world. Ignatius Kilage's *My Mother Calls Me Yaltep* (1980) is a perfect representation of this dichotomy. Although Kilage's purpose is passionate and ethnographic, it is the "poetically evoked landscape, the reality of his imagination and the imaginative mental world which has its bases both in the oral language and in the written world that is of paramount significance."[33] It is the confrontation of unanswered questions that Kilage attempts to portray in his book. The problem of the unanswered questions remains the most enigmatic aspect of the book. The people are immersed in the world of magic, dream, fantasy, imagination, and the supernatural: "This world counter exists with the world of reality, facts, and with concrete objects such as mountains, landforms, landscapes, floods, and rain." Man is in between these worlds and "seeks both protection and inspiration. He understands his environment and makes it possible to perceive the supernatural world within it." One must observe the spiritual and physical attachments to man.[34]

Papua New Guinean writers are already attached to a place. They find both spiritual and physical attachment, as a necessary condition of explaining their history, culture, and values. The re-reading of our texts and making sense out of them begins at this juncture. In re-reading these texts we come to know the silenced world of our ancestors, their traditions, values, and beliefs. We come to know ourselves better by discovering ourselves. Soaba describes the space as the "cosmological womb" in which our people define themselves. These definitions are the controlling ideas of poetry, rhetoric, and politics. Sometimes this space of poetically evoked landscape is described as the silenced world. It is a silenced world of Lomo'ha and St. James Nativeson. Writers must uncover the textualized world of this silenced world. The best critics of any writers' works are the writers themselves.[35]

It is within this cosmological womb that writers discover themselves and project outward their own sense of identity and history. In re-reading *Lomo'ha I Am, in Spirit's Voice I Call* (1991) Soaba reminds Papua New Guinean writers about the cosmological womb that gave birth to us in the first place: "Everything that is our poetry, and our literature as a whole, must be hidden in the deep unconscious of that womb of Melanesian cosmology that surrounds us. We only need to visit that cosmological world again and again to unearth the reality that will endow us the blessings of our sense of place, our sense of time and space, and our sense of history."[36]

One other way of discovering ourselves is through the use of our people's languages. Many of our people are afraid to write. They argue that their written English is substandard. Why should anyone be afraid to write in English, when the options are manifold? If Tok Pisin or Hiri Motu cannot do the job, then our indigenous languages are there. The capturing of our thoughts and desires in our own languages is in itself political. One does not have to fear or be ashamed of what one is. There is a sense of completeness. This desire has found its root in the ever-changing flame of the Campus Writers group of the University of Papua New Guinea. The Campus Writers' group's publication: *Savannah Flames* (1993) offers new insights and inspirations. The collection of promising young Papua New Guinean writers show raw taste of literature, but with more choice in the language of writing.

In *Lomo'ha I am, in Spirits Voice I Call* (1991) the narrator is trapped in the language spoken after his arrival from death.[37] Lomo'ha's language did not belong to the living, but to the dead. The villagers refused to entertain him. The villagers proceeded to end the dead people's language and bring back the language in which they could accept Lomo'ha as one of their own. The apologetic Lomo'ha has no choice, but to submit to the wishes of the people: *that him and us, must return to the people by speaking and writing in the people's language*. We do not have to succumb to the languages of the dead and become estranged. We have our own languages to write in. A colleague once argued that the language, which he used to craft his narrative, was better than Lomo'ha's. The fallacy, if not, a bad judgment on the colleague's part, does not place him in the same situation as Lomo'ha's narrative, which transcends the semi-autobiographical narrative of the colleague, immersed in the unrealistic pastoral novel, insinuated by a language which even the people written about cannot understand. Even then, Lomo'ha's transcendence and acceptance as the true orator comes because he infuses the different languages to make his world more meaningful. It is such experiences of Lomo'ha and its narrator, which this paper is advocated here. Stella points out that it is an attempt to infuse the traditional past with today's contemporary society. That it is the re-affirmation of cultural heritage and the depiction of the "alternative world view [that] has been "interiorised" by the west."[38]

Papua New Guinean writers have to recognize the uncompromising situation where languages encounter each other and where a text is determined by the dominant language of power and authority. It does not follow, however, that writers too are forced to accept the subject position. Instead it privileges a writer's position, so that he/she can establish dialogue between different texts, between the old tradition and the modern, and between the early and new Papua New Guinean writing. It is a position that promotes liberated consciousness and healthy writing. Bakhtin describes this process as a dialogic imagination. It is within this situation that a writer establishes dialogues with other texts. We see this happening in Soaba's *Maiba* (1985) where Yawasa Maibina is forced to establish a dialogue between the different forces of power, and between those who are dominant and those who are dominated. Maiba's silence and tolerance is interpreted as persistence of a will to survive.[39]

There is no such a thing as passivity for our writers. Instead, there is a major task to be undertaken and that is to confront the world, which describes us, defines us, and constructs us. We need to radically challenge such a world rather than to accept its imposition. Papua New Guinean writers need to open up a dialogue, which places them in the center of discussion on Papua New Guinean literature. Our aim is to capture politically acceptable conditions where we can negotiate for greater respect and understanding of our cultures, our societies, and ourselves. The only way we can call ourselves literate is to be writers of our own lives, of our own identity, and of our own destiny. We will not be literate if we allow all the ideas of dominant discourses to discriminate us, detour our thought patterns, and replace our rich linguistic inheritance.

CONCLUSION

The main argument in this chapter is that cultural literacy is a process by which productive knowledge is transmitted. Only when the negotiated classroom is in place then the dialogic relationship between various forms of cultural knowledge is exchanged. The process of mental decolonization is only possible when learners question and articulate their cultural differences as a way of making sense of their identity. Without basic cultural knowledge a learner continues to remain illiterate. The literary culture of Papua New Guinea is as important as traditional cultures. Most of us tend to think of culture as something that is traditional, oral, and that it consists of artifacts, songs, and dances. Culture is a generic term with many branches developing their own conditions of emergence. Whether we speak of culture as an orally transmitted knowledge or as a written expression of a society, we need to keep one thing in mind: *Culture is always in a flux and continues to accommodate the changing times and conditions.* As such it is impossible to argue that a total return to the ideal culture, the traditional past, or the village pastoral culture is necessary. On the contrary, a blending of the aspirations to retain culture and maintain continuity is challenged by the social, economic, and political needs of a particular community. In the formal education system, culture should form the basic tenet of education of a nation's youth who constitute a collective force to remould a nation in the vision of its educators and learners. A vision, expressed, for example in my "Date With Destiny" a mural poem on the wall leading to the University of Papua New Guinea students' mass.[40]

Our arrival is a celebration
From the time of our ancestors
To the moment of nationhood
In whatever visions we have
Our journey onward continues

Children of this land search
Every valley, rivers, and oceans
For the colours of every dream
They hold close to their hearts
The world must know you

Golden is our land
Embrace the time we have
The smiles of our souls
Drawn from a spring within
The depths of our hearts

The feast of our nation
Is sung in the tunes we know
Passed down from our ancestors
We can dance in a single rhythm
As a nation united in difference

Leaders in corridors of power
Discuss the destiny of this land
While we wait for tomorrow
Our hope is to be strong and free
From all forms of oppression

March on youths of this land
The end of the road is near
You will find on your path
The answer to your quests
It is your date with destiny.

3

TRANSITIONS AND TRANSFORMATIONS

Much of what I read influences my way of thinking and writing. I have read all works written by Papua New Guinean writers. My early reading of PNG writing in 1978 persuaded me to follow a literary life. Literature existed for me at that time as expressive arts, which in many ways were reflected in my active participation in school theatre performances. This served as the basis of my education and transition into the Papua New Guinean literary culture.

I first read PNG writing in 1978 as a Grade 7 student in St. Xavier's High School. Our school library had all the issues of the literary journals *Papua New Guinea Writing* and *Kovave*. I read these with avid interest. I read Paulias Matane's *Aimbe, the Challenger* and Vincent Eri's *The Crocodile*. Aimbe served as a cultural hero who took the challenge to learn new things and better himself. Aimbe was, for me, someone who was on a quest to know everything there was to know. Hoiri Sevese, the Moveave man in Vincent Eri's *The Crocodile*, was the typical character who shared the same fate as my grandfathers and father. He was forced into accepting his condition as a subject of colonialism and its aftermath of psychological rearrangement of the indigenous psyche to one of disillusionment, trauma, and paranoia. Hoiri is left to accept his psychological disturbance as natural, which to me has always been problematic. It reflects the general unquestioning attitude that we inherited from the colonisation experience and that affected my own parents' lives. I could not accept the conditions under which my parents lived as colonised subjects.

Creative narratives led me into accepting writing as the vessel of a life-long journey. Kumalau Tawali's 'The Bush Kanaka Speaks', for example, sparked off my interest in writing poetry. In that poem Tawali pokes fun at the colonisers for their outrageous sense of dilution or cultural rub-off from those they colonised:

The Kiap shouts at us
forcing the veins to stand out in his neck
nearly forcing the excreta out of his bottom
he says: you are ignorant

He says you are ignorant,
but can he shape a canoe,
tie a mast, fix an outrigger?
Can he steer a canoe through the night
without losing his way?
Does he know when a turtle comes ashore
to lay its eggs? ...

He says: you'll get sick
eating that fly-ridden food.
Haven't I eaten such food all my life,
and I haven't died yet?
Maybe his stomach is tender like a child's
born yesterday. I'm sure he couldn't
eat our food without getting sick.[1]

I admire Tawali for his courage to stand up and speak out against the colonisers for looking down on us as people needing their help.

Trevor Shearston challenged the false myth of the untainted world of the coloniser in his collection *Something in the Blood* (1979). This made me realise how twisted the experience of colonialism was and is in my life. Even today I am constantly troubled by the violence brought about by colonialism in Papua New Guinea. My distaste for that white mythology was greatly reinforced by John Kasaipwalova's 'The Reluctant Flame'. Kasaipwalova's fiery nationalism and call on us to explode like magma out of a volcano and fill the land with the lava of our experience as Papua New Guineans has remained a lasting image in my literary life:

Where is that flame!!! Where has it gone!!!
The acid in my heart kicks with volcanic tremors
My veins, my arteries, they bulge with swelling resentment
I tremble in frenzy to smash open
To let the acid, the fire and the boulder in my throat
Spew outwards into every direction of havoc cyclone and
Thunder! ...

Green mountains will boast their size and their forgiveness
A passing eye will sing their permanency and solidness
But inside each mountain lies a tiny flame cradled and weighted
by above
People will live, people will die
But the tiny flame will grow its arms and legs very slowly
Until one day its volcanic pulse will tear the green mountain apart
To allow pent up blood flow and congested vomit spit freely.[2]

The power of this poem is its challenge to my generation to speak up without fear of punishment or shame of being who we are. Colonialism has created a permanent place in our conscience through its repressive ideological apparatuses. As a generation of Papua New Guineans born in the colonial period and celebrating independence we have a responsibility to question the values of colonialism. We must erase the stigma born of the colonised experience.

In addition to Kasaipwalova I came across the writings of Frantz Fanon, Ngugi wa Thiong'o, Chinua Achebe, Richard Wright, Ralph Ellison, Langston Hughes and others with similar experiences. They had a significant effect on my work. As a young writer I realised that there were many people in the world with a similar history of struggles to mine.

In the late 1980s and early 1990s the call for the decolonising of the mind had become an empowering one for me. Ngugi, for instance, inspired me to write about what I experienced and in the style that I chose to write in. At the same time I realised that writing alone was not enough. I chose to teach at the university where I could have the space and opportunity to write and articulate my experiences. I had to go beyond the B.A. degree in literature, philosophy and history. I wrote and published my work while I studied for a Masters degree in New Zealand and a Ph.D. in the USA. It was more of a challenge to continue writing while pursuing my academic interests.

Consistently in my reading and writing I have explored the various genres available in literature. I am comfortable writing poetry, short prose and essays. I began writing in 1983 as a student in Aiyura National High School. The Education Department allowed schools to offer optional courses beside the main core subjects. My optional subject was Creative Writing. In that course I read *Hamlet, Nineteen Eighty Four, The Lord of the Flies*, and *The Old Man and the Sea*. One of the assignments in that course was to write a poem. I had no idea of the difference between a poem and a short story. My attempt at writing poetry turned out to be a short story of a quarter of a page. The subjects of my stories were childhood life and stories I had heard as a child in my village. A lot of short stories published in *Papua New Guinean Writing* and *Kovave* were about village life and about the changing urban environment, which I felt drawn to. The immediate impulse was to write similar narratives that captured my own experiences.

Drawing on real-life experiences I infused imaginative ones into the stories. My first short story, 'A Good Man's Death', about village life was published in the literary magazine *Ondobondo* when I entered the University of Papua New Guinea in 1984. This story was the one that was supposed to be a poem. My first published piece in *Ondobondo*, however, was a poem, 'Shriveled Shrine in a Smoke Crowned House'. In this poem I explored my cultural and social world. Most of the early poems written at this time were published in *The PNG Writer*, published by the Papua New Guinea Writers Union, and in *Bikmaus* and *Sope*, journals published by the Institute of Papua New Guinea Studies. This phase of my literary life was one of discovery and experimentation with forms and structures of poetry. 'The Dancer' is one such poem:

> In solitude with the spirits
> A silhouette
> Dances against the blaze
> Letting words and chants re-echo.
> Fingertips of flames
> Race to every part
> Calling sleepers to return
> To life with the dancer.
>
> As the fingers of flame
> Returned to the beat of the drum
> The dancer sweated and panted.
> Sweat fire, breathe smoke
> Sleepers awake! Join the dance.[3]

The University of Papua New Guinea with its literature courses, literary activities such as the Ondobondo recital nights, the *Ondobondo* magazine, and the centre for visiting writers opened up the world of literature to me. I read my poetry alongside elders such Kumalau Tawali, Arthur Jawodimbari, John Waiko, John Wills Teloti Kaniku, Nora Vagi Brash, Russell Soaba, Bernard Kaspou and William Takaku. In later years I came to meet Paulias Matane, Vincent Eri, Michael Somare, Rabbie Namaliu and Bernard Narokobi. It was the time I came to share in the emergence of a new generation of writers including Regis Stella, Nash Sorariba, Loujaya Kouza Dunar, Adam Delaney, Sam Ngwele (the Vanuatu writer), Gideon Ginkawa, Jacob Kila Harry, Toby Kagl, Michael Mel, Joyce Kumbeli and William Tagis.

The decision to make the study of literature a career began after my first international exposure as a Papua New Guinean writer in 1986. I attended the First World Black Literatures conference organised by the University of Queensland. I also attended the Association for the Study of Australian Literature conference in James Cook University. I read my poetry in both places alongside renowned writers such as Sonia Sanchez, Daniel Kunene, Faith Bandler, Archie Weller, Garry Bostock, Thea Astley, Mark O'Connor, Antigone Kefala and Dimitris Tsaloumus from Australia and around the world. I also met inspiring postgraduate students of literature who encouraged me to pursue literary studies as a career. My journey into the literary culture of Papua New Guinea grew out of a passion for what I do best — writing — and out of an insatiable appetite for intellectually creative experiences as a writer-scholar in the Pacific. The 1980s for me was exciting because of the literary and cultural activities of the period. There was the National Literature Competition organised by the Institute of Papua New Guinea Studies, the National Broadcasting Commission's drama and young people's program, various cultural festivals, touring drama performances by established theatre groups, and the opportunities to publish in *Ondobondo*, *The PNG Writer* and *Bikmaus*. All three journals have now folded.

My first collection of poetry, *Lomo'ha I Am, in Spirit's Voice I Call* was published in 1991 by the South Pacific Creative Arts Society, Fiji. The opportunity to have my first collection published came about with the support of Ron and Marjorie Crocombe. I had met Ron Crocombe at the University of New South Wales in 1988 when I attended a conference on Australia's relationship with the South Pacific. When my collection of poetry came out I was then studying for a Masters degree in English at the University of Canterbury, New Zealand. It took another ten years before the Institute of Pacific Studies published my second collection of poetry, *Hembemba: Rivers of the Forest* (2001). This collection was prepared during the period of my doctoral studies at the University of Minnesota. The poems in the collection were written in New Zealand, Papua New Guinea, and the USA.

My first collection of poetry reflected some of the themes and issues that confronted me at that time. To make sense of my life as a writer who was part of a literary tradition and a colonised history, I made reference to earlier PNG and Pacific writers. For example, the poem 'Different Histories' contained a reference to Albert Wendt's *Sons for the Return Home* and Russell Soaba's *Wanpis*; to Steven my 'The Missionary and the Unpainted Mask' to Leo Hannet's story 'Disillusionment With Priesthood'; and 'Today Reluctant Warrior' to Kasaipwalova's 'The Reluctant Flame' and Kumalau Tawali's 'Monument'. These references suggest that my work has to be viewed in relation to such works and others that have transformed my thinking about the world that I live in today.

I share the view of Chinua Achebe that whatever language I use must bear the burden of my experience. Most of my work is written in English, but I allow that language to bear the burden of other languages that I speak. English provides the structure of literary experience by which I am able to create a tapestry of my experience. In *Hembemba: Rivers of the Forest* the importance of language in my work stands out more clearly. A whole section is written in Tok Pisin with translations provided alongside the poems. I also attempted for the first time writing in Nagum Boiken, my mother tongue. It is difficult for me to express myself fully in my mother tongue. This is a result of learning English at the age of nine and using it more throughout my entire education. But English will have to coexist with the other languages that I use in my life. The coexistence has proved more productive and opened up a lot of possibilities in my literary experience. It reflects the postcolonial hybridity that is ever-present in contemporary Papua New Guinea.

The concern with language is also captured in my poem 'Nais Moa'. The Tok Pisin version of 'Nais Moa' is in one stanza whereas the English translation is in two:

Olsem long draipela san taim em i stap long opis
Dispela mama i wok hat tru long pulim pis
Na watpo bai prais i go daun long wanem
Em i gat inklis na work long opis i gat ekon
Ating sapos mama Tok pisin long yu
Olsem meri Hailens i save salim buai long
Gerehu maket bai yu save pasin bilong maket
I no olsem pasin bilong opis.

The woman who speaks English forgets
That she is not in her office
The market mother sweats her guts fishing
Why should the price be lower
Because she speaks English
And works in an air-conditioned office?

Perhaps if this mother speaks Tok Pisin
Like the Highlands betel nut vendor
At Gerehu market she will know
The market trade is not like the office.[4]

Compositions in both languages, with their conscious structural differences, are a way of reflecting all my experiences; they are necessary to the process of self-definition.

I am very conscious as a writer and scholar of inheriting a legacy of cultural capital from a body of writing that represents a successful first literary emergence in the Pacific. It's a legacy that successive generations can use to understand, develop and transform themselves. The references in my poetry to other PNG writing that has influenced me help build a bridge of the creative spirit and reinforce the sense of a relationship to a community of writers. Through such interactions we come to view ourselves collectively as a unique group of people.

Albert Maori Kiki's *Ten Thousand Years in a Lifetime* (1968) began the transformation by representing the self involved in linking various fragments of cultures, belief systems, historical conditions and transitional experiences among the Papua New Guineans who built a nation in their own vision. The process of transformation was consolidated in Vincent Serei Eri's *The Crocodile* (1971), with its description of Hoiri's transition from an innocent villager to one who discovers that the world outside Moveave is a difficult and alienating experience. Eri captures a society caught up in the web of social, political, cultural, and economic change. Entrapment, disillusionment and betrayal are the consequences of a society making a transition from its precolonial to a postcolonial stage. These books share one powerful message: how have we imagined ourselves as a nation? Did we end up like Maori Kiki or like Hoiri in the last chapter of Eri's book? Papua New Guineans have continued to tackle these questions in the literary culture they have produced over the succeeding years.

Rabbie Namaliu and John Kasaipwalova are said to have quickly realised that drama and fiction can be used as 'a basis for commentary on their country and the new nationalism, with particular reference to colonialism as they understood it'. Kiki and Matane achieved the status of 'grand old men of letters' while Kasaipwalova and Soaba assumed the role of 'token rebellious youth'. But such labels served to pamper their creative impulses more than to build up the recognition accorded by any nation to its writers. Papua New Guinea has forgotten its early writers. They have been abandoned, just as happens to the character Jimmy Damebo, the writer-figure in Soaba's *Wanpis*. The death of the Jimmy Damebo in *Wanpis* can be viewed as signifying the death of any serious support for the development of literary culture in Papua New Guinea. The birth of PNG literature in the late 1960s and its development in the early 1970s had the full support of the Administration of the Territory of Papua New Guinea. In Papua New Guinea today the scenario is one of neglect. Access to publishing opportunities, writing grants and support groups is very limited in Papua New Guinea. Russell Soaba often reminds me that the life of a Papua New Guinean writer is a difficult one because the society itself is a difficult one.

Those who attended school in the 1970s were fortunate enough to read the literature produced by the early PNG writers. The student readers of this literature became the second generation of writers. In the early years of my writing life I often felt the responsibility of bridging the literary gap between the first generation of writers and my generation. The uniqueness of my generation is that we wrote out of the need to make sense of ourselves, our lives, and our history. I see writing as a way of contributing to the development and understanding of my society. I write out of the need to make sense of the world that I found myself in. Coming from a village society to one that is modern, I have had to adjust to the changing times. I am conscious of being a university-educated member of my community. If I have to contribute anything to my society it has to be my writings. I feel that I have to give back something valuable and lasting. I see this in literature. I want to see that the generation after me reads what I have written in the same way I read early PNG writings.

These days I associate myself with the South Pacific region community of writers, most of whom I have met and most of whose works I have read. They include Albert Wendt, Vilsoni Hereniko, Epeli Hau'ofa, Konai Helu Thaman, Jully Makini (née Sipolo), Sam Alasia, Julian Ma'aka, Subramani, Vanessa Griffin, Sia Figiel, Regis Stella, Caroline Sinavaiana, Nora Vagi Brash, Satendra Nandan, Sudesh Mishra, Larry Thomas, John Pule, Russell Soaba, Teresia Teawa and Sam Ngwele. Through my association with such writers I am able to contribute to the expressions of a regionally collective community that strengthens the position of South Pacific literature as the newest literature in the world.

The journey one makes to become a writer and live as a writer is a lonely and often a misunderstood one. But from the beginning I made up my mind to build my life as a writer. I wanted to be a good writer who can write works that are read by many people. Writing is for me the only way I can have control over my life. And I have constantly reminded myself that I would not die like Jimi Damebo.

4

CONSTRUCTING INDIGENOUS POETICS

This chapter considers the construction of Papua New Guinea through written poetry. Poetry is used to paint new perspectives of the world. In their efforts to describe their worlds Papua New Guineans used poetic forms present in their societies. The writers considered in this chapter appropriated traditional poetic forms, songs, chants, and cultural expressions to give new meanings to the experiences of growing up in a society undergoing sporadic changes in ways of life and belief systems. In many ways through poetry Papua New Guineans attempt to locate their epistemological base to begin thinking about their own systems of thought and knowledge about the world.

NATACHEE: PNG POET LAUREATE

Allan Natachee, the PNG "Poet Laureate" published a collection of traditional poetry in 1965. The collection entitled *Aia, Mekeo Songs* was published under the banner of Papua Pocket Poets. The collection features Mekeo war songs that Natachee remembered from his childhood.[1] Natachee translated these Mekeo songs into English after his meeting with Ulli Beier in Port Moresby. *Aia* is translated as God. *Aia* is a traditional mythical figure`living alive and living forever, `above the water', and `above the darkness!' According to the Mekeo, *Aia* is the creator of the earth and their homes.

The poet grew up as an orphan in a nuns' convent. The Mekeo influence in his poetry flows out from his early childhood with the people of Amoamo village. Natachee's sense of poetry was picked up from listening to his grandfathers hum everyday. Natachee is at peace whenever he sings these songs in his Mekeo language. He says: "I loved very much to sing with rustle of leaves of the nearby coconut palms and the betel nut trees." He is also the son of a peace chief of Amoamo. The first song is called *Falaela*, sung about traditional war:

Aia kearaie vea	Aia walks on the road
Aia iv ruvuai	Aia all naked
Kearai e vea	Aia walks on the read.[2]

Mekeo poetry is sung with the intensity and senses of traditional rhymes. His "Love Charm" consists of three lines, but is effective in its performance in the traditional context:

> I shall come and enter your heart, woman!
> Leaf of *kapok* shall entice you!
> Weeping leaf of *kapok* shall entice you.[3]

The first line 'I shall come and enter your heart' refers to the spiritual possession in the subject. The subject in this case is the person to whom the charmer directs his utterance. It is assumed a 'leaf of *kapok*' is used as a sacred cultural plant evoking magical utterance targeting a particular person. The powers of the *kapok* leaf 'shall entice you.'

Natachee's knowledge of the Mekeo society is registered in "The Sun God". "The Sun God" is narrated in the third person. It is about the sensuous relationship between man and spirits. In this case Kirope Karope is the Sun God. The man in this poem is referred to as 'Enemy', which the Sun God crippled and buried. His grave remains the mystical place the narrator is searching for in the last stanza. Kirope Karope, the Sun God is said to bury him (the enemy) in the sky, after chasing him to the East and West. The obvious pattern evolving in traditional poetry is very clear. The first few lines are general in their approach. The climax of poetry is reached towards the end of the recital.

The climax is reached through repetitive lines, which makes the poetry rhythmic and enjoyable. Natachee is said to be 'fascinated' with the English language. He had written all his verse in English, but with direct cultural influences from his Mekeo society.[4] Natachee has appropriated the English language with his own Mekeo tradition to create a unique style of poetry. Indeed, whether Natachee understood such an approach for the construction of his poetry is another matter. Natachee was conscious of his role as a poet: "I confess I am a poet in my own right because those who know me intimately will tell you that I am a lover of music. There is always music in my heart, musical in my political and public life and music is poetry."[5] If music is poetry and has political implication, then Natachee has simply achieved the ultimate goal of the postcolonial poet as someone who insists on writing in his own language and contexts. Poetry is a unique form of performance that Natachee used as an instrument of "music and peace of mind."[6]

Traditional poetry has different functions and performative conditions. Some concentrate on a lamenting pattern where each verse is a complete story. Sometimes the rhythm is in the form of repetitions, which is important to stress a deep feeling, for instance of sorrow at losing a child. The important aspect of traditional poetry is the warm relationship between man, nature, and the supernatural world of Melanesians. The mythical and natural worlds are formed

Allan Natachee's poetry collection: *Aia* published in 1965.

as one through the performance of poetry and song. Natachee demonstrates the special feature of traditional poetry in his writings. These features include repetition of words, themes of everyday lives, and the supernatural and their inter-reactions with mankind. Peace and harmony are achieved in performance poetry.

Natachee was a fascinating men according to Ulli Beier: "Natachee's English versions cannot capture, of course, the hypnotic effect of the chanting by his elders, but they do achieve a serenity and stark beauty that forms an extraordinary contrast to the bathos of Natachee's own celebration of the atomic age."[7]

SIGNS IN THE SKY

Kumalau Tawali is one of the greatest poets of Papua New Guinea. Tawali took up poetry as a genre to represent his experiences as a Papua New Guinean. Through poetry Tawali made the transition from being a 'bush kanaka" in his Manus province to an educated tribesman in the country. Tawali published his first poem "The Bush Kanaka Speaks" in 1968—one of the earliest indigenous expressions of feisty anticolonial sentiment ever recorded in the Pacific.[7] Tawali had lived up to his reputation as one of the greatest Papua New Guinean poet. He published numerous poems during his life-time. His first collection of poems *Signs in the Sky* (1970)[8] was published to a very receptive audience: "his poetry is made by art and intended ultimately to be enjoyed as art... Tawali, a son of Melanesia, is a poet of the pacific seascape and delicate nuances."[9]

To discuss Papua New Guinea poetry without making reference to Tawali's work makes our discussion mediocre. In many ways Tawali had remained true to the poetry genre until his death in the turn of the century. He had published two collections of poetry. The first collection *Signs in the Sky* (1970) was followed by the second collection *Tribesman's Heartbeats* (1978).[10] The first collection was published five years before Independence arrived in Papua New Guinea. The second collection was published three years after Independence. In the second collection he affirms the views he held at that time. Tawali uses poetry to transmit important messages of hope: "That message ...is to awaken the people of this nation and the Pacific to face the forces which now threaten their lives as a free people."[11] The reference here is to colonialism, militarianism, and various forms of Eurocentrism in the Pacific. Like a fearless leader, he tells his people to be strong and free: "It is, and will be, a continuous struggle, which asks for sacrifices to be made now in time of peace, before it is too late for us. The sacrifice is the sacrifice of our pride, hatred and fear. This I take to be supreme task of those who love their land and thirst deeply for peace and unity."[12]

The prophetic visions of Tawali expressed here had concerned him for as long as he had lived. He loved his people, culture, and land so much that his poetry changed little in their concerns even after the 1978 publication. The love of the land and the pride of the Indigenous traditions had the strongest impact in Tawali's life. Tawali wants all educated Papua New Guineans to revisit their traditions and knowledge systems to reequip themselves to resist the temptations of the modern world. He calls for writers to perform the function of being "the conscience, the inspiration and the prophets of a new world order" without submitting themselves to a process of total assimilation or subjection.[13] Tawali's own life moved from the radical nationalist in the early student days in the 1970s to the more active participant in the Western Christian culture in his later years. One would ask how Tawali would contradict himself. The very person who dismissed the Western colonizers way in 1968 had now joined forces with the Westerners to reinforce their belief system imposed on Papua New Guineans. How did Tawali balance himself in his cultural psychology then?

Tawali always maintained his locatedness in the Manus culture and another in the modern changing Papua New Guinea. He says: "I therefore believe that those who have offered their artistic might to the remaking of their nation should burn with revolutionary flames to lead their nation and humanity into fresh thinking and living."[14]

The remaking of a nation is a powerful process of conscious constructions in artistic and ideological terms. The reimagining of the nation, community, tribe, and state has to come from those who constitute it, from those who attest to the affirmation of a common belief, cause, and vision. The constructions of the kind of nation its constituents want is manifest in their constitution in the first instance, but is displayed in the diverse social, cultural, and political activities that a community actively pursues to achieve such a goal.

In his life, Tawali pursued, like other contemporary Papua New Guineans, the remaking of the nation, through artistic and intellectual activities. He remained committed to the project of reimagining the nation in its transition from a colonial society to a postcolonial nation state. Outside of the two published collections he published various poems in the literary journals of Papua New Guinea. Tawali had a mural wall poem celebrating 50,000 years of civilization in New Guinea. Some of these individual creative productions have more power as single poems to radically alter the perceptions, mind sets, and transform consciousness of Papua New Guineans. He also became active in the intellectual production of some of the ideals of national discourse and pan-regionalism. He worked as a lecturer in philosophy at the University of Papua New Guinea at one point, teaching a course in Melanesian philosophy.

THE BUSH KANAKA SPEAKS

In his 1968 poem "The Bush Kanaka Speaks", he had fore-shadowed the important tasks of educating the Europeans about Melanesian ways and indigenous knowledge systems:

> The Kiap shouts at us
> forcing the veins to stand out in his neck
> nearly forcing the excreta out of his bottom
> he says: you are ignorant
>
> He says: you are ignorant,
> but can he shape a canoe,
> tie a mast, fix an outrigger?
> Can he steer a canoe though the night
> without losing his way?
> Does he know when a turtle comes ashore
> to lay its eggs?

Kumalau Tawali's poetry collection: *Signs in the Sky* (1970)

The kiap shouts at us
forcing the veins to stand out in his neck
nearly forcing the excreta out of his bottom
he says: you are dirty

He says we live in dirty rubbish houses.
Has he ever lived in one?
Has he enjoyed the sea breeze
blowing through the windows?
and the cool shade under the pandanus thatch?
Let him keep his iron roof, shinning in the sun,
cooking him inside, bleaching his skin white.

The Kiap shouts at us
forcing the veins to stand out in his neck
nearly forcing the excreta out of his bottom
he says: you'll get sick.

He says: you'll get sick
eating that fly-ridden food.
Haven't I eaten such food all my life
and I haven't died yet?
Maybe his stomach is tender like a child's

born yesterday. I'm sure he couldn't
eat our food without getting sick.

Every white man the gorment sends us
forces his veins out shouting
nearly forcing the excreta out of his bottom
shouting: you bush kanaka.

He says: you ol les man!
Yet he sits on a soft chair and does nothing
just shouts, eats, drinks, eats, drinks,
like a woman with a child in her belly.
These white men have no bones.
If they tried to fight us without their musiket
they'd surely cover their faces like women.[15]

These are sharp distinctions between the Papua New Guinean tribal living and European way of life, manners, and attitudes. The binary oppositional reality between western and non-western cultures is brought out in this poem at the dawn of nationalism in Papua New Guinea. Tawali, Kasaipwalova, Waiko, Hannet, Eri, Soaba, Benjamin Umba, August Kituai, Nora Vagi Brash, Peter Kama Kerpi, Earnest Mararunga, Kiki, and others of that era pounded the Australian administration with powerful imagery, contrasting the writers' cultures with that of the European colonizers. The concern with privileging the Indigenous cultures and knowledge systems filled the artistic and intellectual activities of the period. The 'Bush Kanaka' spoke hard and in a language that was heard and understood by the colonizer.

In the years that followed Independence Tawali and others moved into the gear of nation building through active participation as teachers, bureaucrats, and politicians. The literary and artistic activities took the back stage; a development that left observers of literature and arts in Papua New Guinea musing over its discontinuity in later years. Few writers like Tawali, Soaba, Waiko, Kadiba, and Kasaipwalova continue writing and publishing their works, without having any major impact on the cultural scene in Papua New Guinea. The problem seems to lie in the shift from prophetic mode to the pragmatics of nation-building. Writers too realized that the dream for independence was achieved sooner than expected. The immediate challenge was to build that imagined community, the nation that was formed without bloodshed or a major coup, one which at its dawn was still gathering its fragmented parts, all too diverse and varied in their individuality, yet malleable enough to acquire the shape its artists, writers, intellectuals, and political elites imagined.

In his second collection of poems *Tribesman's Heartbeats* (1978) Tawali acknowledges the significant contributions the arts and writing made to the emergence of the nation of Papua New Guinea. In the poem "In Gratitude" Tawali is grateful to have been part of a literary culture that had accomplished the goals young Papua New Guineans envisioned in the process of literary representations about themselves:

> The whispers of your inspiration
> Have, like the refreshing voice of thunder
> after the dry season,
> Brought rain to the buried seeds of a force
> Which now blossoms mightily,
> And shall herald the hidden strength and colour
> Of those unseen and unheard
> Chants and charms,
> Those life-giving proverbs,
> Those drum rhythms,
> Those haunting songs
> And those other unwritten,
> Shall now stand on two feet,
> And carry the mystery of a nation.[16]

This poem is also a reference to another contemporary of Tawali, John Kasaipwalova, whose fiery poem "The Reluctant Flame" was one of the most widely read and powerful poem created during the period of PNG literary vogue in the late 1960s and early 1970s.[17] Such an acknowledgment suggests that Tawali and other PNG writers were writing simultaneous histories and parallel lives in the future they imagined outside of the colonial shadows. They also read what their contemporaries wrote. In the poem "The Final Battle" Tawali writes:

> Titanic forces of global magnitude,
> Economic, ideological and perverted
> Now upon us creep treacherously,
> Gripping our given treasures,
> And squeezing hungrily from us
> The fire of life,
> That joy of yesterday's simplicity
> Leaving us rootless victims
> To a world of lifelessness.
> O children of your fathers' greatness,

Will you choose in yourselves
To be reduced to nothingness?
Or is there left in us
That eternal touch of spiritual prowess,
Which will rise
From the depth of our listening souls,
And burn to oblivion
The temples of dark alien forces in our hearts,
And mould unbuyable men—
The true fighters of the new state.[18]

The Tawali we encountered in the 1960s had become the leader of the cultural survival fighters in the new nation. These fighters are the educated elites of Papua New Guinea positioned precariously between a tradition about to change in a radical way as it confronts the powerful forces of globalization, influenced by global theories of economics and ideological persuasions. The watchful Tawali warns his followers to attend to cultural consciousness and adhere to the ways of knowledge present in the traditional societies of Papua New Guinea. The awareness of the trauma and disenfranchisement of people experiencing sweeping change is the only way to handle the imposition of new ideas and ways of doing things. In Tawali's eyes, accepting these changes must go hand in hand with self-respect and open-ended conscience guided by the spirit of the *Constitution* of the Independent State of Papua New Guinea. In the poem "Joy of Togetherness" Tawali expresses the spirit of the community again:

Simple folk of yesterday
Did work in peace and joy of a kind,
Joy of a kind that came from togetherness.
And no minding of how much to produce,
But enough as is promised for the day.
And no demand for more and more
That leads to blinding exploitation,
Which annihilates the powerful, delicate
Will of this.[19]

One of the most memorable poems in Tawali's 1978 publication is "Who Holds the Steer?"[20] Tawali is at his best in using the imageries drawn from his Manus cultural and maritime environment to make a statement about the future of the country he helped to form as a writer. The question posed in the poem is about the leadership and wisdom of those who will lead the country onward. He writes:

A canoe now sets for sailing,
Her sails hang like huge claws in the calm
lagoon.
I hear the sounds of its conch shell,
And the voices of the men
Who will sail it through unknown waters.
May they travel back in hearts and minds,
Our ancient seafarers millenniums before Cook,
Their compasses, the stars, winds, tides
and currents,
But above all each other.
That canoe out there has not even lifted
its anchor,
Yet its crew are at each other's throat.
Not in mutiny,
But as to who should hold the steer.
I, the old man who sees into the past
And into the future,
See storms out there to fight
And treacherous reefs
With their ceaseless mocking smiles to avoid.
They must decide.
The evening sky is blotted out.
The anchor has come aboard.
They will sail.
Careful, careful, O youth of adventurers,
The sea has a voice
According to our ancient literature,
And it must be listened to.
"Togetherness, togetherness,"
Says the voice in the still sunset sky,
"That is your secret."[20]

Tawali has, since, taken a back stage in most of his life working as a theologian and teacher in a Christian college until his death. He stood back and watched the country move through the many challenges of a new postcolonial society, from a calm society into the open rough seas. Political changes and leadership became stranded on the reef of the sea. Papua New Guinea changed from a new nation of hope to one struggling with issues of national definitions, political uncertainties, and a society that brought itself into a postcolonial nightmare of corruption, greed, and a state tested by the winds of changing political climate around it.

Tawali's poetry is like the endearing call of the Chauka, a special bird in his Manus society as featured in the poem "The Heart-Beat of the Tribesmen."[21] It is like the familiar sound of the conch shell or the tribesman's heartbeat that keeps a tribe in check, a community in secured environment, and with its members playing their part in maintaining peace and harmony. The chants, the stories, the ancient knowledge, and the wisdom of its elders and ancestors, all form the bedrock of a society build in strength and cultural values able to stand the test of time. Whether Tawali is writing about his own Manus society or Papua New Guinea, or the South Pacific Island communities, there is always the sense that Tawali's poetry is drawn from the depths of the seas and the colours of the reefs around it, making poetry feel like a soothing advice or sound wisdom to guide travellers on a journey of discovery and arrival at the destiny of one's vision. In his final poem "The Reflections" Tawali inscribes the rules of nation building:

Untamed mountain peaks
And rivers wild and swift,
This land of a thousand tribes,
Its two million give it life
In colorful, mighty colourful tongues;
All this wealth, stirs in my soul
a patriotic cry.

I tremble for a land
Which now stands in full measure on its feet
And drums to the world it birth.
But with *taim bihain* [future] to be unfolded,
I cry out.

O are there eyes to see
And prophesy the pure truth
Of a land whose hope must lie
In passionate humility
To reach that assured destinations!

O my people, do you see
Through the great creator's mirror...
The reflection of a nation amongst nations,
Steered by statesmen of consecrated
and dirt-free hearts,
Whose low lives must grow like huge tropical suns,
To give growth to a land unshakable![22]

This poem remained buried in the pages of Tawali's second and only collection published three years after PNG Independence. Such timeless advice and foresight would have guided Papua New Guineans to develop a sense of internal self-consciousness as a society, listening to the advice and wisdom of its seers and poets. Tawali died without being heard or read by Papua New Guineans, even those who are highly educated with university degrees. Most Papua New Guineans who pass through the universities have never read the writings of Papua New Guinean poets, novelists, or scholars. The thoughts and words of Tawali are written in slabs as guiding rules of nation building.

WELI NIMOU: AN INDIGENOUS POETIC DISCOURSE

Paschal Waisi published *Weli Nimou*, a collection of poetry in the 1980s.[23] Waisi's poetry attempts to bridge the indigenous poetic discourses with contemporary poetic forms. Waisi's little known collection of poetry is a fine example of work drawing inspirations from traditional poetic forms. The work is based on his experiences in Lau'um, a linguistic group in the Lumi district of the Sandaun Province of Papua New Guinea. The collection makes use of basic sayings and expressions of women in Lau'um. Waisi's work has its roots in the Laufi culture. The Laufi society is made up of Lau'um speakers of the Olo language. The work reflects a philosophical view held by the Laufis.[24]

The *Weli Nimou* poetic form is based on Lau'um women's empirical experiences. "Weli Nimou" means 'torchlight'. The Olympian torchlight is a metaphor for light and guiding moral principles in the Laufi world. The Laufi chant the *Weli Nimou* during times of feasting, singing, and dancing. The *Weli Nimou* provides light for them to attend singing and dancing before returning home.[25] The torchlight is likened to the guiding principles of the country enshrined in the National Constitution of PNG.

Waisi presents the unique experiences of his people through poetry in concert with his scholarly interests on Melanesian philosophy as espoused in his scholarly work: *The Laufis World-View: An Attempt to Locate its Metaphysical Base* (1982).[26] The bases on which the Laufis understand the mythical, ancestral, and environmental cosmos is through their own indigenous epistemological concept called *Pingis*.[27] The full understanding of the spiritual world in relation to the ability to prepare gardens, hunt, tell seasons, making gardens, harvesting, and hunting of animals is expected of all the members of the society. Villagers also have to know the names of animals, plants, trees, insects, mountains, and rivers. Knowledge, as Waisi explains, is also the skillful remembrance of the clan history, the recitation of myths, legends, and the genealogy of the clan.[28]

Waisi writes about the spiritual affiliation the Laufis have with their spirits' worlds. In "A Mother's Lament" Waisi reconstructs an oral chant in English:

'I' walk in the bush in bare feet.
—saw no spirit
'I' walk through the 'black forest'
—saw no Being
'I' wash 'my' body in mind
—'My' mourning garment

Memories of 'my' loved one
-passed away on a faraway plantation
—lingers on in 'my dream
—see vivid and strong his spirit vomit blood
'I' ask: Can this world 'I' am in now
—Seeing immediately turn on its head.[29]

The chant is about the grief experienced by a Laufi woman on losing her loved one. The woman is grieving over her husband who left her stranded to face the world alone. In her lament she seeks a reunion. Originally it is a love chant: *Nouti Munge*, chanted about a husband's death on a plantation:

she 'walk the bush with bare feet'
'through the black forest'

Her sorrow could possibly,
'turn this' world'
'on its head.'[30]

Waisi selects the theme of women's experiences within the Laufi's perspectives. In "Childbirth Lament" Waisi portrays the pain and endurance of childbirth as expressed by women in his society:

'I wailed and 'I' wailed,
Till the sunsets,
'I' long for the rope to hang 'myself'
'I' want to communicate the pain,
But no one would listen
Bring 'me' the bark of a 'yelu' tree
strain the bark in water and wash 'me'
Fetch some water from the gentlemen's house
Whose 'evil' spirits haunt and hold up 'my' delivery
Bring all the children 'I' have closer
Let them see 'me' in 'my' departure
For 'I' will not nurse the life's pleasure.[31]

The poem has the power to move the reader with deep emotions. It is about a woman's anxiety about going through childbirth experience again. She longs to die and free herself from the painful experience. In the poem, the woman in labour pains is also the victim of male sorcery and subjugation in Waisi's society. In the poem: 'Humanity', Waisi looks at the subjection of women in Papua New Guinea. He paints the picture of the domesticity and low views men have of women in many Melanesian societies:

> This bedrock of defined role
> Strips one part of her soul
> Day and night she cooks for him
> While he chews betel nut and be merry
> The children she carries to wash sago
> She returns with child on top of her load,
> Her back heavy with pain
> The night she lay awake massaging her back
> Talk to her about reciprocity
> Talk to her about humanity
> This talk is too 'heavy'
> This talk is too mysterious.[32]

The collection is a stunning presentation of traditional chants written in contemporary poetry forms. Waisi's poetry is embedded right in the core of sociocultural relationship among men and women of the Lau'um society. Waisi's poetry is drawn from the experiences of his own people in the Lumi district. Using the vicarious experiences of people he creates chants that are about people's lived experiences. Through the process of writing these Waisi re-presents these experiences in a way that resonates the experiences of others in Papua New Guinea.

Elements of humour are intertwined with a love scene in some of the poems. This is carefully threaded with metaphor and figurative languages. Waisi presents sexual scenes in disguised poetic language. Open discussions of sexuality are prohibited in Waisi's society. It is offensive and creates disharmony and unacceptable social behaviours. In public performance the reciter employs the use of metaphor, allusions, images, parables to describe the secret world of human sexual relationships. In 'First Blood', Waisi constructs humour with an actual experience:

> A husband walks into her bedroom
> Ask her to smoke in a happy mood
> Were it not for the light from the moon

She would have mistaken him for someone new
And would have chased him with a broom
They stayed on smoking through the night
They had never smoked in their life,
They continue exploring without the light
Morning came the wife saw her first blood.[33]

The references to sex are slight, but effective: "'they continued exploring without the light" and "morning came the wife saw her first blood". Waisi is skillful in his evocative use of language and creates new expressions that remain memorable. The selected expressions are evocative of the experience described, whilst enabling the writer to go beyond the immediate cultural boundaries of his work. Waisi uses metaphor and other figures of speech in his poetry in effective ways.

The beauty of language lies in the careful usage of language without compromising the cultural innuendoes. Poetic language is beautiful and much cherished if metaphors and similes are incorporated. Memorable of these metaphors are the following: 'Exploring without the light' — to describe the sexual intercourse between a man and the woman; "Her first blood" — expressing the act of deflowering of a virgin and 'They have never smoked in their life', which expresses the idea that the couple never had sex before in their lives. Waisi also uses images like: "Shape like eagle egg", "Like a bird of paradise", "like a cowboy in Hollywood", "Like the symbol on *limbun* wall", and "Men act like clowns". These are borrowed images linking the traditional indigenous world with the outside world as members become exposed to the modern western culture. Lexical borrowing and appropriating common expressions and everyday metaphors are normal processes of linguistic growth and enrichment.

The uses of metaphors in Waisi's work establish a rich source of poetic syntax. In the Laufi society, rich metaphors and figures of speech allow a philosophical and expressive dimension in their viewing of the cosmos. The world around them is viewed through a poetic or symbolic representation of concrete images. Through poetry the Laufi construct a deeper knowledge of their concrete and metaphysical world. The Laufi men also become imaginative in their everyday dealings and social exchanges. They construct their experiences in song or poetry. Waisi uses this process to create his poetry without letting imaginations supersede the empirical experiences. Waisi also borrows similar experiences from other cultures to help explain what his views are. There is no distortion as far as the meaning of a poem goes.

The *Weli Nimou* allusion to the great Olympic Torch links the Western culture with the Laufi world. The young man who tries his luck on a girl is rejected. She thinks 'he dresses like a cowboy in Hollywood'. Other instances of appropriation are 'one single 'B' minor tract' of a symphony and the reference to the 'Holy waters spring'. The borrowing of non-Laufi terms strengthens the power of his poetic expressions. The continuous use of traditional images from his own Lau'um language and the syntactic borrowing from other languages opens up new ways of looking at something or other ways of describing an experience.

Poetry in the traditional culture are composed and recited to suit the moods and the situation of the composer or reciter. The reciter can invent and recreate certain atmosphere to suit the time of the recital, audience's taste, reception, and other expectations. The reciter also selects and finds materials that have beautiful and rhythmic sounds that appeal to his audience. By rewriting traditional poetry Waisi uses images and allusions to suit the desires of his readers. In his poem: 'Becoming', Waisi employs an interesting technique. He repeats the last syllables of each line.

Moto wape naule nulu ku
(a real woman she came she saw 'us')

Toa naule nulu ku
('Devil she came she saw 'us').

Riril naule nulu ku
('Soul' she came she saw 'us')

Waute naule nulu ku
('ancestor' she came she saw 'us'

Moto wape nweitei nire toa
(A real woman she becomes she as it were devil)

Moto wape neitei nire riril
(A real woman she becomes as it were Soul)

Moto wape nweitei nire wautei
(A real woman she becomes as it were Ancestor)

Moto wape nwitei nire toa nolomen?
(A real woman she becomes she as it were Devil. She how?)

Moto wape nweitei nire rirl nolomen?
(A real woman she becomes as it were Soul. She how?)

Moto wape nweitei nire nautei nolomen?
(A real woman she becomes as it were Ancestor. She how?).[34]

This is a sacred chant used by women in Laufi in association with a female mythical spirit to acquire knowledge, wealth, and power. Waisi is experimenting with different literary devices, both in his language and the English language. His poem 'Common Expressions' is another example with a rhythmic pattern:

'I was told to make sago with 'my"etif'
And sweep rubbish with a 'tinif'
But never was told to cook 'Kai' in a 'milif'
For fear the colour of 'my' hair is 'ketif'
When you brought 'us' the 'Weli Nimou!
'We' never knew it symbolizes your 'nimou'
Otherwise we'll feed chicken with 'mou'
Catch the fish with a 'raimeref'
Cook the food in a 'wenglef'
Let 'me' check a 'emeref'
For this fish is 'naref'
Ne neli naite nimbu kupol
Ne neli kare youtif ringol
Ne naltei wolu lafo faingol
Pe peli kare kulpou
Ne neli nalowi wnglef — olou
Le laloi saukei molou
Ku neli morsi morou.[35]

The first four lines of the poem ends with "f", followed by 'mou' in the next three lines, then another four lines with 'ef'. This rhythm is an interesting composition with English words, except for the last words. He uses the same style in the Olo language by ending with a rhythm pattern "ol" and "ok".

Waisi code switches from the Lau'um language to English so as to retain the meaning of the poem. Losing the meaning in translation does injustice to the traditional form of chanting poetry. Written poetry is a product of different circumstances. Traditional Lau'um poetry has its origin in magic and rituals together with dance and music. Written poetry is an outcome of recent social and historical development and manifest more directly than prose fiction.[36]

Weli Nimou is written in two different contexts. One part of it is derived from the Laufi worldview. The other context draws inspiration from the experiences outside of the traditional society. Waisi's work will remain a class of its own in the literary map of Papua New Guinean literature.

The harvest of literary culture in Papua New Guinea calls for a feast in Russell Soaba's collection of poetry. *Kwamra: a Season of Harvest* (2000) brings together poems spanning three decades.[37] Some of these were published and translated in various literary journals. This collection bridges Soaba's last novel *Maiba* (1985) and his current preoccupations.[38] Soaba is aware of the significance of continuity in his work. In getting the collection published at the dawn of the new century Soaba asserts his position as the foremost Papua New Guinean writer. Soaba weaves his craft consciously to capture the temporal and spatial conditions that Papua New Guineans are confronted with throughout their lives. The publication of *Kwamra* is viewed as the metamorphosis of a writer who might have been considered death in the savannah literary silences, but who has proven his critics wrong. This new collection makes the point that writing is a life-long experience and through it a writer contains him or herself. The suggestion here is also that Soaba revises the various literary positions that concern him over the years. *Kwamra* brings to the fore Soaba's prominent literary position in Papua New Guinean literary culture over the last three decades. A writer, according to Soaba, is someone who searches for and finds meaning in the various social productive forces of society.

Indeed we could think of *Kwamra* as the door into much of Soaba's literary concerns. *Kwamra* published by Anuki Country Press includes a preface by the author, previously published poems and new creations. The preface by the author serves the purpose of guiding readers into Soaba's oeuvre. The preface directs as well as challenges readers to be conscious of the act of reading. Soaba is known as a very subtle writer. Readers can easily misread Soaba's writings: "And when that happens, when both technique and device converge as complimentary if not 'contemporaneous' components of aesthetic judgement in our consciousness, we know we are experiencing the true nature of *maiba* itself."[39]

The collection begins appropriately with "Return of St. Nativeson" (the reference to Jimmy Damebo of *Wanpis* fame) and ends with "Biriko in Moonlight", a new poem. In between them are poems captured in the tradition of *maiba*, the Anuki form of communication of truth through parables and contemporary utterances: "a *maiba*...lies in the form and not content of an idea. Even if it appears as a character or an instance of personification, it still retains its original significances as a parable."[40]

A number of poems stand out as representations of this Anuki poetic tradition. Contemporary forms of expressions, syntactic fusing, and glossary added expressions are suffused with Anuki forms of communication. Soaba attempts to translate some of the words, ideas and expressions, but only in-so-far-as they serve to amplify the dominant idea of the poem. "Biriko in Moonlight: An Anuki Children's Folk Dance" is characteristic of this type of poems:

Hus gowin to da mun?
Not mi;
Ai kamin from dea, mon:
Kwarureregi, kwarureregi;
Kwarureregi, kwarureregi.

The children join hands
In a biriko ring;
Fingers stretched, clasp, hold firm.
The dance the biriko
To the right, to the left;
Kwarureregi, kwarureregi
Kwarureregi, kwarureregi.[41]

In this poem the writer uses traditional Anuki song patterns, local popular expressions, child-play songs and repetition to achieve the rhythm of the work. The writer describes poetry in motion in a vivid way that it leaves a reader to visualize the action of the dance. The deliberate negation of stanza type poem suggests that Soaba is abrogating the conventional forms of poetry and insisting on writing his poetry in a style that is closer to ethnopoetic forms of expression. In his explanation of the *birijo* dance Soaba considers it as a lively dance that flows in most child play rhymes.

In another poem Soaba demonstrates his deep attachment to his culture and his society. The poem, "Siapa" written for Romney Gaesasara II, Soaba mourns a certain loss of persons, people, culture, and ways of being:

"For you, Romeni,
and all the Warakouta
Gaesasara, Bogerara
Kerina, Matasororo
Gone, I mourn."

"Oimada."

A dynasty lay deep,
Forgiven, An old woman
Saw, remembered, spoke.[42]

This is a long poem, perhaps Soaba's most elaborate work, in this collection. In his glossary on this poem Soaba writes that *Siapa* is an important Anuki elegy sung to commemorate heroic deeds:

An elegy sung by a poet-singer to the heir of the *Gaesasara* commemorating the heroic deeds and times of the later's predecessors. The heir to whom such elegies are sung does not have to know all the historical detail being imparted on him, the idea here being that he must grow up unconsciously knowing what is being sung to him as knowledge and wisdom…The *siapa* is often sung by the grandmother to the heir. The siapa, however, is not restricted to the members of the Warakouta aristocracy as members of the other classes also sing such elegies as part of their children's education.[43]

The glossary works at situating the poem in the Anuki folk tradition. Soaba, like other postcolonial poets, is at liberty to leave untranslated words in their works to maintain the significance of a word or expressions in the original language. Poems that are similar in themes are: "The Cassowary Dance", "Magororo", and "Egara".

Soaba is also conscious of his responsibility as a writer in a postcolonial society. In many of his poems Soaba drives home the point that our societies cannot remain untouched by what is happening in the world. In the poem "Roominations: Big Bro" Soaba captures the experiences of a life that imitates no one. This particular poem was written in the 1980s as a poem used to defend himself against the criticism that Soaba has become one of his fictional characters. Those who came to know Soaba of *Wanpis* days view this poem as a classic of the writing style in the existentialist tradition that Soaba was so fond of:

And who knows? It could be because
Of him that we are happy and secure now.
He could be fighting for our rights
While we sleep.[44]

The new collection consolidates Soaba's respected stature in the literary culture of Papua New Guinea. Soaba continues to pen memorable poems that bridge the earlier generation's concerns with the present generation's concerns. *Kwamra* testifies to Soaba's greatness in the literary community of the world.

CONCLUSION

The poets of Papua New Guinea considered in this chapter wrote out of different sets of experiences with different visions. All poets draw inspirations from their own cultures and environments. They are products of their own societies and times. The perspectives and views expressed in their writings serve to remind Papua New Guineans to listen to their inner spirits, inspirations, and collective visions. These writers use their indigenous traditions and epistemologies to view the world. By using the inspirations found in the traditional cultures and knowledge systems, these writers have build a bridge between the written and unwritten cultures, between the past and the present, between the illiterate villager and the educated elite running the country.

CREATIVE SPIRIT AND POLITICAL ENERGY

The masses are in search of a centre, a point of reference to begin or to return to for a sense of unity. The fragmentary experiences lived now seem to present an urgency. The masses remain pessimistic. Gramsci probes the role of intellectuals in different phases of nationhood: "The intellectuals of the old generation, who have so much historical experience, who have seen the whole tormented development of our people over these last three decades, would fail in their duty and mission, if, precisely in this culminating phase, they stood aside and were unwilling to contribute to clarifying, organizing and centralizing the ideal forces which already exist—which in other words, do not need to be brought into existence (that would be utopian), but merely to be centralized and given a direction."[1] The same concerns that Gramsci raises are those that concerns artists and intellectuals in Papua New Guinea.

POLITICAL RESPONSIBILITY

Creative and intellectual activities are locked in institutional spaces. Literary activities, artistic productions, and theatrical performances in Papua New Guinea are often linked to educational institutions. The University of Papua New Guinea, the Administrative College, the National Arts School, the Goroka Teachers College, and the PNG University of Technology played a key role in the germination and proliferation of art, writing, and drama between 1960s and 1970s. These institutions served as the cultural hub of creative expressions. The issues of representation, cultural decolonization, and intervention into negative structures of thought inherited from a colonized history fuelled the continuity of literature, writing, and artistic representations through works of art and theatre performances.

The need for political responsibility is unavoidable. The masses, as Gramsci says need a direction and central point of reference, from which they can question the structures of thought that continue to colonize them. The artists and intellectuals of the post-independence era have yet to apply the critical eye on some of these structures of thought represented in the literary and artistic works of Papua New Guinea.

Cultural decolonization happens only when Papua New Guinean writers and intellectuals interrogate the negative structures of thought inherited from the colonized experience. Without interrogating the structures of thought Papua New Guineans will continue to remain voiceless participants in their nation's history. The birth of a literary culture in Papua New Guinea offered an opportunity for Papua New Guineans to participate in the decolonizing process. Young Papua New Guineans attending the University of Papua New Guinea and other higher education institutions in 1960s and 1970s seized the opportunity to be part of the new literary culture under Beier's leadership.

LEGACY REMAINS

Before his death Ulli Beier wrote *Decolonising the Mind,* describing his role as a catalyst in the emergence of Papua New Guinean (PNG) literature in the late 1960s and early 1970s.[2] The book reveals all that Ulli and his wife, Georgina, had worked so hard to see happen in Papua New Guinea—especially their tireless commitment to see that Papua New Guineans use literature and arts as weapons of resistance to colonialism. That the chosen title comes from the work of the renowned Kenyan writer and social critic, Ngugi wa Thiong'o (*Decolonising the Mind*, 1986) is also apt, as it leads us to consider the strategies that Papua New Guineans employed to decolonize themselves, even before independence arrived.[3]

Under Ulli Beier's guidance, young Papua New Guineans used writing, drama, poetry, and arts to capture national sentiments and to promote PNG cultures. *Decolonising the Mind* is not just a memoir that recalls the Beiers' time in Papua New Guinea; it also tells of the activities and people with whom they associated during the period leading up to independence. It covers the vibrant period of literature, art, performance, writing, and publishing at the University of Papua New Guinea (UPNG). This was a time of quick planting and harvesting of the literary and artistic talents that the Beiers stumbled into, waiting as it were to be nurtured, given impetus, and made to bloom.

From subtle nationalism to fiery anticolonial resistance; from imagining one's own community to living in one that is about to be independent—those were the moods of the period. Those Papua New Guineans that the Beiers influenced—such as Albert Maori Kiki, Vincent Eri, Kumalau Tawali, Leo Hannet, Mathias Kawage, Akis, Taite Aihi, and Ruki Fame — have all shown that the arts and literary culture have a purpose to serve the people of Papua New Guinea. The main thread of the book is about the impact of the university on culture and identity in Papua New Guinea between 1971 through 1974. Ulli wants to tell us his story about what happened in between those years. After spending many years working to promote the art and literature of the Yoruba people of Nigeria, the Beiers came to Papua New Guinea in September 1967.

Here, Ulli took up a UPNG lectureship—excited with the possibilities of embracing, nurturing, and promoting a rich artistic and literary culture.

One of the first Papua New Guineans they met on their way to the country, late at night in the departure hall of the Brisbane Airport, was Sir Albert Maori Kiki. Ulli recounts that encounter: "On the plane we had a brief conversation. His name was Albert Maori Kiki, he said. He had been a patrol officer to the Australian administration, but he had recently resigned from that position in order to become the secretary of a new political party. I asked him what part of the country he was from and he said: "Well, you wouldn't have heard of it, it's a very small place on the Papua Gulf called Orokolo."[4] Such openness on the part of Maori Kiki led Ulli Beier to help Kiki publish his autobiography, *Ten Thousand Years in a Lifetime* (1968), a book that would trigger a wave of excitement, not only in Papua New Guinea, but internationally as well.[5] The second autobiography that Ulli had a hand in was Sir Michael Somare's *Sana* (1975).[6] Somare served as PNG prime minister from independence in 1975 until 1980, from 1982 until 1985, and from 2002 to 2011.

Ulli Beier also passionately recounts his work with pioneer UPNG students, then referred to as the "boys' university." He discusses establishing a relationship with Allan Natachee, the Papua "Poet Laureate"[7] (12-19), developing the UPNG creative writing course, and starting a publication series called the Papua Pocket Poet series (43-50).[8] From the creative writing class, Ulli recalls: "One of my first and most fascinating students was Vincent Eri. He was a mature student, 31 years old, who had been an education officer. He had twice visited Australia and had been to a conference in Teheran. In 1966, he was sent to Malaysia to represent Papua New Guinea at a writer's conference. This experience inspired Eri to write his first and only novel, *The Crocodile* (51-60), which was also Papua New Guinea's first novel, published in 1971.[9]

Then, in later years, Ulli was inspired to establish the Institute of Papua New Guinea Studies. Ulli was supported by his wife, Georgina, on his mission to accomplish this dream—or perhaps it is better considered an awakening. Georgina provided mentorship and guidance to artists, sculptors, and textile designers in the studio behind their house. This was the beginning of what later would become the National Arts School, an icon of an era rich with artistic flowering. The Beiers also helped to foster the work of pioneer artists at the Center for New Guinea Creative Arts and formed a close relationship with the center's Mathias Kawage, who became the most original and prolific of all PNG artists and brought contemporary PNG arts to the world.

ULLI BEIER'S INFLUENCE

Ulli Beier's role in the birth of Papua New Guinean literary culture is common knowledge. Teaching creative writing to Papua New Guineans, Beier made it possible for Papua New Guineans to publish their works at both local and international levels. He was a very skilled editor. Beier was very enterprising in the promotion and circulation of writings by Papua New Guineans. Brash describes three most significant features of Beier's influence: (1) "The discovery of potential writers and artists", (2) "the opening of channels for publication of the work of local writers", and (3) the introduction of the creative writing course at the University of Papua New Guinea: "Mr. Beier convinced both the University and the Department of Education that such courses were valuable, and in the case of the University, academically respectable. Fortunately, he found firm support from Dr. K. McKinnon and Professor F. C. Johnson.[10] Through the University courses came for example: *The Crocodile*, by Vincent Eri and *Five New Guinea Plays*, by Leo Hannett *et. al.* and other literary productions. The short courses conducted in Rabaul produced stories for *When the Moon was Big* and poems for *Words of Paradise*" (1974: 36-7).[11]

The creative writing course was the factory of writing. Beier set up publishing projects and arranged with publishers to have some of these writings published. According to Brash "the initial barriers have been broken; both public and publishers have accepted New Guinea Literature and the possibility of more New Guinea Literature."[12] Talents and enthusiasm by Papua New Guinean writers pushed the literary culture to sprout from the hallways and forums of the educational institutions.

NEW CULTURAL PATHS

Beier introduced the Papua Pocket Poets series as cheap pocket size booklets featuring individual writers and coauthors. The Papua Pocket Poets was successful in producing more poetry collection and posters featuring art and poetry.[13] The principle behind the success is that more people would have access to writings and artistic expressions of Papua New Guinea. These cheap publications had a sense of aesthetics to them. The flurry of literary activities organized by the Bureau of Literature within the Department of Information and Extension Services enhanced the development of Papua New Guinean literature in a lot of ways as well.

Writing embodied self-expression in the 1970s. Papua New Guineans used writing to re-describe the imperious imaginings about them. The young writers and intellectuals used writing to assault the epistemic violence against them. Writing became a process for the colonized to reimagine themselves. Papua New Guineans abrogated and appropriated the Western culture of writing and adapted the English language to represent their own experiences. Writing, Subramani argued opened up "new cultural paths" in Papua New Guinea and elsewhere in the Pacific. The sense of discovery of these new cultural paths led to uncovering new possibilities of understanding cultural knowledge implicit in the cultures and experiences of Oceanic peoples.[14] Indigenous cultural forms and structures of experience enrich them to understand the kind of world they live in.

THE PROPHETS AND THE BULLS

The writers on the University campus were regarded as the "prophets" and the political enthusiasts across the campus at the Administrative College (Institute of Public Administration) were regarded as the "bulls" (to use Ken Goodwin's description).[15] Their combination was radically assertive and antagonistic toward continued colonization of Papua New Guinea. The creative spirit and the political energy, however short lived, accomplished so much that is now a milestone. The contributions of the prophets and the bulls to the development of a literary culture were significant. The political destiny and overall creative enterprise of the young Papua New Guineans reflect the innovative and productive spirit of Papua New Guineans.

The writers wrote and said what they wanted without fear, sanction, or political persecution. The literature produced in this period is regarded as "nationalistic, angry, protesting, lamenting a huge loss…. The literature attempts to reconstruct what has been lost or changed. Consequently much of it is a fabulous storehouse of anthropology, sociology, art, religion, history, dance and music."[16] Anti-colonial literature and literature of cultural representation emerged together. The literary culture served as a structure of an imagined community: "If the nation is an imagined community, then this is where it is brought into being. In this, its true and essential domain, the nation is already sovereign, even when the state is in the hands of the colonial power. The dynamics of this historical project is completely missed in the conventional histories in which the story of nationalism begins with the contest for political power." [17]

The production of literary culture enabled a mass circulation of the collective experiences to end up in the hands of many people. The views of educated Papua New Guineans became the collective voice of the people. The emergence of a formative literary culture was in a way the process of transformation in the lives of Papua New Guineans. Papua New Guineans read about themselves through the printed cultural form. Papua New Guineans wrote about their traditions, customs, and folklore.

IDEOLOGY AND NATIONALISM

The relationship between national identity and the literature of Papua New Guinea is a significant one. The concept of "Melanesian Way" contains an essential world-view of a collective ideological expression. This concept has its foundations in the old colonial society. It is often used as a focus for national and political sentiments. The concept is related more to the needs and values of the affluent and the middle-class than to the great majority of the population. Melanesian Way offers a set of principles to reframe identities in our societies. As an ideology, however, it is dismissed as a 'beautiful lie' in ideological terms since it stands as another excuse for colonialism. Its use in the present society is tarnished by the imposition of foreign values.

Contemporary Papua New Guinean society is now in a state of change, engaged in recreating, restructuring, and reconstructing its history, culture, and traditional values. It is a society struggling to maintain a national identity, through its political, social, and cultural systems. With three official languages and more than 854 indigenous languages, a country like Papua New Guinea faces the inevitable problems of language difficulties and communication. Cultural differences, provincial, and regionalistic attitudes make a single ideology more difficult. With a history fractured by forces of colonialism, the attempt to rebuild a new history is a daunting task.

Looking back over the years to the escalating moments of self-consciousness and political awareness during the 1960s and the early part of the 1970s, we see the earliest development of nationalism. At that time, Papua New Guineans were expressing their aspirations and dreams. They rejected colonial images and impressions about them. This literature of Papua New Guinea concerns itself with nationalistic sentiments, colonial antagonism, and cultural re-evaluation.

The attempt here is to critique the construction of the "Melanesian Way" as an ideology, specifically as an ideology of nationalism. The critique of the term as an ideology provides a different perspective on ideological development and nationalism in Papua New Guinea.

THE MELANESIAN WAY

The Melanesian Way is a cosmic view of the world. It represents a fusion of traditional values, modern culture, and the history of the people. Narokobi first sounded the Melanesian Way in these lines:

Our Melanesian ways stem from the unquestionable fact that we are an ancient people, born to liberty, born to ancient culture and civilisation.

We are not one year old, nor are we 200 years old. We are thousands of years old. We might be new to modern institutions, but we are not new to human persons' strengths and weaknesses.

We have a right and indeed a duty to call on the wisdoms of our ancestors. Collectively we possess the treasures of time tested and proven strengths. This

69

we can use in times of stress and strain to liberate ourselves from oppressive circumstances, of whatever nature or magnitude.

As Melanesians, we are a spiritual people. Even before Christians came onto our shores, we felt and knew the forces of a source greater than ourselves. That was our divine power, the Melanesian Way.

We can and should call on the strength of that source. We have a right to demand interpersonal dialogue with the forces at work to change us. We have a right to be here, not as carbon copies, but as authentic Melanesians.

From our spirituality, we had a communal vision of the cosmos. Our vision was not and is not an artificially dichotomized and compartmented pragmatism of the secular society. Ours is a vision of a totality, a vision of cosmic harmony.[18]

The Melanesian Way is a highly political concept. It is an ideology developed as a counter discourse to the discourses of colonial ideology. It works as a dual ideology: First, as an ideology of nationalism and second as an ideology of rationalism. This duality insists on categorizing people according to physical, biological, psychological, and cultural traits. Where similarities exist, a viable concept is necessary so that easier interpretation is possible — a characteristic of early European anthropological, scientific, and sociological studies. Thus, the Melanesian Way has that touch of categorization that is of concern here.

COLONIAL LABEL

The Melanesian Way has its origin in the colonial discourses. It reflects a western perception of the society. It is problematic to consider it as an ideology of nationalism. The Melanesian Way as perceived by proponents of that concept today was invented to categorize and class people of distinct ethnic and cultural traits. What has been described imperialistically has again become the redescription of our people. Narokobi points out that the Melanesian Way "comes from the European language and probably means negroid or black.... native or kanaka."[19] In the colonial discourses the concept of 'Melanesian Way' was coined as a term to describe the dark-skinned people of the 'dark islands' who occupy the Northwest Islands of the South Pacific, and are "dangerous and blood thirsty savages" who "are all cannibals, frightfully cruel and terribly treacherous".[20] They are preoccupied with "head hunting and the practice of offering human sacrifice on even the most trivial occasion." These 'dark islands' are Papua New Guinea, Solomon Islands, Vanuatu, New Caledonia, and Fiji. Papua New Guinea, known as New Guinea in the colonial period, was shaded black on the map and called the "Islands of the Bad People."[21] This chain of islands share cultural, linguistic, and geographical similarities, but with different political and historical circumstances.

Such impressions of the Melanesians proliferated in the imperialistic literature of travel, adventure, and administration of the colonial period. The imperialistic literary discourses provided Europe with the debating ground for colonialism and missionary activities. The brutality and violent exchanges of confrontation between the intruders and the islanders may have more to do with the negative images of the islanders. The missionaries used it as comparison to Medieval Europe engaged in great monarch rivalries and barbarism. The missionaries took advantage of this rivalry between Melanesians and Europeans. They saw the savagery and cannibalistic behaviour of Melanesians as the great testing ground for their philosophy of pacification.

What is seen as the "Melanesian Way" today is not an authentic view, but a label demarcated and created by imperialist occupation: French, British, German, and Dutch. Narokobi's recognition of the concept as derived ideology from the colonial discourse and his defense of it as authentic is not to say that it is a positively inclusive terminology, but one that requires careful consideration. The Melanesian Way like the subaltern consciousness is a "historized political species" and "it implicitly operates as a metaphysical methodological presupposition in the general sense, there is always a counter pointing suggestion".[22] Without critiquing the terminology, we stand to promote a particular kind of consciousness that can easily become a 'negative consciousness' because it is of the oppressors, invented to pacify and oppress the 'dark islands'. The Melanesian Way is ambiguous and homogenizes the many diverse cultural, linguistic, belief systems, and traditional political systems. The reinvention of the concept Melanesian Way as an ideology only serves the basis of repression and demarcation, in the demise of nationalism, it seems in its early formation.

NATIONALIST DISCOURSE

Nationalism has been constructed as a "historized political species" on the basis of the colonial establishment. Our attempts to define ourselves are based on common ideas, belief systems, and distinct cultural identities and psychological differentiations. A critic of the Melanesian Way, Bernard Minol says that the elites of Melanesia have been so dislocated "that such ideas as these provide solace for our disturbed spirit."[23] The politicized concept of the Melanesian Way is identified with the elites who are schooled in western ways and subscribe to Christianity. It also reflects the idealization of the traditional past in discourses of nationalism. Such classification provides the foundations for distinct ethnic grouping and micro nationalistic movements.

The Melanesian Way as a politicized ideology during the colonial period, acted as the negation of the imposed order. Immediately after colonialism the same ideology was used to promote an elites definition. The Melanesian Way is "subject to the cathexes of the elites, and that it is the elites who define what identities they perceive."[24] Present day Papua New Guinean leaders are also caught up in this twin imperative, created by colonialism and Orientalist forces of power, including the activities of missionaries and the other colonial forces. Idealized concepts are enforced by uncritical sympathies of outside views on the part of academics, historians, social scientists, journalists, old patrons, and nationals who make up the part of the population living a bourgeoisie life.

Rejection of village practices is necessary for the advancement of colonialism. Processes that validate colonialism are always at the expanse of the colonized peoples' submission and subjugation. Cabral, writing on the revolution in Guinea says that there is a "paralysis or deviation or even halting of the history of one people in favour of the acceleration of historical development of other people."[25] This contributes to the development of the Western world more than the colonized world. Ngugi wa Thiong'o, like Cabral, says there are two aspects of this process of colonialism. The first is "the destruction or the deliberate undervaluing of a people's culture, their art, dances, religions, history, geography, education, orature and literature, and the conscious elevation of the language of the colonizer."[26] Second aspect is the "domination of a people's language by the languages of the colonizing nations" thereby leading to the domination of the mental universe of the colonized."[27] A situation described as mental colonization of postcolonial subjects.

A problem is created for the post-colonial person to redefine, reconstruct, and re-invent a culture, a myth, or an ideology. The opportunity for a pre-colonial culture is never allowed to develop; it is sacrificed for another more dominant culture or ideology constructed by the colonizers and their successors — the elite class of Papua New Guinea. Furthermore, what is seen as national identity today is either perceived as a ritualised celebration of customs in the form of arts or rhetorics of customs involved with reference to a particular region, group, or province within the postcolonial state.

NATIONALISM IS A POLITICAL MYTH

Nationalism works as a political myth. Its ideological foundations were created during the colonial period to counteract and reject colonialism. Although nationalism works as an ideology of colonial negation, it simultaneously establishes a common bond among the colonized. According to Antonio Gramsci, the subversive group resists imposition by constructing nationalism. Since Independence, however, nationalism has become a political myth. Commenting on the African world, Emmanuel Ngara says: "Nationalism does not necessarily lead to a transformation of society, because the national bourgeoisie often steps into the boots of the departed colonialists, maintaining the same old system and introducing only cosmetic changes, while working in alliance with the international bourgeoisie who control the economy of the country from a distance." [28] Nationalism reflects the elite's dominant calls to repress the dominated, the illiterate villagers, and the silent majority of the people. The subverted group in Papua New Guinea is the simple, illiterate villagers, who do not understand even the concepts of 'nationalism' or the Melanesian Way.

Nationalism has become the very ritualised activity that assumes a lot of things. It is the very ideology of exploitation and suppression. Nationalism is in itself, an inviter of "disassembly, offending individualism, particularity, variety and difference, it is a principle of not only absurd definitions, but repressive homogenization, closure and exclusion."[29] Campbell (1989) notes the lack of a nationalistic outlook in the political system of Papua New Guinea. The "disunity of the nationalist movement" in Papua New Guinea has done little to strengthen a political practice based on ideological lines. In its early days many of the nationalist sentiments were based on regionalism rather than on nationalism "to the extent that some of them advocated secession from the rest of the territory."[30] Instead of national movements, provincial and regional movements emerged, based on regional boundaries, provincial and language groupings. In this system it becomes possible to talk about a Tolai, Manus, Morobean, Sepik, Engan, a Papuan, or a Highlander, but not of a Papua New Guinean, or a Melanesian for that matter. The Bougainville Revolutionary Army on the island of Bougainville used this very argument, to secede and to form an autonomous region type of government. The Bougainville Revolutionary Army fought the state troops, closed down the mine, and demanded self-government. During the 1970s, there were cases of secessionism on the islands of Bougainville and East New Britain. The Matagaun Association (MA) of Rabaul, for instance, wanted its own council. It rejected the multiracial council and demanded the return of its traditional lands. The threat to secede issued by the Islands Regional Council only reaffirms what has been said so far. Where secession and insurgence actively establish protest and negative attitudes, nationalism declines. In such a state, provincialism and regionalism dominate ideological formations.

IDEOLOGY IS A BEAUTIFUL LIE

Attempts to form ideology are very difficult. Ideology serving a social function in one group is also used to dominate and control the other. The same ideology is used with the intent of domination of one class over others, and the economic exploitation that maintains its pre-eminence, by making the exploited accept their condition as based on the will of God, 'nature', or moral duty. Ideology is a 'beautiful lie', as Althusser says, invented by the exploiters to control the exploited and keep them marginalized. It helps individuals of the dominant class to recognize themselves as the dominant class. The subjects accept the domination of the ruling over the exploited as 'willed by God', as fixed by 'nature', or as assigned by a moral 'duty'.[31] This serves as a bond of social cohesion that keeps the members of the same class — the class of exploiters, together. The 'beautiful lie' of ideology has a double usage. It works on the consciousness of members of the dominant class to allow them to exercise their exploitation and domination as natural.

The dominant bourgeois class controls the lower class by creating the ideology of nationalism for their own purposes. The "working class protests against exploitation," but within the very structure of the dominant bourgeois ideology, within its systems, and in large part with its representations and terms of reference." [32] The very nature of the bourgeois ideology is reflected in "the whole history of utopian socialism and trade-union reformism" of the world.[33] The bourgeois class "is so exclusively the provider of raw material (frames of thought, systems of reference)." On the other hand "the working class cannot, by its own resources, radically liberate itself from bourgeois ideology. At best the working class can express its protests and aspirations by using certain elements of bourgeois ideology, but it remains the prisoner of that ideology, held in its dominant structure."[34] These structures, rules, and categories of the dominant class give rise to a discourse of domination and control over others. Althusser describes this as an "ideological struggle" of the working class "against the domination of bourgeois ideology" linking the struggle to Marxist theory and the working class movements.[35]

Like the working class of Europe or the peasants of Kenya, the villagers on the lower strata of Papua New Guinea are experiencing an ideological struggle against the bourgeois ideology. Attempts to redefine the self are always ideological. Such attempts represent nature, society, and the very world in which humans live. The life of humans, their relations to nature, society, the social order, and their own economic and political activities are elements of social control. These ideological representations, however, are false representations of the world. In the Althusserian sense ideological representation is often determined by sociopolitical and economical conditions of society.

Under the ideology of nationalism, the elite pretends to represent the whole society's human experiences or to express the total cosmic view of our society. The ideology of nationalism, however, has become a process of domination over the less privileged, illiterate, racial minority. It is a valorized ideology based on colonial negation, agitation, and mythology. Considering the underlying racial and colonial sentiments of the past, the duality in ideology can never be eliminated. The ideology of nationalism is borne out of the deeply felt antagonism to colonial conquest, colonial power, and its consequences such as land alienation, culture uprooting, and neo-political control. Out of the need to recognize and destabilize negative influences a counter discourse needs to develop. The urgent need to restructure its systems of organization is seen in the formation of Papua New Guinean literature.

LITERATURE, IDEOLOGY, AND NATIONALISM

Literature constitutes ideologies that express "the way men live, their relation to their real conditions of existence, and which will thus look beyond its strategies of containment to its roots in history. Literature reflects a writer's interactions with nature, the spiritual world, and society. The relationships between ideology and literature are explained by the national dreams, visions, and aspirations. Literature is about people who make up a society. Ngara points out that "literature enables us to see the nature of ideology of an epoch because it is socially conditioned."[36]

The rise of Papua New Guinea literature in the 1960s concentrated on political views, the colonial situation, and political self-determination. The period is marked by the establishment of institutions of higher learning (Administrative College 1964, University of Papua New Guinea 1965, Goroka Teachers College 1967), and the development of political consciousness among Papua New Guineans. Students at these institutions were encouraged to talk or discuss ideas about the country's political, social, and economic development. This gave rise to a literature written with a national flavour.

The literature between the period 1968 and 1974 concentrated on the negation of colonial rule and the absurd values inherited from the dominant culture. Ideas of resistance and recreation of new ideology, culture, and history dominated the themes of their writings. The Papua New Guinean writers of this period were politically attuned to the world. Through literature, Papua New Guineans found a powerful medium of expression. So much is expressed in the literature of this period. The emergence of Papua New Guinean literature is closely identified with the university, and has its basis in the Literature Department. This created another problem of literature being identified with the educated elite and institutions of higher education. Furthermore, the language in which this literature was expressed in was English — the language of the colonizer. Clearly, the use of this world language was at the expense of the local Papua New Guinean languages. Even though Papua New Guinean literature was university-centered, written in English by a few intellectuals and idealists, it became an important instrument for self-expression, protest against colonialism, distaste for colonial imperialism, and the rejection of the imposed value systems. The young writers of this period lived with what they preached about in the later days of colonial rule. The very people who wrote during this period moved into the newly independent nation's bureaucracy and the private sector in the new nation.

Literature carried the tag of being an elitist preoccupation, written in English and circulated among intellectuals and higher learning institutions only, at times centering around Port Moresby as its only place of distribution. In the 1972 conference John Waiko, a Papua New Guinea writer, spoke on the place of literature in the education system.[37] According to Waiko, the education system had produced a portion of the educated Papua New Guineans who occupy the top echelons in the society. He lamented the awkward position of the national writers and intellectuals in the country. Among other things he was concerned that the literature produced was not reaching the village people. The literature produced was for a different audience, the colonizers and the elite. Waiko argues that ideological concepts such as the *wantoks* and 'pay back systems are destroying our lives and causing misunderstanding amongst Papua New Guineans. The elite class is "fit for continuing and taking over from the whites, and (in ignoring) the traditional values," they were only competent in the white man's ways of doing things, and understanding things, even if it means oppressing their own people.[38]

No consistent ideological foundation has developed out of this initial literary development. Literature is a committed activity and is "a passive product of historical condition, a passive reflection of reality," which influences and helps shape reality. It is "a social force which with its emotions or ideological weight, shakes and moves people."[39] In *Decolonising the Mind* (1986) Ngugi wa Thiong'o argues that a "writer's handling of reality is affected by his basic philosophic outlook on nature and society and his method of investigating that nature and society, whether, for instance, he perceives and therefore looks at a phenomenon in its interconnection or in its dislocation; in its rest or in its motion; in its mutability or immutability; in its being or in its becoming; and whether he sees any qualitative change in its motion from one state of being into another."[40] Ngugi adds:"a writer's handling of the material can also be affected by his material base in society, that is his class position and stand point."[41]

The writer who once upon a time joined nationalists to challenge the imperialist ideology has now become the ruling elite of Papua New Guinea. Where political ideology and nationalism took an anti-imperialist approach in the first half of 1970s, these subsided into a different activity by the later half of the 1970s. Nationalism in Papua New Guinea gave way to regionalism and secession, while ideology became a 'beautiful lie' used by the ruling class as an excuse to dominate the illiterate villagers. In these moments of silence, the nationalists have stepped into the corridors of power and economic exploitation. The writers, too, no longer see literature as an important element of their lives. Literature has ceased its vibrant energy to challenge forces of power, perhaps because the forces of power have absorbed the writers.

The creation of new ideas in Papua New Guinea is constructed within the framework of colonizers, elitists, and capitalistic systems of thought and practice. Ideologies have become exploitative and only affirm the elitists' concerns or the bourgeois ideology of the new national elite. The ruling class created false excuses to exploit and dominate the ones who are worse off than them. There is no denial that there are disagreements, denials, and criticisms on certain inherited, reinvented, re-described concepts. The "Melanesian Way" or other concepts, with their basis in the colonial discourses have to undergo critical analysis in order for anyone to accept their purported basis of representation.

Conclusion

The development of a literary culture in Papua New Guinea remains in a continuum, but with a closer link to institutions, especially with universities and the higher education institutions. From *Papua Pocket Poets* (PPP) to the *Savannah Flames* many challenges and visions remain locked up in the minds of people. Without the support of institutions, publishing houses, and patrons, the literary culture of Papua New Guinea will continue to remain undeveloped. Literary culture is an important element of national development. Literary journals have served as the publication venue for most Papua New Guinean writers. The artistic and intellectual contributions in the literary journals have often been overlooked. Intellectual and artistic contributions are cultural capitals produced by Papua New Guineans about themselves. Cultural capital is used by a nation to define, differentiate, and promote itself in the world.

The construction of authorship, the patterns of publishing, and the emergence and continuity of a literary culture to the socially productive relationship need a critical reading. Stella challenges readers of PNG literature to reconsider their approaches and critical evaluation of the literary culture: "I believe that critical evaluation is vital and necessary because it nurtures the growth of literature, both aesthetically and functionally. It is like applying fertilizer at different stages of a crop's growth in order to produce a better yield. From this perspective a critical model to appraise Papua New Guinea literature, one that encapsulates the different orientations — for example, orality, orature, cross-culturality, and its marginality is necessary".[42] Stella's argument is that our approaches to critical evaluation of the PNG literary culture must consider the various discourses and discursive practices produced in that culture. The call is for critical scholarship on the formations, transformations of knowledge, identity, and ideology within a culture. The instituting of critical scholarship on the literary tradition of Papua New Guinea is needed to map out the different concerns, thematic strengths, and the emergence of a Papua New Guinea novelistic tradition.

6

DOUBLE CONSCIENCE WITHOUT THE INSTRUMENT TO LIBERATE

Information disperses and circulates following the rule that society is structured on power relations. The distribution of power allows social relationships to develop thereby allowing communication to be possible. Without the
process of self-definition we are dependent on the influence of a colonized
power structured history. Such a history has created a notion of double consciousness in our lives. I argue that this double consciousness can be erased
with effective instruments. Papua New Guinean writers are intervening into
this situation to secure a place in nation, development, and identity debates.

On a trip from Minnesota to Papua New Guinea I found myself in discussion over the new government of Bill Skate. The conversation took place in
Manila International Airport while waiting for Air Niugini to fly me home.
The fellow Papua New Guineans in conversation were returning from their
sojourn in the United States, Europe, and Asia. In our time overseas we relied
on the news accessed through the Internet system. We are an informed generation about the current affairs of Papua New Guinea. The utterances we make,
however, are still over sentimentalized. We have not distanced ourselves from
sentimentalized expressions and considered where we draw the line between
sentimentalism and rational arguments on how we produce and disseminate
knowledge. In what sense are the utterances we make of ourselves through
speech and representation in our literature of any value? The literary culture
we created as we thought of forming our nation has become the least of our
concerns in the age of technological culture. How are we to reignite the literary
flame to burn again?

COLLECTIVE EXPRESSIONS OF DIFFERENCE

How do we develop as a community that collectively expresses itself through
its literary culture? Our literary culture develops by emphasizing a national vision: "while the difficulties in the way of achieving a wide national acceptance

and enjoyment are great (low literacy rate, multiversity of languages, etc.), they do not constitute excuses for not trying to do so."[1] Papua New Guineans are not reading their own writings. Through interpretation of its literary culture a community realizes its goals and visions. A community is shaped each time its members recognize the collective expressions of difference through their literary culture.

Where a nation struggles to liberate itself from the double consciousness syndrome a causation argument enters. The education system is blamed largely for institutionalizing the double consciousness syndrome. This double con-sciousness is sometimes described as mental dependence: "we are to a large extent dependent on the metropolitan 'experts' to instill into our minds what they think is best for us or what they think we should do to achieve rapid and effective westernization and/or modernization."[2] Indeed such a view instigates antagonism. A few Papua New Guinean intellectuals and writers are critical of this view as it negates any aspiration to formulate their own theories and ideas based on their cultures. The basis of locally constituted knowledge is realized through a dialogic process. The social positioning of a writer between the village experience and the contemporary urban setting already presupposes a mediating self.

The underlying antagonism by Papua New Guineans is an ideological one. The "nationalistic ideas of resistance and recreation of new ideology, culture and history" are rethought of in relation to the way in which history has shaped its existence.[3] A "collective interpretation" is agreed on the grounds that "the world of texts seems to encompass and constitute reality, or at least the whole world of discourse."[4] An effective instrument of a collective expression in Papua New Guinean writing is insurrectionary against the established order of dominant discourses. Erasure of mental dependence and colonized conscious-ness is possible through strategic literary interventions.

In speaking of the double consciousness there is one that blames someone else for our problems. Another we carry around with us. The latter works as the subject/object reality, which we constantly struggle to understand why there are people who have control over our lives. In the same confusion we continue in silence about the world described for us by others. The world described is a world colonized since having the power to describe is having knowledge over something. We are still the objects of knowledge, exhibition, and control. The absence of critical Papua New Guinean discourses only extends the orientalis-ing descriptions. The failure on our part to liberate us from the object position is partly obscured by the general inability to articulate our experiences. What is at stake here is Papua New Guinean collective identity that must pass through self-negation as witnessed of Abel Willborough in Soaba's *Wanpis* (1974). The shifting self within a difficult society is partly explained by the historical condi-tions that shaped such a character.

Waiko suggested a disruption of the double consciousness in the 1970s. A pragmatic like Waiko rhetorically negates the agenda: "The problem is how can we do it, because many of our people have become part of the system, including myself."[5] In reality the double consciousness makes it possible for individuals to respond vaguely when questioned. The responses inherited from the colonized experiences have been internalized that they are unconsciously reproduced when referring to those seen as representatives of the former colonizers. These responses reflect a negative structure of consciousness that reaffirm duality in our way of thinking thereby allowing binary oppositions to be legitimated. Some of these binaries are thought of in terms of race, ethnicity, religion, class, and gender. Cultural oppositions are also viewed as the negative reflections of each other. The consequence, of course, is the expansion of the rift that already exists after confrontation between opposing cultural practices fail to compromise.

LITERARY BRIDGES WITHOUT HONOUR

I noted two responsibilities of the Papua New Guinean writer.[6] Now I extend the responsibilities to include the importance of narratives speaking about the past, the narratives of contemporary everyday, and the recognition of narrative structures that constitute our heterogeneous experiences. The writer is aware of the conflicts, contradictions, and confusion that promulgates into discursive cultural consciousness. By centering such issues Sorariba informs Papua New Guineans about the depressing situation in the society.

A few conscious Papua New Guineans see PNG literary culture as an instrument of mental decolonization. A collective effort by Kakah Kais and Bernard Minol with illustrations by a local artist saw the narrative of a Manus culture hero presented in written form. The publication *Pokop of Pohyomou* was endorsed by the politician Stephen Pokawin: "With the new skills in reading and writing, it is in our communal, cultural and provincial interests that we write the stories that have survived through time and the new stories that have come about our time for us to enjoy now and at the same time leave them for those of the future"[7] By the same token the Aimbe series authored by Paulias Matane would not have profoundly celebrated our history if the author had not written without the present generation of Papua New Guineans in mind. By privileging the Papua New Guinean literary culture one subscribes to the view that the author is politically situated in the Papua New Guinean society. Anyone who has read Eri's *The Crocodile* would have noticed that Hoiri Sevese, the protagonists in the novel was the prototype Papua New Guinean caught up in the dilemma of a colonized history. That very condition is described as fixed by the nature and will of God. The argument is already problematic because of a colonized history. The more obvious demonstration of this colonized history is recollected in Papua New Guinean autobiographies like Kiki's *Ten Thousand Years in a Lifetime*, Somare's *Sana*, and Abaijah's *A Thousand Coloured Dreams*. The real life narratives of these people suggest a shift away from the stagnant reality into the modern condition of the technological culture.

Cultural literacy is necessary in a nation's development. The reading of autobiographies of national leaders and literary works of Papua New Guinea opens a window into the world of possibilities. We learn from our own kind to rise above the ordinary to respectable status in society. Leaders too learn how to govern with sincerity the affairs of the country by knowing about the real struggle and pain of its people. Without such a system there are no informed government and responsive citizenry.

DIALOGUE AND NEW ALIGNMENT

Identities are consciously negotiated in the Papua New Guinean literary culture. The literary culture is often forgotten as a nation struggles with ideas of national development and technological progress. We ignore the view that the "written history of our society is no longer in the domain of those who control the means of production, but with the writer who is caught up in the conflicts, contradictions and confusing moments of a nation in crisis with itself."[8] What is critical now is for Papua New Guineans to form new alignments with themselves by centering dialogue on differences rather than on sentimentalized impressions about the nation.

The last two decades saw the continuation of the Papua New Guinean literary culture, emerging as "an integrated national culture and true national consciousness."[9] There is a continuum in Papua New Guinean literary culture. The continuum reassures the Papua New Guinean writers to continue producing knowledge for a nation already faced with the contradictions and disillusionment, making it vulnerable to all the negative ideas infiltrating its cultural values. The value of Papua New Guinean writers is succinctly expressed by the late Ignatius Kilage: "The peculiarities and sensibilities of our nations can be expressed by our own sons and daughters as an innate offering of the immortal values of our people, in words that can change our changing mood."[10] For me, literary works have influenced the way I view Papua New Guinean nationhood (since the politicians' rhetoric is too hard to remember).

To gain progress as the nation reconfigures its journey to reach the national goals and objectives it must listen to its writers. A writer's journey is a long and difficult one, conditioned by a collective national experience of high expectation. The condition that the Papua New Guinean writer is challenged by is the frugal and often-dubious relationship established with the nation. A relationship shattered in tragedy of the writer figure like Jimmy Damebo in *Wanpis* and resurrected as Lomo'ha, the orator in *Lomo'ha I Am, in Spirit's Voice I Call*.[11]

The responsibility we bear as Papua New Guinean writers is realized through our commitment to write. Through our writings we intervene in areas where the conscience of a nation is damaged by sentiments that imprison us from thinking constructively. Papua New Guinea's literary culture embodies the collective expressions of Papua New Guinea, thereby allowing the individual writer to be re-invested with the authority to represent a people by giving voice to the subaltern experience in our society. The subaltern experience therefore becomes the basis of questions related to the politics of representation. Since representation is problematic who indeed is interested in articulating the Papua New Guinean experience? I suggest we look into the literary culture already produced by Papua New Guineans. The writers have been mediating the differences by producing knowledge that reflects heterogeneity, plurality, and collectivity.

Through the literary knowledge the relationship between myth and reality, fiction and non-fiction, ideas and materialism are understood. In the short story, "Where Is Mummy?" Sorariba intervenes into some of the myths created in a Papua New Guinean's mind. The author questions some of the inherited ideas, values, and tradition. For example, on the issue of sexuality and purported violence, Sorariba observes that the "fault lay in the traditional Melanesian values of male dominated society. A terrible misconception reinforced by the introduced ethics of early missionaries which gave way to a confused perception that shorts or long trousers were only meant for men, and that the women were supposed to be well covered by missionary dresses or long skirts."[12]

Such misconceptions are juxtaposed against traditional Papua New Guinean views of sexuality and dress code. Sorariba then asks: "So what sort of men would these be? Behaving as if they had never seen a woman? What sort of men were those that had no sense of morality and had no sense of guilt or shame to go around harassing women in public?"[13] The writer's social conscience sets up the evaluation of the morality question. The difference between the negative consequences of modernity and traditional societies is mediated through Sorariba's text. Sorariba reveals a society constructed by a double conscience mentality. The potential to liberate the double conscience is increased when a writer encounters the everyday by questioning the very fabrics of social, political, and cultural constructions.

Nash Sorariba juxtaposes the urban experiences of modern Papua New Guineans with traditional values. His short stories are centered in a particular social context. His fiction conveys the burden of a unique PNG experience. Sorariba's work acts as the guide into the ever-changing society. His short stories focuses on introduced culture and challenges readers to interpret the fictional experience with reality: "You are an expensive bitch, a whore, a Whiteman's concubine. It's in your blood; that's what your kind are. Spreading your legs for Whiteman's money"[14]

Sorariba is critical of the changes taking place in Papua New Guinea. He portrays what may be an actual experience, resulting from culture conflict and confrontation. The abrogation strategy is more profound and clear from the way Sorariba rejects the introduced culture and returns to those values that are embedded in the Melanesian culture of respect, family obligation, and responsibilities in the society. The *wantok* system culture is also represented in most Papua New Guinean short stories. Minol argues that PNG short stories focused on themes of "change taking place, the romantic memories of village life, the pains of the growing urbanization and lately the criticisms and protest of the forces in power.[15] Sorariba's "Waiting for Botol" is an allegory of the abandonment of Papua New Guinea values and customs of caring and sharing. Simi the old man in the story represents the old ways, values, and the voices of the others in the Papua New Guinea villages.[16] His silent death on the eve of the country's Tenth Anniversary of Independence symbolically portrays modern Papua New Guineans neglecting the most respected ways of their ancestors. It is also about the shedding away of old ways and accepting new ways, while maintaining their identity.

Sorariba's will to write in English challenges the perceived notion that it is difficult to write in English. Sorariba fulfills his desire to write and to tell a simple, common everyday story to other Papua New Guineans. Through his stories Sorariba educates Papua New Guineans about their disastrous fate of social ills and ignorance of cultural values inherited from their indigenous communities. Through this process Sorariba embodies in his text the synchronized culture and effectively binds the oral and introduced western traditions of Papua New Guinea.

The tendency to replace village orators in post independent Papua New Guinea is also a task that writers seem to aspire to. The Papua New Guinean writers seem to think the independence dream is sour: "Pan Melanesian identity seems a dead letter while daylight hoodlums (affectionately known as rascals) patrol the streets."[17] Writers shifted their attention to the evaluation of change as it sweeps through the communities in Papua New Guinea. Papua New Guinean writers became "the conscience and the watchdogs of the nation". The writers celebrate the cultural diversity and unique traditions that hold people together. Even in the midst of gloom and postcolonial anxiety the writers are able to provide the positive imagery needed to mobile people to see themselves as blessed with the many things others don't have.

Nash Sorariba's *A Medal Without Honour* published in the 1990s, is a first single author anthology in Papua New Guinea. Sorariba began publishing short stories and poems in *Ondobondo* literary journal and other magazines in the 1980s. Sorariba follows the path many Papua New Guinean writers have taken and that is to have another salaried job while writing. This path requires great endurance and strength to deal with the difficulties and struggles within a society that is unwilling to honour its own writers. To live like a writer is to demise oneself in the skin of bureaucratized intellectuals, work as a public servant, and still perform the role of an agency of knowledge production. The bureaucratized intellectuals are like some of the prominent characters in Sorariba's literary society. These are Papua New Guineans with a sufficient level of literacy and numeracy skills, but are unable to think outside of the role described as public servants.

The making of a writer takes time and is a continuous activity. Writing demands patience and endurance. A Papua New Guinean writer begins the journey of discovery from the joy of having the first published writing to the satisfaction of having the first book published in one's own name. The limited publishing incentives, high mortality rate of the few literary magazines, the infrequent literary incentives (such as the National Literature Competition and kind newspaper sponsored pages), and the general lack of government support deny the existence of a writer.

Sorariba's collection of short stories represents distinctive Papua New Guinean experiences. In bringing the different voices together within the confines of a text, Sorariba celebrates the feast of diverse social, cultural, and political discourses of Papua New Guinea. Sorariba deals with pertinent themes and cross-cutting issues in Papua New Guinea. The collection features published stories as well as Sorariba's new work. The stories are exciting, provocative, and sensitive. The reader is able to find familiar experiences captured in the stories.

Sorariba's work has depth and texture. On the surface Sorariba gives us a good story. Beneath that lay an array of discourses that undercut the discursive formations of a society. Some of these discourses contest against each other. Others disperse in directions that are naturally progressive, but which ends up forming new discourses. Moreover, Sorariba manages to show some of the contradictions and confusions inherent in postcolonial Papua New Guinea. Sorariba represents the many voices and experiences of a heterogeneous Papua New Guinea society.

Papua New Guineans learn to deal with the contradictions and shortcomings of their society caught up in the ocean of modernism (the technological age influenced by the dominant global economy) and also tangled in passionate ways with the traditional village societies, customs, and values. Some of these values have crystallized into an obscure ideology, known as "Melanesian Way." Sorariba touches on this ideology in most of the stories, especially in "Melanesian Policeman," "Nogat Wantok-Nogat Wok," "He Was My Brother," "Sons Don't Return," and "Where is Mummy?" Sorariba represents a society torn by ideological confusions. Papua New Guinean societies are already over influenced by ideas impressed upon them by some obscure processes:

The struggle of people trying to live a city life baffled Charles but he was caught in it. The cheating, lying, stealing, black markets, marijuana, sex and money, was at first too fast a life for him. But eventually he had to come to terms with them. This was what they called-The Modern way of life.[18]

Such realities signal the direction of the society. Modernization on the shores of Papua New Guinea means transformation of the traditional society to a modern cash economy. The lifestyles and cultural traditions change in this process as Papua New Guineans make the difficult transition from village society to an urban one. The emphasis in political authority, too, shifts from the wisdom of village elders to the flamboyant rhetorics of modern politicians. Yet what is at stake here is democracy that is easily manipulated by a few powerful individuals within the society. In "The Home-Made Guns of Siruvaya," Sorariba writes about recurring problems of land ownership and compensation that has stifled the country in more ways than imagined:

When the landowners approached their representatives in parliament, they were told that the national government back in the capital city, Port Moresby had not released the funds yet. The 'National Lands' Minister had told them that the matter had been settled, between the companies and their representatives in Parliament, and that it had nothing to do with the national government.[19]

Contemporary Papua New Guinean societies are riddled with all kinds of excuses. Politicians and top bureaucrats use all kinds of excuses to embezzle money from public coffers. Effective delivery of government services to rural people is appalling. The nation's elite enjoys higher socioeconomic status while majority of the people struggle everyday. These are scenarios that are real in Papua New Guinea. Most people have come to tolerate the inequality and difficult times faced over the years.

These stories remind us about the ugly picture of development, social change, and upward mobility. The community seems to open itself up to all kinds of social infections. As a society does so, the individual in it struggles to liberate him/herself from such social inequality. The truth unveiled to us is that of human suffering endured within a largely uncaring society. In "Waiting for Botol" Simi, an old man epitomizes the experiences of a premature independence:

There are many like him, men, women and children. Empty bottles are the currency of Moresby's under world society. It keeps their hearts and bellies full. Those whose existence are never acknowledged by the rulers of the country: The illegitimate children of independence.[20]

The individuals in Sorariba's stories face conflicts between individualism and societal expectation. Individuals are forced into making decisions that hurt and destroy their sense of commitment to the society. The conflict is existential in nature, but out of individual martyrdom (like that of a writer) differences in the uneven distribution of power is visible.

In the story "No Daddy, No Baby, No More," Sorariba reveals the different levels on which power is exercised. Those with education and employment have more authority to make decisions than those without. Ironically, in the story "Nogat Wantok-Nogat Wok" the University educated Papua New Guineans also faces the same fate as urban drifters. We employ ideological signifiers to make connections with concepts such as the "Melanesian Way" or Papua New Guinean ways such as those loosely clustered under the "Wantok" system.

Papua New Guineans have yet to realize their dreams. The message in "The Sordid Affair," is about double standards in our changing society, which causes more social problems. The contestation for physical space as well as for maintaining PNG cultural values in two different systems results in alienation. Alienation already makes it possible for violence. The sense of community is threatened: fear and suspicion of unexpected terror dominate the consciousness of a people. Free movement of people and free expression of a society respecting itself is reduced to a society crippled by its own confused sensibility.

From "Geno and Karo," to "Waiting for Botol," insanity and hopelessness are faced every day in Port Moresby and other urban centers. Just like the son of a dying father in "Sons Don't Return," many Papua New Guineans are unable to return to their villages, their roots, and their people. Papua New Guineans are people on their way to forgetfulness and alienation in the modern world. The lack of trust and betrayal is no longer a game, but a depressing moment in Papua New Guinea history.

Sorariba's work draws attention to our responsibilities as writers. The first responsibility is to tell the truth without being repressed into a sanctioned fear of moral banishment. In this case, writers find themselves being forced into limiting their will to truth within a state that homogenizes its politics on faked nationalism, too often controlling the national conscience by institutionalizing its power over the individuals. The second responsibility is to make literature a symbol of cultural consciousness. A nation celebrates its nationhood if it can have collective symbols represented in works of art or literature, which reflect the consciousness of its people.

Once Papua New Guineans recognize these two responsibilities they can reach their visions as Papua New Guinean. The free conscience of a nation is the challenge of the national writer. Since PNG society is polycultural, the differences in voice require a dialogic process to emerge, whilst also acknowledging the crucial task of a distinctive practice that forms within the realm of knowledge formation. The written history of Papua New Guinea is no longer in the domain of those who control the means of production, but with the writers who are caught in the conflicts, contradictions, and confusing moments of a nation in crisis with itself.

Sorariba situates himself within the nexus of time and place in the history of Papua New Guinea. Sorariba's writing proves that Papua New Guinean literature has not waned, but is taking a new course in its literary history. Sorariba explores deep personal relationships to community loss brought about by the introduced lifestyles.

INTERVENING NEGATIVE STRUCTURES

Writing encounters embedded consciousness and renders them visible. Papua New Guinean writers are intervening into the internalized negative structures of thought that sustains a double conscience. The concern that Papua New Guinean literary culture is often about the negative consequences of modernization is immediately dismissed. With such a dismissal the political position of a Papua New Guinean writer is exposed. The necessity to articulate the Papua New Guinean experience is instituted concurrently with localized calls for indigenous knowledge production.

Positioning a Papua New Guinean writer in such a situation is very problematic. First, Papua New Guineans have to reaffirm their collective identity through individual differences. Cultural differences are therefore expressed in a structural literary form with its own ideological influences. Second, the liberating scheme involves the tools that effectively assault the dominant discourses by insisting on representation from within the culture of a writer. For such a project to work, Papua New Guinean writers must question the position from where the assault is staged and articulated: "To remain unwilling to rethink one's politics on the basis of questions posed is to opt for a dogmatic stand at the cost of both life and thought."[21] Hence, remaining unwilling to write activates silence, which invites distortion and misrepresentation of a heterogeneous Papua New Guinean experience. Such a practice is similar to Malagasy literature as observed by Manoni, though criticized by Fanon. The nameless Arab troublemaker in *The Outsider* by Camus is considered a representative of the silenced voices of the Arab world. [22]

Critical discursive activity formulates a collective identity freed from institutionalized colonialism. The internalized double consciousness is then questioned further to achieve a liberated society. The inability of Papua New Guinean writers to do so directs attention to the inconsistencies of the Papua New Guinean literary culture. Some of these inconsistencies owe their origin to the early Papua New Guinean writers's shift away from literary activities: "that some writers who had been prominent around 1970 had since ceased to write (only temporarily in many cases, as we learned later) and it ignored the fact that new young writers were springing up everywhere and that there was merely a change of emphasis and of outlets."[23] The Papua New Guinea literary culture of the 1980s and 1990s developed with renewed interests influenced by Papua New Guinean writers themselves. The slow publication of books in the 1980s did not mean that there were no literary works produced in Papua New Guinea. Literary activities were pursued by the Young writers pursued their writing interests in literary journals like *Ondobondo, The PNG Writer, Bikmaus, Sope, Mana Publications, Manoa, Meanjin* and the *Savannah Flames,* to name a few. A good survey of such a trend would reveal remarkable evidence that Papua New Guineans are writing, but are not exposed enough. Positive commentary and literary criticism by indigenous intellectuals have yet to develop. Soaba argues: "Perhaps we should begin by looking at ourselves as writers, the sort of writer that believe we are, and the qualitative aspects of that writing that we have been producing in the last three decades or so then look at the society we live in to see what sort of find there ourselves."[24] Soaba is hinting that literary culture is made up of three elements: writers, readers, and critics. All are involved in giving shape, depth, and voice to a literary culture.

The literary production centers too have shifted to other government institutions such as the National Broadcasting Commission, the national and local theater companies, the Institute of Papua New Guinea Studies, the National Research Institute, and private publishing houses such as Oxford University Press, Dellasta Pacific, and Kristen Pres. With works already published in literary journals mentioned earlier what kind of action will salvage them from their obscurity? A question that Regis Stella ponders in the collection of short stories: *Moments in Melanesia.*[25] If the question seems problematic what is the appropriate action? Do we seek publishing outside of Papua New Guinea in the way Stuart Watson did with new writings by Papua New Guineans in *Lost In Jungles Ways*? For me the literary culture of Papua New Guinea will remain obscured by our inability to intervene consciously.[26] More depressing is the lack of interests in the literary culture by Papua New Guineans themselves.

The call for intervention into this neglected scenario of its history comes with the belief: that action as a collective force must begin within a structure of experience. Such an intervention is based on the belief that a nation is founded on a collective expression of solidarity imagined simultaneously with change and development. The literary culture of a nation supports its nation's visions as "an imagined political community and imagined as both inherently limited and sovereign."[27] The political significance of a literary culture evidently reflects the social and cultural behavior of a nation. Papua New Guinean writers are already situated in a localized setting that is both creative and intellectual: "they prove that these local, specific struggles haven't been a mistake and haven't led to a dead end. One may even say that the role of the specific intellectual must become more and more important in proportion to the political responsibilities which he is obliged willy-nilly to accept." Whatever is produced through creative or intellectual labor goes towards the establishment of truth "by virtue of multiple forms of constraint" which enables power to be experienced.[28] All societies have their own forms of discourse to express their collective struggles.

Papua New Guinean literary culture has only to reconfigure its emphasis on how it develops the discourse about itself. Crocombe highlights such a phenomenon in relation to book production in the South Pacific: "So while government almost universally give strong emphasis on encouraging their indigenous languages, and while every effort should be made everyone concerned with book publications to respond to that wish as far as possible, it should be recognized that there will be significant constraints on it being achieved as fully as governments would wish."[29] The place of the Papua New Guinea writer has to be reconstituted in terms of its knowledge producing function.

WRESTLING WITH THE WORD

Short stories published after independence in several literary journals and anthologies are considered in this chapter. Short stories published in journals and anthologies received little critical attention.[30] Many Papua New Guineans write short stories than novels or autobiographies. Russell Soaba, Benjamin Umba, and John Kadiba of the first generation published short stories in journals such as *Bikmaus*, *Ondobondo*, *Imprints*, and *Meanjin* right into the 1980s. Another generation of writers in the likes of Sally Ann Pipi Bagita, Rex Okona, and Nash Sorariba maintained the continuity of writing in Papua New Guinea. The *Ondobondo* generation of the 1980s, include Regis Stella, May Paipaira, Joyce Kumbeli, Andrias Wabiria, and this author. The *Ondobondo* generation consists of students at the University of Papua New Guinea in the 1980s. Very little exists in terms of critical treatment of the short stories done between the period 1980 and the present.[31]

The innocent taste of creative writing shows in many student writings published in school and literary magazines. The impressive and unique designs of their cultures and imaginations are captured in writing as students attempt their first creative pieces. An Expressive Arts teacher at Kerowagi High School discovered that students began their artwork without any suggested models to aid their creativity.[32] The artistic expressions in Oceania "reflect the present nature of their societies, their beliefs and aspirations. The ethnic diversity of the region, as well as the vastly different environments and social circumstances of the people, means that their forms of creative expression encompass an enormous range of styles."[33]

A similar observation is made of the written narratives by Papua New Guineans. Chatterjee argues that most short stories written by Papua New

Guineans lack a literary device to hold them together.[34] What then do we make of works that are the same in their nature, meaning, purpose, and styles? The emergence of creative writing in Papua New Guinea aroused self-consciousness, self-assessment, and realization of the people's unique experiences. The writers felt the need to "give credibility and authenticity to our humanity and our sovereignty."[35] Writing in the period leading up to Independence was used to proclaim from every mountaintops, ridges, valleys, and seas the richness and varieties of the Papua New Guinean cultures.[36]

Post-Independence short story writers expressed their disillusionment with the colonial madness and nightmares. Anti colonial protests and fights for self-autonomy too were over. The tone of "fiery" language ceased all of a sudden after the attainment of independence. The post-independence writings of Papua New Guinea, especially in the 1980s centred around urban experiences, loss of tradition, and the consequences of change in the lives of Papua New Guineans. Papua New Guinean short story writers, like their Solomon Islands cousins, are writing about their people, "seeking to overcome the cultural dichotomy which presently faces them as they find themselves stranded by inroads and subjected by the twin imperatives of change and the need to preserve an image of itself."[37] An inevitable process of appropriation of the introduced written cultural knowledge and tools is taking place, which makes their writings as important contributions in the literatures of the postcolonial world.[38] Through the process of appropriation writers " reconstruct in writing, a culture of group of cultures which are very different from the one from which English emerges."[39] Reconstruction is actually taking a given form and converting the form for new uses.

Conclusion

The Papua New Guinean literary culture establishes frames of thought used as instruments to liberate the double conscience. It therefore follows that a community to reimagine itself must erase the double consciousness through aggressive articulation. The literary culture is therefore fundamental to the development of a society in contest with its national priorities and cultural development. The Papua New Guinean literary culture establishes frames of thought used as instruments to liberate the double conscience. It therefore follows that a community to reimagine itself must erase the double consciousness through aggressive articulation. The literary culture is therefore fundamental to the development of a society in contest with its national priorities and cultural development.

7

LISTEN MY COUNTRY

A vacuum exists in the critical study of writings by or about women in Papua New Guinea. This chapter discusses emergence of women writers in Papua New Guinea. The discussion attends to the issues of gender representations and the difficulties women writers face in their efforts to write and publish their works. Our discussion here is limited in scope. It is our attempt to establish some perspectives on the involvement of women in the production of a Papua New Guinea literary culture.

The story of women writers in Papua New Guinea is better described in Tok Pisin as *Meristori* for its slow development, together with the shyness exhibited by women in participating in the production of literary and cultural life of contemporary Papua New Guinea. Women are influenced more often by the existing structures and prevailing customs and traditions. The patriarchal traditions and the 'bigman' system of social political organizations have an overbearing on how women are treated in Papua New Guinea societies. Women are kept in the background and expected to participate according to the traditions of the society. Our discussions of women's participation in the literary tradition of Papua New Guinea is an effort to highlight the absence of women in the early period and the lack of participation of women in the production and amplification of the literary culture in Papua New Guinea.

In the 1970s and 1980s several women writers made their marks in Papua New Guinea literary history. Few women participated in the higher education system during the 1970s. Linda Thomas Kasaipwalova, Rita Mamavi, and Nora Vagi Brash published poetry, short stories, and plays. Adeola James describes their voices as "strong and unequivocal" against the male dominated Papua New Guinean society: "there is a quality of dynamism that permeates their work whether it is at the very topical plays of Nora Vagi Brash or the short stories of Sally-Ann Bagita; or the quiet, poetic reflections of Mary Toliman, Rita Pearson Mamavi, and Joyce Kumbeli. A pulsating energy characterizes the writer is experienced in the poems of Loujaya Dunar."[1]

Women writers of the 1980s and 1990s such as Sally-Ann Pipi Bagita, Loujaya Mojii Dunar (Kouza), Joyce Kumbeli, and Mary Toliman struggled to establish themselves as writers against domestic expectations and stereotype roles in a Melanesian society.

The international women's movement of the 1960s had an impact on many women in Papua New Guinea. Many educated women demanded equal rights and self-assertion in the development of the country. Yet, these demands and aspirations have achieved little to nothing in changing their lives or those of their sisters in the country. Papua New Guinea is still a male dominated society where political decisions and national priorities are far from making a difference in the lives of women in the country. The educated women folks make up a minor fraction of the total population.

Most women are still trapped in the age old traditions of Melanesian societies of bigman and male centred activities in areas of domesticity, politics, social production, and economic distribution of wealth: "within less than two decades after independence, the movement for change is not noticeable in the number of working women in the urban areas, or increase of female students in schools, colleges, and tertiary institutions, but also in the general attitudinal changes among women everywhere throughout the country."[2] One such woman is Gayum Kaman of the Simbu province, whose life is exemplary to others: "I was like a donkey or a workhorse. I was tired of that life and was going to break that tradition and work to improve my status."[3] Many women writers in Papua New Guinea realized this predicament. They tried to capture their experiences as well as of others in their writings.

Writing their experiences down allowed them to speak for themselves about their conditions and their plight to escape from the traditional structures and boundaries that bind them to servitude, cultural slavery, and subjected to male dominance. In their writings expressions of hope and change recur in as much as their encouragement to other women to take action to change the attitudes and perspectives of the male counterparts in their relationship to women: "the women writers are preoccupied with the recurring themes of change taking place in their society, their hopes for the future, and the types of Melanesian men and women that the forces of change should produce."[4]

The construction of women in the writings of Papua New Guinean male writers also needs critical attention. Women were described in lopsided images, playing secondary roles to their brothers, husbands, and male relatives. These stereotype images work at perpetuating the gender biased status of women in Papua New Guinea societies. Male writers handled the treatment of women poorly in published poetry, song, prose, and drama. Women are viewed as domestic house wives, commodities in bridal payments, over modernized and over educated, prostitutes, disillusioned members of the society, victims of male power, and as the most vulnerable members of the changing society in the modern world. These images legitimate the subjugation of women in Papua New Guinea societies.

RESPONSIBLE WOMEN

A women's literary tradition is far behind their male counterparts. The responsibility to do a feminist critical reading of Papua New Guinean writing remains with women writers and scholars. Women critiquing women's writing or writings by men is absent in the country. Male writers and scholars dominate all areas of critical study. In the 1980s a number of women took up powerful roles in the social and political spaces of the nation. A number of women took on political offices with high status in the public service. The number of women entering the higher education system increased dramatically. Kelep-Malpo writes that in "the last 30 years women have increasingly taken up the challenge and contributed to this country's development alongside their male counterparts despite the increasing law and order problems."[5] At independence Papua New Guinea accepted as one of the national goals and directive principles: "we declare out second goal to be for all citizens to have an equal opportunity to participate in and benefit from the development of our country." The increasing number of women leaders attests to the slow unfolding process of political participation of women leaders in Papua New Guinea. Kelep-Malpo lists some of these women leaders with exemplary lives: "Ms. Margaret Elias, the former Secretary for Personal Management, Dr. Naomi Tulaha, the former Commissioner for Higher Education, Mrs. Anne-Marie Kona, the senior inspector for National Capital District [sic], Dr. Anne Dickson Waiko, from the University of Papua New Guinea, Mrs. Winifred Kamit, a businesswoman who was once an ombudsperson, Ms. Maria Kopkop, the Principal of Kopkop College, Mrs. Tess Sition Chan, a former Registrar of the PNG University of Technology, late Margaret Nakikus, former Director, National Planning Office, Ms. [Dame] Josephine Abaijah [sic], a former Parliamentarian, late Alice Wadega, the first female Parliamentarian, Ms. Kathleen Sakias, Executive Director provincial radio stations, Dr. Rona Nadile, First Assistant Secretary, DRD & EP of the Labour Department, Ms. Francesca Semoso, the Deputy Speaker of the Autonomous Bougainville government, late Elizabeth Yip, the first national woman to head secondary schools in the country in the 1970s and many others."[6]

The exemplary lives of the pioneer women leaders created interests in the representations of women in Papua New Guinea. Women began to question themselves in relation to their men folks: "a study by Turner (1993) revealed that Dr. Naomi Tulaha who was one of the prominent female leaders focused on in the study and was the Commissioner for Higher Education said she did not encounter any problems from her male colleagues while she was their leader. Similarly, Mrs. Anne-Marie Kona, who is now a senior school inspector, shared how she rarely received negative remarks from her male colleagues and students when she was a head teacher of several schools in the national capital district."[7] The most poignant of the relationship borne out of the colonial system is that of Dame Josephine Abaijah. She recounts what had changed her:

> "I had been as unprepared for the violent assault on my mind by blacks in London as I had been for the bitterness of colonialism in Port Moresby... I was a reject of the whites at home," thereby leaving her no choice but to "steer a middle course."[8]

CHANGING LIFESTYLES

The changing lifestyles of women in society inspired women writers to offer commentaries and criticisms of their lot in literature. Few women writers have attempted to bring this aspect out to the rest of the world. The ever-inspiring Nora Vagi Brash leads in this department in the dramatic representation of women. Her most performed and read play is *Which Way Big Man*, which captures this aspect in a persuasive and influential way. Ann Turner describes Nora Vagi Brash as an unpretentious person with a good sense of humour, which she deploys in her plays to ridicule the elites in her society:

> "...a completely unpretentious and egalitarian person, Nora accepts people for their basic worth and is unaffected by wealth and social status. She appreciates being able to live in material comfort, but does no regard money and possessions as among the most important things in life. She has wit, humour, and a strong sense of fun. She is able to see the contradictions and irony in many social situations. She exploits this insight in her writing to attack those whom she sees as being pretentious and hypocritical. She tries to see herself and her work objectively but, in fact, underestimates the influence her personality and writing have on others."[9] When probed about whether there is a need for literature by women that addresses the problems women face in Papua New Guinea, Nora Vagi Brash makes the significant point that her work does not seek to address the women's issues alone: "I think there is a great need for that kind of literature and there are people who write about those issues. There are definite problems about women that writers can focus on."[10]

Nora Vagi Brash takes the position that in "nation building, there are many problems, so the way I see it you just can't afford to promote one and leave one behind."[11] Nora Brash is aware of the issues that women face in PNG, but she has opted to remain distanced from the influence of feminism developed in the West. Brash explains that the "only time I am faced with this subject is when I go to various conferences and I get to sit on the panel with feminists... I write about everybody, men and women."[12] Brash is uninterested in the kinds of demands Western feminism make on women writers around the world: "There is a definite woman's point of view which can be explored in writing about women's issues, but I am just not cut out to do that. This is a pity, really, as I am the only woman in my family; I have five brothers."[13] Brash has always maintained this principle throughout her writing life. Though feminism is not her cup of tea Brash is at her best when issues of race, class, and elitism inspire her to write with vigor and dynamism. Brash remains committed to her writing. She does occasional readings and performances of her work in Port Moresby and overseas.

The women who wrote about their experiences recognized the need for self-representation as well as the need to express themselves in a medium, which is shared by other women. In her interview with Adeola James at UPNG, Loujaya Mojii Dunar Kouza was asked about her views on the problems women encounter in Papua New Guinea. Loujaya responded with the conviction that it will takes years before the mind-set of men is changed to respect women:

> "I don't have that kind of approach whereby I go to a woman who is being abused and tell her that she must do this or that. All I can do is to talk about myself and what I have gone through and just be an example. It will always be there, the abuse and so on, and it will be more so because we are going through a transition when our men folk are feeling threatened. Their position in the house is no longer a sole responsibility. Women are also questioning their responsibility and asking, "Why don't we share that responsibility?" As long as we have women thinking for themselves and having their own ideas, we will always have that problem. But we are the ones to educate our men by the way we conduct ourselves. It takes years. We have to get through to our men. The way to do it is to start with our children because if we can't get through to our adult male population, at least every mother can try getting through to her sons. Then the next generation will be considerably better people."[14]

Through writing women create a dialogic environment in which their experiences as Papua New Guinea women are given significance. Women are able to talk about their feelings and experiences as women, their struggle against the male dominated world, and their consciousness as women in the contemporary world.

As women, mothers, housewives, and aunties women writers give significance in their lives: "I think that we as writers in Papua New Guinea today should address these issues, especially wife-bashing, wife-insults and other evil behaviours that come under the topic treatment of women in our society. The drinking problem is related to the problem of wife bashing — that too should be declaimed."[15] Women writers provide different perspectives to that of their male counterparts in Papua New Guinea. For example, Nora Vagi Brash explains why she created a character such as Sinob in her play *Which Way Big Man?*:

> Her grandmother was my grandmother's sister. That is why I noticed the change in her attitude straight away. I felt that a statement of some sort needed to be made about this state of affairs for, if she does this to me and I am her equal, how does she treat grassroots people? My immediate reaction is, how does she react to the village people? That is what started me thinking about the character of the old man in *Which Way Big Man*?[16]

In her autobiography, *A Thousand Coloured Dreams*, Josephine Abaijah presents a lucid account of her life that began from a humble beginning to one that propelled her into a colonial and postcolonial political life. In her narratives Dame Josephine unashamedly talks about her early struggle as a girl coming to terms with the colonial world. In that world she moved between the educational institutions and from her career to the formation of the Papua Besena political party. She recalls Papua not as a place for a young Papuan woman:

> It all started at the native village of Wamira on the northeast coast of Papua. My mother, a young, grass-skirted bride of seventeen, was at full term in the village. My father, seven years older, was away working 'trade' for the Australian foreigners — the colonial masters who manipulated our lives, our thoughts and our gods to serve their ends.[17]

Abaijah was brought up in the 1930s. After the war years she was sent away to school in Australia. The colonial times were very difficult times for Abaijah, but with courage and strength she moved through them: "the colonizers introduced their religion, their language and their materials when they colonize a country."[18] Abaijah spent 18 years of her early life on Missima. She attended the first government primary school in 1950s. She was the only girl in her class, finishing the first four years of crash course, and later sent to another crash course in Australia, after finishing another year on the mainland. She studied for another four years in Australia before returning to her country. She began her career as a medical assistant to her mentor, Dr. Parker. He sent her, to the first Papua Medical School in Port Moresby, for her medical and nursing education.[19] It was here that she confronted what would become the most influential moment of her time:

> A few of us had been suddenly caught on the crest of the wave of Australian decolonization and we were carried on by an energy that we could not control. I lived in a peculiar world in which everything was a first. At no place was

there any past. No successes, no failures, no honour rolls of past, students or distinguished dead. No end, no beginnings. We did not know where we were going and we scarcely knew where we came from. There was no history, no past, no heroes to salute or worship. Nobody has ever been there for us. We were a ghost army on patrol in an unknown land, marching toward tomorrow.[20]

Abaijah's pioneer experience is unique in Papua New Guinea. Unlike many other women in Papua New Guinea, Dame Josephine is lucky enough to gain the experience that propelled into the world outside her own society. Most women are still unable to break away from traditions and societies that bind them. The suggestion here is also about writing by women.

Mary Toliman observes the lack of interests Papua New Guinean women have on writing down their experiences:

There are probably many reasons for that. One is that there is certainly a lot more emphasis on encouraging men to write. Women in this country should really take an active interest themselves, in this process. Maybe we need more workshops to focus on women's writing. There has not been enough encouragement for girls in schools to explore this area of their talent. I see the problem falling into different categories, but what is most important is that women themselves take an active interest in writing. For example, I see how Nora Vagi Brash is developing as a writer. She should be an inspiration to our young girls.[21]

Loujaya Kouza Dunar views the writing life of women as a positive experience:

Right now in Papua New Guinea we are in a time when people have a lot of problems and people are looking for direction. I like to portray, not only in my poetry but also in my music that we suffer and we can feel pain but we can take it in two directions. We can continue to wallow in regret and live in the past, but that sort of thing will not get us anywhere. Or we can build on all those sufferings and become a better people and try not to let it happen to our children and try to make the world a better place.[22]

The inconsistency in the writing life of Papua New Guinean women writers is no different to their male counterparts, though individuals may have specific struggles related to their writing life. For Joyce Kumbeli, her writing caused her some difficult domestic problems: "I think it is because being married creates some problems. At least in my own case, my husband doesn't like me to write. I think he is afraid that I'll expose what is happening in the family."[23] For Nora Vagi Brash, writing is a continuous activity, but the problem with publishing seems to be the biggest problem:

People tell me they were writing but they have no outlet. If I am living here, I will go and read in tabari place. I have tried it once and it worked. We also tried reading at Koki market and it worked. You just can't sit down and wait for publishers to come to you. You've got to do something to give to them. I suppose it is also discouraging when people write and write and can't get published.[24]

Mary Toliman's problem is finding the time to write:

The main problem is finding the time to sit down and write. The second problem is playing the two roles of writer and mother at the same time. The most difficult time for me is in the evening when I come home, and the kids want attention. It may be a time when I am at the point of finishing a poem, when a child falls sick and I have to rush him to the hospital. That is certainly one of the most difficult challenges of being a writer and a mother. On the one hand I think it is also beautiful.[25]

These Papua New Guinean women writers direct us to the need to recognize problems, struggles, prospects, and challenges women in Papua New Guinea face in their everyday experiences. Toliman's resistance to easy categorization of women under the conceptual framework of feminism directs our attention to the unique experiences of women in Papua New Guinea. The experience of women in Papua New Guinea is different to women elsewhere in the world. Women in Papua New Guinea are conscious of their links to their traditions and their status outside of tradition. Women are aware of the predicament they face in Papua New Guinea as mothers, daughters, aunties, grandmothers, and professional persons. It is easy to be anyone of the pronouns, but it is not that easy to be a writer, a thinker, or a person totally cut off from Melanesian traditions.

In the poem "The Woman" Loujaya Kouza Dunar expresses the life of women as mothers in the country:

The woman that was brought forth
From the womb of mother nature
Was bound by the umbilical cord
Of labour and suffering

She was born, raised, bred
And sold like a pig to a buyer
Her husband;
For him must she slave and
Sweat to feed his empty bowels
To fill him with satisfaction

She would get nothing in return
But a child within her.

A child to be suckled and fed
And later torn from her sides
Leaving her empty, a barren
Woman seeming nothing more
Than a slaving animal.[26]

In a poem we can see that only women can write more honestly about their experiences, their views, visions, and struggles as women. The importance of women's voices and experiences are captured in poems, short stories, autobiographies and novels.

LISTEN MY COUNTRY

Papua New Guinean women were in parliament since 1961. A simple Papua New Guinean village woman made history that even some of the history books, except for Eric Jones' book on Dame Alice Wedega, have no records of.[27] PNG women have been asking their country to listen to what they have to say about themselves. We have not been listening. We have been assuming their voices all along. In so doing we have denied women to speak for themselves.

In her autobiography, *Listen My Country*,[28] Dame Alice Wedega answers one of the moral question of our time asked by Gayatri Spivak: Can the subaltern speak?[29] Can PNG women speak for themselves? In her life and in her book, Dame Alice, pleaded with her country to hear the voices of women. The book was published in 1981, a first by a Papua New Guinean woman. Dame Alice was born in 1905 to Wedega Gamahari and Ema of Alo Alo village in Milne Bay province. She went to school at Kwato mission school led by Cecil Abel of the London Missionary Society fame. In a book on colonial impact between 1884 and 1984 Dr. Anne Dickson Waiko and Professor Tony Deklen made scanty references to Dame Alice's part in the 1961 Legislative Council.[30]

Dame Alice did so much in her lifetime by speaking for our women in international gatherings in New Zealand, India, Sri Lanka and in Europe. A pioneer member of the Legislative Council between 1961 and 1964, she was one of the nine native representatives during the Australian colonial administration. Dame Alice's life story is exemplary of a colonised Papua New Guinean woman's ability to rise above the ordinary to transcend all expectations by participating in a political process dominated by white Australian males. She worked with Sir Cecil to bring Christianity to Abau and parts of Central province in 1935. She founded the Ahioma Training Centre in the early 1960s to train women welfare assistants in Papua New Guinea. In 1952 she represented women's rights at the Pan-Pacific women's conference in Christchurch, New Zealand. Later in 1952 she led the Moral Re-armament Group to India and Sri Lanka.

Her story is brought up again in Deklin's discussion on the Constitutional development, especially for a home-grown Constitution, in PNG between 1962 and 1975. Following World War II Papua New Guineans played no part in decision-making in terms of Constitutional changes until 1964. During this time the Legislative Council, created by the Papua New Guinea Act 1949, was the body advising the administrator on the running of the territory administration. This Act was the basic colonial constitution until it was repealed in 1975.[31]

Only three Papua New Guineans were nominated on the Legislative Council of 29 members since 1951. The Legislative Council Ordinance 1951, however, prohibited them from voting or being elected on the grounds that they were "natives." This remained until 1960 when nine additional members were added in the new Legislative Council. The significant constitutional change in 1960, according to Deklin, was "the principle of indirect election of native members of the Legislative Council authorised by the Legislative Council Ordinance 1960."[32] The climate in the early 1960s was such that the Australian government wanted the indigenous representatives to vote with them on any major legislative changes because the administration chose them for such purposes. Of course, we now know, that Dame Alice did vote if she felt it was right. She voted against the administration if her conscience wins, as was the case against the Bill on Liquor Licensing in 1962.

In the Legislative Council of 1961 there was the sense of feeling that Papua New Guineans must take control of the future development of the Constitution. As a member to the Legislative Council, Dame Alice had the opportunity to vote for any legislative changes that would have a dramatic impact in the lives of Papua New Guineans. One such important vote was on the formation of the Select Committee on political development on March 9, 1962. Of course, later in the political development of PNG, in the 1964 and 1968 House of Assembly new constitutional development committees were formed, headed by Sir John Guise and Paulus Arek, respectively. The last, but most important committee, known as the Constitutional Planning Committee of 1972 was chaired by Michael Somare and later by John Momis. By this time, Dame Alice was out of the political scene. She resigned from the Department of Welfare Services and went back to missionary work in 1972. She was awarded the MBE (Member of the British Empire) that same year. Be it national politics, public service, or missionary work, Dame Alice had been a stout ambassador for women's voices in PNG for many years.

The current efforts to have women members nominated to Parliament have come under a lot of scrutiny from the public, politicians, women's groups, and NGOs. The decision to have women nominated to Parliament or voted in remains a political hopscotch.

WOMEN IN PARLIAMENT

The national election is important for women of Papua New Guinea. Before the 2012 national election the parliament rejected the proposal to appoint women into Parliament. The proposal failed to get the vote it needed to become a statutory law enabling women a place in the decision making chambers of parliament.

That leaves women in Papua New Guinea to challenge their male counterparts in the 2012 election. In that year's election a number of women have taken the call to prove their worth just as the male folks.

Total number of women nominated to contest was more than previous elections. Some of these women are contesting as Independent candidates. Others are supported by the political parties. Two women lead political parties as their leaders. Some of these women have contested in previous elections. Others have just raised their hands to be noticed.

It was hoped that the results for women in the 2012 National Elections would change the political history of this country. Having more women in Parliament will shift the political culture to another level. It is difficult to see any shift without including our women folks in the Parliament. Women should be given the opportunity to lead through our votes.

Consider the information on women in parliament presented in Eric Johns' *History Through Stories: Book Two* (2006): "Only one Papua New Guinean woman, Ana Frank Gaudi, with two Australian women, stood for the first House of Assembly elections in 1964, and only an Australian woman stood for the second House of Assembly elections in 1968. No women were successful in either elections. Josephine Abaijah was the first women elected to the national parliament, in 1972. When Abaijah, Nahau Rooney, and Waliyato Clowes were successful in 1977, it seemed that a breakthrough had been made for women. However, in 1982, only Rooney was re-elected and no women were successful in the elections of 1987 and 1992. In 1997, Abaijah was returned, along with Carol Kidu, but in 2002 Kidu was the only woman elected."[33]

Dame Lady Carol Kidu was reelected in 2007 until the end of the 2012 Parliamentary term. Dame Lady Carol Kidu has retired from active politics to pursue other interests. If no women were elected to parliament in 2012 then parliament will have no women representation, leaning towards a male only parliament.

Over the years the number of women contesting the elections had increased, but the results were against the women folks. In 1972 four women contested, but only one woman (Josephine Abaijah) was elected. Of the ten women who contested in 1977 only three women (Josephine Abaijah, Nahau Rooney, Waliyato Clowes) were elected. For the 1982 election, only one (Nahau Rooney) of the 17 women who contested was elected. It seemed to have gained more interests around 1987 when 18 women contested, but no one was elected. The same result was produced in 1992 when 17 women contested the national elections.[34] Veteran female politician Josephine Abaijah and new-comer Carol Kidu were elected to Parliament in 1997, which saw the highest number of 55 women contestants. The poor result of 1997 did not do any better at the elections in 2002 when 60 women contested the elections. Only Dame Lady Carol Kidu won in that election and again in 2007.

With this statistical analysis I am ambivalent about the results in this election. The change in mind-set and will to change political culture is needed before any women can be elected into parliament. I also think that women candidates contesting this (2012) election needed more than popularity to win. It seems some candidates are contesting in big ponds while others in small ponds where chances are good. Nonetheless their fates lie in the voter psychology and desire for change.

It can never be argued that candidates who stood before can never win. The cases of Abaijah, Rooney, and Kidu have proven that voters are intelligent enough to want the best person for a leader.

Or it can never be argued that Papua New Guineans are unwilling to change their often too male concentric perspectives of women leaders. There is a change, but at a snail's pace, we observe.

Eric Johns asked the question that begs to be answered: "Why have so few women been elected? Although conditions are not the same throughout the country, the majority of Papua New Guineans still believe that women should not be leaders or make important decisions because that is the work of men. Many women who have achieved success in the public service, private enterprise, universities and other fields, have come into contact with family or community members who believe that women's work is the home. There is even more criticism of women who wish to enter the national parliament. Unless these attitudes change, women will continue to find it almost impossible to be elected, thus excluding half of the country's population from having any say in important decisions that affect everyone."[35]

Many of us will agree that the women who were elected or nominated to parliament were exemplary leaders. Some of them have written their autobiographies that Papua New Guineans have benefited from reading about what makes a great leader. In her autobiography *Listen My Country* (1981) we learnt Dame Alice Wadega was the first PNG woman knight (1982) to be appointed to the Legislative Council (1961). In Dame Josephine Abaijah's autobiography *A Thousand Coloured Dreams* (1981) we learnt that she founded the political party Papua Besena (Hands off Papua), and from Dame Lady Carol Kidu's we learnt of her courage to marry a young Papua New Guinean lawyer, and making the incredible journey to the land of the unexpected, where she became a political leader and exemplary Pacific leader in her own right.[36]

Someone who had formed her own political party was Waliyato Clowes known as Panal (Papuan Alliances) when she was elected to Parliament in 1977. Clowes was quoted as saying: "A lot of men think we are rubbish and take no notice of us."[37]

CONCLUSION

Women writers in Papua New Guinea need a lot of support, encouragement, and recognition. Many women are writing without seeing their works published. The autobiographies of Dame Wadega, Dame Josephine, Dame Lady Carol Kidu are revealing in that the struggles these women leaders have gone through tells a million stories of women in Papua New Guinea. These autobiographical narratives have one important role: they serve as the inspirational narratives to women in Papua New Guinea. It is important women write about themselves as a way of promoting their cause and encouraging others to rise up, to speak up, and to be counted.

8

A NOVELISTIC TRADITION

Papua New Guineans began writing out of the necessity to express themselves in the written form. The entry into the literary world marks the investigation into the self, society, and history. Papua New Guinean writers wrote out of a deep inner necessity. They used structures of writing from their own traditional cultures and from the written tradition. The literary production in Papua Guinea is intertextual since the "subject of the text is composed of discourses" to form "a signifying system."[1] This dynamic process brings into context a unitary system that is structured on the basis of various textualities played out against each other. For the Papua New Guinean writer, literature in the general sense is a serious business. Through writing Papua New Guineans discovered their recent history, its turning point, and its future. A natural desire to create, invent, and reconstruct a new written culture out of the colonized experience took on more urgency.[2]

The entry into the literary world is significant. An indigenous author faces the challenging tasks of mediating between the oral culture and the literary culture. European English literature was part of the Literature courses at the University of Papua New Guinea. The Europeans' manipulation of the environment in relation to the manners and morals of the colonials of the period could have helped trigger the literary flame as well. The emerging tradition of novels in postcolonial world also triggered the urge in Papua New Guineans to write their own books. The motivation to write emerged out of the need to make sense of the "problematic relationship both to the mechanics of writing and the specificity of an indigenous language, with all the constitutive intellectual and emotional forces concentrated in it." Through writing Papua New Guinean writers "mediate between the opposing forces, generate a space for new and more appropriate reasons of personal and domestic development." The mediation provided "a vantage point for satiric examination of foibles and vices in all the contextual systems of knowledge."[3]

The early Papua New Guinean writers constructed their texts using models and forms available in their unwritten cultures. They used the tools and knowledge of the written culture to express their unique experiences as Papua New Guineans. They used their traditional cultures and way of life to juxtapose against the Europeans cultures and way of life under the control of Australians. Early writing in Papua New Guinea shows "evidence of such critical awareness." Many early writers of Papua New Guinea wrote "without much thought of the superficial words and genres of the book knowledge."[4] The important issue is that for the first time a concentrated effort in writing had begun to shake the foundation of the colonizers.

The desire to express their problematic position in a changing environment also motivated Papua New Guineans to write. The novel provided the canvass on which they painted their complex historical, linguistic, cultural and political backgrounds. The "structures, imagery and rhetoric"[5] of the novel serve to enforce an ideology reflecting an entirely new unaffected response, perhaps, primordial, and free of the expectation of the literary conventions.

Papua New Guinean novels are sometimes criticized for being inadequate and experimental in nature. A common assumption is that there are no Papua New Guinean novels or a literary culture active enough for critical study. For our sake we argue that the Papua New Guinean novel is part of a literary culture that has developed over the years. This literary culture is a significant aspect of the contemporary Papua New Guinean culture. The novel encompasses the polycultural, multilingual, and diverse experiences of the pre-colonial, colonial, and post-colonial experiences of Papua New Guinea. The concept of a "novelistic discourse" as used in Bakhtin's dialogic imagination is useful to this discussion. The novel has several stylistic elements that are heterogeneous in style:

1. Direct authorial literary-artistic narration (in all its diverse variants);
2. Stylization of the various forms of oral everyday narration *(skaz)*;
3. Stylization of the various forms of semi-literary (written) everyday narration (the letter, the diary, etc.);
4. Various forms of literary but extra-artistic authorial speech (moral, philosophical or scientific statements, oratory, ethnographic descriptions, memoranda and so forth),
5. The stylistically individualized speech of characters.[6]

These five basic types of compositional stylistics are relevant to our discussion on the various narratives and literary works that Papua New Guineans created since they began publishing works literature. These elements of the novelistic discourse will help us to view the literature of Papua New Guinea in a way that frees them from the criticism of failing to meet the requirements of traditional

European structures of a novel. Our discussion follows Bakhtin's explanations of what a novel is all about:

> The novel can be defined as a diversity of social speech types (sometimes even diversity of languages) and a diversity of individual voices, artistically organized. The internal stratification of any single national language into social dialects, characteristic group behavior, professional jargons, generic languages, languages of generations and age groups, tendentious languages, languages of the authorities, of various circles and of passing fashions, languages that serve the specific sociopolitical purposes of the day, even of the hour (each day has its own slogan, its own vocabulary, its own emphases) — this internal stratification present in every language at any given moment of its historical existence is the indispensible prerequisite for the novel as a genre. [7]

The point here is that the novel is structured in every sense of it that analysis must take into account all the relevant elements taken into the construction of a work of literature. The novel is artistically organized based on the rules of internal structural constructions. Bakhtin's ideas of the novel appeal to our investigation of the PNG novelistic tradition: "The novel orchestrates all its themes, the totality of the world of objects and ideas depicted and expressed in it, by means of the social diversity of speech types [*raznorecie*] and by the differing individual voices that flourish under such conditions." [8]

It becomes clear in this chapter and elsewhere in the book our investigation of the PNG novel is about many of the notions of the novel in the Bakhtinian sense. We are interested in the authorial intrusion in the text, " the speeches of narrators, inserted genres, the speech of characters are merely those fundamental compositional unities with whose help heteroglossia [*raznorecie*] can enter into the novel, each of them permits a multiplicity of social voices and a wide variety of their links and interrelationships (always more or less dialogized)." [9] The Papua New Guinean novel consists of many of these features and more, each of them forming important intertextual relationships that form a novelistic discourse: "These distinctive links and interrelationships between utterances and languages, this movement of the theme through different languages and speech types, its dispersion into the rivulets and droplets of social heteroglossia, its dialogization—this is the basic distinguishing feature of the stylistics of the novel." [10]

THE PAPUA NEW GUINEAN NOVEL

Papua New Guineans write autobiography, semi-autobiography, novels, novellas, short stories, plays, and poetry. The style is a combination of actual historical accounts, personal anecdotes, vicarious experiences, and various life stories worth writing about. The Papua New Guinean novel has a mixture of styles, influences, and traditions. It is a source of strength and vitality, and not the cause of weakness and diminution of insight. The critical question to consider is the direction the Papua New Guinean novel took since the publication of Albert Maori Kiki's autobiography, *Ten Thousand Years in a Lifetime* (1968).[11]

Their newfound talent and the acquiring of knowledge of the written culture offered an important opportunity for Papua New Guinean writers. The writers celebrated their newfound talent in various genres. They transferred their cultural, social, and political beliefs into a powerful form of art. It was a radical reorientation of the indigenous mind, from passive acceptance to indignation that led to a critical reassessment of national identity and self-consciousness in the process of nation formation. Their writings consist of a reflection or a sense of nostalgia for traditions, cultures, and values lost during the time of colonial invasion. Traditional village situations are idealized and celebrated as time-immemorial customs. The belief and knowledge systems of Papua New Guineans are given significance in their work.

Early PNG writers considered the new identity brought about by the social, political, and cultural changes in their societies. Papua New Guinean writers dealt with "growing up in a country controlled by unsympathetic foreigners, the experiences of competing cultures, victimization through racial prejudice, the sense of alienation, the struggle for independence, the establishment of an independent nation, and the movement to the political and social revolution."[12] Such a popular use of the subject among writers conveyed to fellow nationals and to readers from the colonial powers, the nationalistic feelings of against the colonisers.

In almost all Papua New Guinean novels a "good deal of care is often expended in the early chapters explaining the local tribe or village scene to those unfamiliar with it."[13] Nearly all Papua New Guinean novels are constructed in this manner. The writers utilize the rare opportunity to include and define certain words, phrases, images, metaphors, and linguistic elements. This is done through various strategic processes identified by post-colonial literary theorists. These strategies include features of appropriation such as glossing (parenthetical translation of individual words), untranslated words (selective lexical fidelity and leaves some words untranslated in the text is a more widely used device for conveying the sense of cultural distinctiveness), interlanguage (fusion of two languages' linguistic structures as interface signs to foreground cultural distinctions), syntactic fusion (intermarrying of local language syntax to that of the lexical forms of English), code switching and vernacular translation (the technique of switching between two or more codes to make dialects more accessible).[14] All these strategies are combined with the storytelling mode and the various elements of the written culture.

There are three stages in the development of Papua New Guinean literary culture. The first stage in the literary evolution of the Papua New Guinean novel is basically anticolonial writing. The period between 1968 and 1978 marks the first phase in the development of the Papua New Guinean literary culture. Second, writings done after independence are personal or self-conscious articulations. The period between 1979 and 1989 marks this phase of development. Third, writing became a kind of light entertainment rather than a committed activity. This phase is marked by the period in between 1989 and 1999. Soaba criticizes the last stage as inadequate in maintaining consistency in its development. These stages are based on Soaba's concern for the ultimate direction of Papua New Guinean literature. Soaba fears the silent withdrawal, by serious writers, into a vacuum of inactivity and a lack of inspiration for future writers. Soaba is concerned about standards and styles of writing. The principle of forms, through time, transcends those initially committed to open creativity. In this sense "the real problem is not that of being restricted by rules-or the absence of such a restriction-but the necessity of inventing forms of expression, or merely finding them not ideal forms, or forms derived from a principle which transcends the enterprise itself but forms which can be used immediately as the means of expression for a determined content; the question of value of these forms cannot reach beyond the immediate issue." [15]

Papua New Guinean writers experimented with the forms available to them. The forms of expression are already there in the culture. Papua New Guinean authors have only to use the forms and styles for their own purposes. It is within this conceptualization that a writer comes to recognize the multiplicity and diversity of inheritance. These conceptual apparatuses governed how we see ourselves and others with whom we interact with. A dialogic space is created for multiple discourses to interact, to contest, and to negotiate with each other. "This space is not a territory staked out by exclusionary practices," says Lionet. "Rather, it functions as a sheltering site; one [that] can nurture our differences without encouraging us to withdraw into new dead ends, without enclosing us within facile oppositional practices or sterile denunciation and disavowals. For it is only by imagining nonhierarchical a mode of relation among cultures that we can address the crucial issues of indeterminacy and solidarity."[16] Lionet further illuminates the nonhierarchical connection. This link "encourages lateral relations: instead of living within the bounds created by the linear view of history and society." Papua New Guinean writers seized the opportunity "to interact on an equal footing with all the traditions that determine [our] present predicament."[17]

Autobiographical writing describes the colonized people or that of any similar historical experiences. There are disputes on what autobiography really is, and to what extent it is to be recognized as art. It is argued, however, that there are many differentiated forms of autobiography.[18] Pascal in confronting this question goes further to distinguish autobiography proper from other literary forms and branches of the autobiographical genres such as letters, memoirs, diaries, and confessions. Autobiographical and semi-autobiographical genres have developed in Papua New Guinea over the last five decades. Most prose narratives by Papua New Guineans are written as conventional autobiographical writing or as semi- autobiographical novels.

THE AUTOBIOGRAPHICAL NARRATIVES

Papua New Guinean authors have a strong bond with the autobiographical literary tradition. The historical and psychological origins of the genre and how it began is not our concern here.[19] Our attempt here is to discover through the autobiographical tradition the considerable textual practice of Papua New Guinean authors. Papua New Guinean writers have used the autobiography model to redefine place, persons, and cultural backgrounds of their people. The autobiographical form as a textual system of thought gives, in the Bakhtinian sense, "voices" or "dialogism" which take shape from an immediate "event or situation of experience" that "take on almost physical particularity, so that 'life' with which logic must be connected appears to be composed of unique experiential moment."[20] Autobiographical works "represent the self in and through its relationships with the outer world." This "involves the recollection of the movement of a life, or part of a life, in actual circumstances in which it was lived." A story is constructed out of a "pattern on life" as it evolves in a writer's life. Autobiographical writing "establishes certain stages in an individual life, makes links between them, and defines, implicitly or explicitly, a certain consistency of relationships between the self and the outside world."[21]

As the mediator of the past and present, an autobiography uncovers significant aspects of a person's history and life. Indeed, the Papua New Guinean author is at the very core of this activity. Pascal's sense of an autobiography, as a genre is used as a tool to read Papua New Guinean narrative discourses. Stull offers three distinctive branches of autobiography as followed in the Europeans literary tradition: a) the classical or conventional autobiography (as in the case of Grillparzer), in which the author's sole concern is to present the story of his life as factually and "objectively" as possible; b) "Poetry and Truth" as in Goethe and Wordsworth where the factual autobiographical experience is sacrificed or at least subjected to the artistic intent; and c) the autobiographical novel (often referred to as *Kunstlerroman*) — Goethe's *Werther*, and Rousseau's *Nouvelle Héloïse* — in which an occasional glimpse of the author's personal experience is discernible, but which, because of its primarily fictional character, must be relegated to the genre of the novel.[22] Stull's theoretical perspective is relevant here.

In the conventional or classical autobiographical tradition we have Albert Maori Kiki's *Ten Thousand Years in a Lifetime* (1968) and Michael Thomas Somare's *Sana* (1975). These autobiographies were written by themselves and edited by Ulli Beier. One can easily identify them as personal narratives about their life and journey to the present day.

Russell Soaba's *Wanpis* (1977), Paulias Matane's *Aimbe, the Pastor* (1979) and Ignatius Kilage's *My Mother Calls Me Yaltep* (1984) are semi-autobiographical works of fiction. Russell Soaba constructs his narratives through the controlled nameless character in *Wanpis* (1978). The existential position of the nameless character is more ambiguous than the famed national poet, who is perceived as a shadow hero of the novel. All other characters take their inspirations from this controlled nameless character. A considerable amount of information on Soaba's own life experiences appear in the first two sections of *Wanpis.* Soaba attempts "to produce an intimate sense of the determination and despair of Papua New Guineans educated into a system which cuts them adrift from their pasts but establishes no ideals for future."[23]

Paulias Matane and Ignatius Kilage's novels operate like Soaba's *Wanpis.* The books of these writers reflect their own experiences as children growing up in their traditional societies before making their way out of that society as a result of the colonial process. This exposure to the outside world is represented by the characters recruited as laborers to work on plantations, becoming Christians, attending elementary schools, and becoming part of the colonized history. Matane and Kilage's own experiences show them as victims of the twin imperatives created by cultural invasion (as in Matane) and by the contact dilemmas (as in Kilage). These novels set up the foundations for other Papua New Guinea novels.

Umba's *The Fires of Dawn* (1979), Jim Baital's *Tali* (1979), Kituai's *The Flight of a Villager* (1979), Michael Mel's *Kumdi Bagre* and Toby Waim Kagl's *Kallan* (1984) fall under the semi-autobiographical novel categories. In general these authors utilize the autobiographical experiences as the foundation of their writings. Papua New Guinean authors' participation in the art of writing, their different methods of presentation of the past, and the distinctive quality of recalling that part of their experiences is worth considering. The autobiographical literary tradition is an overall expression of a national literature. Chatterjee observes the "typical PNG author writes a single inspired autobiographical story or novel and then moves over to other spheres of life."[24] The autobiographical structure is a distinctive textual practice of Papua New Guinean writers. Through the autobiographical style a novelist reflects on the Papua New Guinean reality.

Benjamin Umba, August Kituai, and Jim Baital collectively published an anthology of their short novels in 1976.[25] Umba's *Fires of Dawn*, Kituai's *The Flight of a Villager* and Baital's *Tali* were published together as *Three Short Novels from Papua New Guinea* (1976).[26] No other similar collection appeared until the mid 1980s when Michael Yake Mel and Toby Waim Kagl, collectively, published *Two Highland Novels* (1984).[27] Paulias Matane published a series of short novels: *Aimbe, the Challenger*, *Aimbe, the Magician*, and *Aimbe, the School Drop-out*. Joseph Aguang published *Sorcerers* (1993) with the National Research Institute. Short novels or novellas dominated the publishing scene for two decades from 1970s to 1990s. Most short novels form a cluster of literary works differentiated to the full novel by structure, word limit, and compositional elements. The thematic concerns are often about village life, colonial setting, or the journeys out of the village into the complex modern world. The short novels fulfilled the literary desire for creative output in Papua New Guinea, especially the period between 1975 and 1980s.

THE THREE SHORT NOVELS

Benjamin Umba's *The Fires of Dawn* starts with the first contact in the Highlands of Papua New Guinea. The period is one full of serious confrontations between the Highlanders and the Europeans and their coastal policemen and carriers. This led to a society disturbed and fragmented as in August Kituai's *The Flight of a Villager*, where the village youth attracted by the seductive city life escapes from the rigid rules of the village. *The Flight of a Villager* is a story about the first experiences of contact societies and the illusions that follow such exposures to the outside world.[28]

There are subtle differences in Umba and Kituai's depiction of the village life. Umba sees the villagers reacting violently against the church and missions. The villagers simultaneously condemn other villagers who assisted the newcomers. In Kituai's story, however, we see the negative attitudes of the villagers force out the young people into towns in search of fortune and glory. Kituai is suggesting that moving out into towns is the most foolish thing for villagers. Town life is far more damaging to self-pride, moral conduct, and social harmony.

Jim Baital's story entitled *Tali* is about the great return to the village. The story is about villagers alienated as a result of long years of service in the colonial work force. The great return, however, is hardly an easy transition. It is the most difficult thing for someone who has been alienated from the village. The village becomes more negative to those who went away to work in outside in coastal towns. The villagers disapprove new ideas and values. Baital goes further to show how damaging this attitude is for future generations of Papua New Guineans. Individuals become bearers of the residual guilt of their colonial

111

past. Baital embraces possibilities of a nationalist's concern here. He highlights some of the individual guilt and shame in a changing cultural system.

These writers occupy themselves with conflict of cultures, escape from these conflicts, and confrontations with more complicated problems in towns. The village conflicts result from breaking of rules, disobeying elders' commands, forced marriages, or sex related conflicts. External forces augment internal conflicts and tensions of one particular society. Individuals caught up in these tensions and conflicts reject such conditions. New laws, politics, religion, administration, and education are the basis of a new social order and power. These stories emphasize the moments of transition and transformations in the colonial period.

The authors of the late 1960s and early 1970s had significant influences on each other. They discussed ideas of politics and social change in the emerging nation of Papua New Guinea. Writings of this period are viewed as protest literature invested with antagonism and protest against colonialism. The central focus is the ridiculous ambivalence of living in the colonial situation, how this has affected Papua New Guineans, and made them appear contradictory, or at times, vulnerable to forces of destruction within both the traditional and the modern societies. In Umba's narrative there are more violent reactions. Whereas in Kituai's narrative we see the colonized exploit the ignorance of colonizers. The futurist work of Baital shows a future of responsible and conscientious Papua New Guineans. He ironically twists the tone of the narrative to imply abuse and misuse of the inherited colonial values. He sees a society willing to accept the condition of its coloniality, but at the same time resisting that aspect, by hoping for the return to the old traditions and values of the people. This is only an implied aspect of Umba's work. The over-all emphasis is on the disillusionment of the colonized as a result of serious cultural contestations.

The main characters of the *Three Short Novels from Papua New Guinea* are single characters. Each character follows a line of experience, perhaps, parallel to the experience of the three authors. The individual characters are often rebellious youths who are forced to leave the village in search of other possibilities in towns. The qualities of the characters are first judged against the society's view of what are considered good qualities against bad qualities. Good qualities involve respect of customs, elders, observation of village rules, hard work, proper marriage, courting, courage, and strength to fight for the society in times of invasion. These qualities are absent.

The characters in *Three Short Novels from Papua New Guinea* ignore the cultural values and expectations of their elders. The protagonists are accused of either being rebels, betrayers, or outcasts. Although Baital's protagonist attempts to restore self-confidence, he too loses the respect of his people. Hence, all main characters in these novellas, in many ways, accepted their condition as village outcasts and rebels. For instance, Anglum's son Tanawa, in *The Fires of*

Dawn, is murdered for betraying the village and tribe.[29] He is portrayed as an element of betrayal. His own society must eliminate him. *The Fires of Dawn* highlights the contact with the first missionary at Denglagu, the traditional land of the Kukane, which was resented by the Kukane tribe. As we discover later in the story, Tanawa, Aglum's son, accepts the mission's word and works on the mission station. The other Kukane tribesmen take this as a betrayal of trust. Aglum is forced to go to the mission station to persuade his son to return home. Tanawa, however, refuses his father's pleading to return to the village. The villagers burn and kill Aglum, his wife Murangiggl, and their son Koima in their own house. Tanawa is killed on the mission station and burned outside the house, perhaps achieving martyrdom in the Christian sense of being tortured and killed by his own people for betrayal.

Iso in Kituai's *The Flight of the Villager* runs away from his village with a friend to Goroka. Goroka with its hordes of problems, crimes, and seductiveness displeases Iso. He lives a vagrant's life with someone from his own village. They live on leftovers brought by his friend. He eventually gets a job as a house servant (*houseboy*) with a young Australian officer in Goroka. The difficult, often-irresistible, modern life always allures the rebellious youth into voluntary isolation, alienation, and separation from the village. Iso achieves personal freedom as well as personal liberation. He escapes from the village punishment and the tax law of the council. This escape makes it possible for Iso to reflect on the two different worlds in a conscious way.

TWO HIGHLANDS NOVELS

The characters in the *Two Highland Novels* live within the confines of their respective cultural boundaries and societies. Both Kallan, the main protagonist in Kagl's *Kallan* and Bagre in Mel's *Kumdi Bagre* are represented as brave defenders of their societies. The two highland authors chose to write about the colonial era in Papua New Guinea.

The *Two Highland Novels* focuses on the traditional tribal way of life in the Highlands: warfare between tribes, historical incidents involving missionaries, relations between sexes, court cases, stealing, healing of ailments, schools, prisons, police raids, plantation work, returning from plantations, marriage and parent-child relations. Mel's *Kumdi Bagre* is set around the late 1960s and early 1970s, while Kagl's *Kallan* is set around the 1940s and 1950s.

Mel's book talks about young Bagre's life of growing up in the village and receiving his education. It is also about some of the incidents that happened during the Baiyer River road construction. Roads are presented as a symbolic connection to the outside world. Roads bring new forces of power and authority that change the old ways of the village. The roads make it possible for modernity to undermine the traditions of the people. The villagers discuss the outside intervention in their way of life, especially the government agents such as the police:

> These police are here to maintain law and order and not to promote trouble. Why did the kiap come? Before I used to chop such idiots like these policemen and feed the birds. Comrades today these blue uniforms are making them too smart and powerful for us.[30]

The new forces of power and control are indestructible in the eyes of the people. The police represent that new power and authority to maintain the rules and laws of the government. The concern here is with the post-independence social, political, and economic order.

NARRATIVE STYLE

Narrative style and subject matter are similar to both Kagl and Mel. Their techniques are the straight forward narratology, generally preoccupied with bringing the Highlands' spirit and consciousness to the fore. They utilize the storytelling aspect of their traditional societies. The act of intertextuality is brought into focus in these books. Intertextuality involves combining oral traditions with actual historical incidents and events. The very act of blending actual histories with fictional recreation of life during the colonial times of Papua New Guinea is an interesting feature of the short novels. Kagl, for instance, rewrites a segment of the Hagen saga involving the killing of the American Catholic missionary, Brother Frank (Eugene is the actual name of the missionary). Kagl's narrative takes the perspective of the Barengigl tribesmen.[29] Kagl's fictionalizing an actual historical account. Mennin's account or from an expansion of an oral history involving this incident are the basis for Kagl's fiction. The historical account took place in the early 1930s. The memory of the event remains with many living relatives of Kagl that the telling of this event could have been important to everyone in the Simbu society. The killing of the first missionaries, Brother Eugene and Father Morchesheur, led to the administration, under Jim Taylor's leadership, sending in a police troop to raid and bring the culprits to justice. This event also triggered the series of police attitude to any resistance in the early years of contact with the Highlands communities.

PNG STORYTELLING STYLE

The oral storytelling style is evident in all writers' books. A good story is told with more power and intensity. In Benjamin Umba's story we see this technique applied with the passion for storytelling in Papua New Guinean contexts:

Though the world around them had reached the electronic age, locked away behind the Bismarck Ranges were groups of people known as the Kukane. This is the name they called themselves and were called by the neighbouring tribes. They belong to the Old Stone Age. Their everyday life was governed by superstition and sorcery. They were unaware of any world beyond the towering mountains that looked like pillars of ruined temples when silhouetted against the early dark night.[32]

The passage also reveals the external influences on the author. The use of the image "looked like pillars of ruined temples", is odd, but serves as a link between the traditional Simbu society and the modern European culture. Umba then introduces the main character of the story, giving a picture of the type of character and his social position in the society. The protagonist is Aglum, "an old one-eyed and crippled man." He is a disable man, but still commands respect and honour from others in the society.

Oratory and power within the Papua New Guinean societies are interconnected. Kagl, in Benjamin Umba's story, is the great leader and warrior of the village. He exercises his power to instigate the murder of Aglums' family. This is demonstrated in this piece of oratory:

Now, what our fathers want us to do is this and listen carefully. They want us, and strongly ask us, that we kill the white man, and if his followers are too proud to leave him and return to the village, they too must be killed, and I mean *killed*. But first the hawk must be chased away and later the hens may be warned about their fate. This may seem rather a harsh thing for our fathers to say. But this is what we are told to do, that is if we want to live. So it means kill or to be killed.[33]

The impact of such oratory is the persuasive skills employed in the delivery, with allusions to their dead ancestors and spirits. Umba is exploring the influence great orators have on their people. Traditional oratory in the Highlands is a powerful influence in the mind-set of the multitude in most Highlands community.

The contact period radically challenged the authority of these great leaders. Maintaining the bigman status depends on the allegiance and loyalty of their own people. Umba's *The Fires of Dawn* reflects this impact of contact on the tribal people of the Highlands. The survival and existence of these people depended on ritualistic worship, ancestral adoration, and tribal consensus based largely on superstition and magic. We see this more clearly in the conversation Aglum has with his son before their murder:

Our people have been dying off at an unusually high rate. Bokun's uncle died, Kagl's mother died, Kimagl's sister died, Mir's husband died, and many children have been dying at childbirth. Hitherto, these deaths were believed to have been caused by sorcery until Kagl consulted the *giglmogl ambu* about the death of his mother. From her the rest of the villagers have found out that they were not the result of sorcery. They are to be taken as…punishment from our ancestors. You may ask punishment for what, and what has it got to do with us. The answer is *…punishment for your joining the white man.*[34]

The early Europeans and coastal people destroyed their superstitions and ritualistic venerations. The missionaries and the government's power were mightier than the power of tribal ancestors. The missionaries and Australian patrol officers were often seen as tricksters with superior magical powers. The Highlanders saw the white men as sorcerers of great magical power:

This white man can trick us so that the ones who come after him will kill us all or treat us as his boys. They will take our land and make us plough it for them so that they may grow their food. This white man says he comes in peace. True, he doesn't have this strange looking wood with him. However his *mundi* [salt] his *nitnuman* [mirror] and his *maima* [axe] weaken us and make us turn against our own people. Not only do they weaken us but they destroy us completely because many others like himself will come after him, and when they appear you can know that it will be the end of us. However it is not yet too late.[35]

The introduced items were as powerful as the white man himself. Salt, axe, and mirror were some of the items introduced. People were suspicious of the white men's power. It reflects the conflict in the minds of villagers at the time of introduction of these new foreign items. Umba is accurate in his representation of the confused state of mind of the villagers in contact with the outside world. Further sustained contact brought more problems and confusions. New laws, imposition of tax regulation, labour recruitment schemes, and uneasiness with the new laws of the society further confused the people.

NOVELISTIC PATTERNS

The pattern in the short novels is threefold in its construction. The first element involves describing the journey outward to escape from the tribe and the village. The second element features adoption of the colonial situation. The third element describes the great return to the village. This pattern is common in all short novels. The journeys outward are emphasized by external sequences of events that are very much part of the foreign western culture. Journeying out of village societies is considered necessary for acquisition of wider knowledge and self-consciousness. This means that exposure to the outside world opens up new experiences. It makes possible the acquisition of a wider knowledge that enriches the mind.

To a certain extent this is a positive aspect of the short narratives of Papua New Guinean fiction. The journey outward into towns and urban centers is one of discovery and uncovering of the secrets of the outside world. The careers these young villagers end up doing are viewed as significant, however menial the jobs may be. The jobs range from a house servant (*houseboy*) to being a plantation labourer. These are considered the most important jobs in those days. Kituai's story, for instance, talks about Iso being accepted for his first job as a *houseboy* by a sympathetic Australian, who cared less about whose letter of reference Iso showed him:

> The prospect of a bright future revived in him and he thumped his stomach with satisfaction. Now that he was offered a job all that remained was for him to prove how good and reliable he was. He promised himself that he would show he was capable of handling the job of a *houseboy* with efficiency. If he didn't and was sacked he had no one to blame but himself.[36]

The *houseboy* job fascinated most of the early writers. Baital like Kituai brings this *houseboy* job back into his fiction. Kanek, Tali's father, in Baital's story ends his career as a *houseboy*. Kanek returns home after many years away from his village. He is unable to locate his village. The help of his patrons and the co-incidental meeting with his brother in a movie theatre leads him to re-establish his contact with the villagers.

The introduction of the outside world to villagers is incomplete until a return is made. This is sometimes described as 'the great return' to the village, the ideal, often and the original point of movement. Tali and his father, Kanek, return to the village. Although we have age and time differences in that of Tali's age (the generation of the seventies) and his father Kanek (the colonial generation), it is Tali's life, which takes significant focus in the novel. Tali becomes the future of the new Papua New Guinea, but one who is still affected by his father's past, with the negative effects of colonialism and the obscure position of being alienated from the village.

Baital's narrative is more melodramatic in portraying this experience. Quick sketches of the characters make them more artificial than real-life characters. For example, a sentimental, dream-like romance takes place between Tali Kanek and the white girl, Caroline Parker. The introduction of guitar music is associated with romance. The conversation in Baital's narrative takes place on a melodramatic level, but one wonders whether romance between the colonial white girl and black son of a *houseboy* was possible. The colonial law prohibits romantic or intimate relationships between a Papuan New Guinean man and a European woman. Neither was it common or acceptable during the colonial period for any inter-racial relationships to develop.

CONTEMPORIZING HISTORY

The *Three Short Novels from Papua New Guinea* were written based on the experiences of the authors. Like other post-colonial writers, their texts are seen as the medium of expression, which includes language, the cultural contexts of a text, and the very act of writing their own colonized experiences. These authors faced the challenge to wrestle the given rules of the text in the English language.

Mel and Kagl wrote their books during the post-independence period. Their works highlight the same old story about colonial contact, social, and cultural conflict, movement in and out of the villages, and idealized village situations. Kagl, for instance, considers the securing of power and status through language. Learning to speak Pidgin on plantations leads a labourer to acquire social status and privilege in the world of the Europeans.

If one of the labourers already knew a bit of Pidgin-English or had picked up meager amounts from hearing others speak, he was destined for the highly coveted position of overseer or the more prestigious position as the missus' cook in the kitchen as soon as the "masta" was aware of the difference. Those who were identified enjoyed certain privileges and benefits as they had an advantage with their newly acquired language tool over their counterparts.

Mastering language in the colonial plantation economy is a vital part of survival. It also measures an individual's achievement. Language competency is related to the types of jobs a labourer can do in the plantations. Language forms the basis of differentiation among the plantation labourers. A social hierarchy is created using language as a measure of qualifications for each category of work. The power of the new language is deployed in the creation of new social order and power structures.

The very act of writing is a challenge many Papua New Guinean writers consider as a serious preoccupation. This is exemplified in Kituai's *The Flight of a Villager*, where Iso shows the letter of reference to the young Australian to get a job as a *houseboy*. This is a classic representation of writing as an important instrument of negotiation between the colonizer and the colonized. In Kituai's story the signature of the referee and the written aspect of the reference are more important than the person who uses the reference. The process of writing reinforces the power of written word in the colonial world: "In many post-colonial societies it was not the English language which had the greatest effect, but writing itself. In this respect, although oral culture is by no means the universal model of post-colonial societies, the invasion of the ordered, cyclic,

118

and 'paradigmatic' oral world by the unpredictable and 'syntagmatic' world of the written word stands as a useful model for the beginnings of post-colonial discourse." The appropriation of the written word meant "seizing of the means of communication and the liberation of postcolonial writing." This practice is described as "the process of self-assertion and of the ability to reconstruct the world as an unfolding historical process."[37]

The process of writing is what matters to these writers. The writing process has power and authority to speak on a writer's behalf. In Mel's *Kumdi Bagre*, we see Bagre wishing to be like his teacher, Mr. Kila. The father dreams about Bagre's future:

> Dad thought for a while, "Bagre, be a good boy in school and one day you will pay back the hardships I faced against the police, warders, and kiaps." He let my hand go slowly. I turned my back to them and walked towards the main road leading to Rugli. Having walked for ten metres, I turned around, then paused for some time. "Dad!…One day I will do what you want me to do. It's only a matter of time." Dad shook his head and smiled at me. I turned around and began my journey back to school, having a lot of thoughts in my mind.[38]

Education is seen as a positive way to achieve goals, dreams, and aspirations. Education opens up opportunities into the written world. The coastal teacher, the police, patrol officers, magistrates, and prison warders are the agents of the Western world. Bagre's father, a victim of powerful force associated with the written world, changes his mind about the education of his son. He sees in Bagre the hope of revenge and power over those who victimized him.

These authors have engaged themselves in bridging two completely divergent cultures: oral culture on one hand and the written culture on the other. In *Kumdi Bagre*, Bagre, a son of two different tribes, is seen "like a bridge that links two sides of the river". The two sides of the river symbolize two different tribes, clans, and villages. Bagre is also a bridge between the traditional and introduced modern culture.[39] In Kagl's novel, Kallan is on the other side of the riverbank at the time the missionaries were attacked by the enemy tribe. An extended reading of this scene directs our attention to the confrontation between the oral culture and the written culture. Kallan relinquishes the old traditions, values, and history of his people. Although Kallan is removed from his traditional society, like Yaltep and Tali, he returns with new knowledge and skills to improve the life of his people. Kallan learns Pidgin English while away on the plantation in the Milne Bay province. He also matures into a conscientious young man.

All these writers use fiction to rewrite history. The 1970s stories emphasize the contact, conflict, resistance, and hesitancy of accepting the introduced modern ways and colonial cultures. Writers see the act of writing itself as an acquired form of social status and prestige. It is not a privilege, but a form in which sudden transformation of ideas takes shape and immediately represents a source of power and authority. The 1980s writers wrote within a post-independence period, but were still writing about the colonial period. The simple reason is that the experiences of the authors also form that part of history.

WRITING THE POLITICAL UNCONSCIOUS

For the first time an indigenous voice of a colonized man was heard. The autobiography as an authentic representation of the colonized arrested the distorted, exaggerated, crude sketches, and literary straitjackets invented by the expatriate writers on Papua New Guinea. Albert Maori Kiki's autobiography, *Ten Thousand Years in a Lifetime* (1968), is the first book written by a Papua New Guinean. The book marks the beginning of very important events in the political and literary history of Papua New Guinea.[1] Nationalism and the birth of a national literature coexisted in their emergence. The publication of the book generated its own literary excitements and celebration. The work achieved immediate recognition soon after its publication. It was reprinted and translated into several different languages. The book generated a readership for authentic Papua New Guinean literature, both in the country and beyond.

OROKOLO CHILDHOOD

Ten Thousand Years in a Lifetime reveals the true feelings, emotions, and sentiments of Papua New Guineans under the colonial administration of Australia. The book served as a vehicle to transport the experiences of Papua New Guineans from the stone-age culture into the modern western world. In his collaboration with Ulli Beier, Albert Maori Kiki recorded his life as a man who has travelled a thousand years in a lifetime to play an important role in the emerging nation of Papua New Guinea.

The first two chapters of the book concentrate on Maori Kiki's early childhood life. Incidents in Maori Kiki's life with his parents and in the village are recollected. Elaborate explanations are given to various incidents on his journey from his village society to the modern world. Orokolo chants, laments, and myths have also served as the sources of inspiration for the growth and personal development of Maori Kiki. Growing up in his mother's village according to Maori Kiki is a life changing experience:

My mother belonged to the Parevavo tribe, who live in the thickly forested hills on the banks of the Purari river, (also called Pulari). To the North the mountains rise higher and higher, but to the south the Purari river soon enters the swampy plain of the Papuan Gulf land. The coastal people feared the Parevavo and considered them wild and savage and identified them with the notorious Kukukuku tribes who lived to the east of us and whose language and customs resembled our own.[2]

Kiki's autobiography takes us on a journey. In *Ten Thousand Years in a Lifetime*, Kiki makes accurate observations about his society. His cultural background reinforces his later achievements and public stature. Autobiographies based on childhood experiences uncover experiences and capacities that form the later life of an author. Kiki's later achievement, public image, and professional career are the result of a unique childhood and adolescence. By entering into a literary space Kiki has given a snap-shot of his childhood and personal development. *Ten Thousand Years in a Lifetime* offers an honest and truthful account of the massive cultural, social, and political changes that occurred during the course of Kiki's lifetime and that of his parents. Thus *Ten Thousand Years in a Lifetime* enters into a complex system of literature, just as the author entered the complex social, political, and historical phases of his country.

The technique of giving so much detailed description or explanation of life in the village, innocent childhood, and initiation, is an important technique used by PNG writers who write to be read by others outside of their own societies. PNG writers take on the responsibility to teach others about the unique cultures, values, way of life, and the experiences of their people. In doing so a writer accomplishes the goal of linking the oral society with the written society. Through writing about his or her experiences an autobiographer makes the point that self-expression through writing is an effective way to get others to read and understand a writer's world of experience. The autobiographical genre appeals to the greater society. Through the autobiographical eyes, ears, and real life experiences a reader is introduced to a world that exists outside of their own experiences.

The book is about a child growing up in a society where a wide knowledge of the lore, myth, genealogies, and the history of a particular thing or events are considered absolutely important. In the chapter "Orokolo", Kiki gives a comparative view of the two traditional societies he belongs to as a member.[3] Social, cultural, and political arrangements in each society are similar in many ways. Both have a common link with the spiritual, natural, and physical world around them. Kiki moves between his mother's Parevavo people's environment and his father's Orokolo society. He observes many differences between the two cultures, especially in the occupational roles of men and women. Gardening, for instance, is a men's job, while sago pounding and weaving of fishing nets are relegated to women. This background is important to the thread of the book:

> My first impression of Orokolo was that it was full of people. Coming from a tiny Parevavo community that wandered through the thick forest with their scanty belongings, Orokolo seemed like a modern metropolis. There the people lived in solid houses, close together, and the place was buzzing with noise and activity. The vast number of pigs roaming about everywhere also astonished me because my mother's people did not keep any tame pigs, whereas in Orokolo the pig population was larger than the human one. My mother told me later on that she felt a wonderful sense of security in Orokolo, where one could sleep without fearing a night attack by the enemy. But to me the experience was altogether disturbing and worrying. At night I missed the humming noises made by the crickets in the forest was reduced to a feeble chirping there and the cries of the night bird were altogether absent.[4]

Kiki talks about his initiation and acceptance into the Orokolo society. He also explains how he came to be part of the Maori Kiki clan, his father's adopted clan. Kiki presents the categories of people and the ways in which Orokolo people organize themselves into different groups, by a strict distinction of houses:

> In Orokolo we distinguish three different types of house: the *uvi*, or women's house; the *maupa eravo*, or young men's house and the *hehe eravo*, which is the real men's house. The young uninitiated boys like me sleep in the *uvi*, with their mothers and sisters. The men slept in the *hehe eravo* and paid only occasional visits to the *uvi*, because it was considered effeminate and immoral for a man to spend too much time with his wife. After their initiation, the young men moved into the *maupa eravo*, which literally means the house for decorating oneself. By contrast, the *hehe eravo* was the house for decision making.[5]

Kiki's *Ten Thousand Years in a Lifetime* is about the transition from his traditional society to active participation in the political development of his country. It is also about the impact of change and its negative influences. He brings to light some of the dark secrets of his Orokolo society, his growing up in it, and his movement out, into the modern world. We see glimpses of both lives in the basic influences on the Kiki's personality. He lived both experiences through sheer courage and incredible personal commitment.

EUROPEAN ENCHANTMENT

Kiki also describes the education he received from his mother's people. The knowledge he gained growing up in Orokolo before coming into contact with the white man and the white world outside of his own are described here. His fascination, astonishment, and enchantment with the European world are an extension of his people's belief that dead relatives had come back from the island of dead: "We further believed that whenever one of our people died he would walk under the ground until he got to the house of the white man. There his body would be washed, and the bad black skin would be taken off. Once he was white, he would be put on the next ship sailing to the island of the dead."[6]

The false notions of the white man and the world outside of the Orokolo society came to a shattering reality after he moved out of his own society. Kiki began to make sense of the outside world. This brought him into contact with other people, tribes, cultures, and ideas. The school system offered him the Christian religion, and his early work with the administration. Kiki was able to understand and demystify some of the beliefs of his people about the white man and the outside world:

> However, it was not until they dragged me to school that I came into contact with the hard reality of the white man's world. There was only one school in Orokolo then and it belonged to the London Mission Society. Though the administration had no policy about compulsory schooling, the mission made great efforts to bring all of us into school, and since most of us were reluctant to go, they would make periodical raids on the village to snatch truants. When I came down from my mother's village to Orokolo I was already about ten years old and felt reluctant to go and sit on the same bench with younger boys.[7]

As someone immersed in the introduced European ways Kiki attempts to negotiate that world with his own traditional Papua New Guinean world. He wondered whether Europeans consider Papua New Guineans as foolish, child like, and ape like in the imitation of the white culture. For a man who has traveled outside of his own Orokolo society, Kiki considered accessing the "white man's material possessions" as an important move towards understanding the world of Europeans. He encouraged his own people to learn from their friends, the whites to achieve economic and political success: "While we are learning let us do it in all humility without all this fuss and nonsense about envy and hatred."[8]

POLITICAL CONSCIOUSNESS

Political consciousness for Papua New Guineans took its bearing in educational institutions. Sympathetic Australians encouraged the young nationals attending the institutions of higher learning to speak up for themselves by resisting Australian colonialism in Papua New Guinea. Papua New Guinean intellectuals attending the University of Papua New Guinea, Administrative College, and the Goroka Teachers College in the 1960s were urged to think about the future of their country. Public views and opinions were expressed about the administration's rigid colonial policy. A greater awareness of the colonial position Australia was placing on the territory began to take shape. Non-administrative officers, the public back in Australia, and Papua New Guinean students questioned continued Australian presence in the territory.

Albert Maori Kiki, one of the pioneer students in one of the higher institutions, recorded the events and political development of this period in his autobiography. He captured the political expressions of his personal life story and the culture of his people in his autobiography. Early in 1947 Albert Maori Kiki got his first job as "doctor boy" or a medical orderly in Kerema hospital, but freaked out after he was told to carry a patient's faeces. He became a tea boy instead, which lasted only for a year. The next job Maori Kiki did after a year or so was the job of an interpreter for the patrol officer Bill Maddock. After a year Maori Kiki returned to the Kerema Hospital as a doctor boy job under Mr. Albert Speer, the new medical assistant. Under Mr. Speer's guidance and mentorship Maori Kiki entered Sogeri School in 1949 and completed his studies in 1951. In his own words Maori Kiki described this experience:

> I spent from 1949 to 1951 in Sogeri school. It was there that I learned to speak English properly. All our teachers were Australians, with the exception of a few Papuan tutors who were ex-students of Sogeri themselves. I enjoyed my stay in Sogeri very much. It was away from the coast and was real forest, reminiscent. I enjoyed games like baseball and cricket but was most keen on the debating society. I can remember a debate argued against equality. I was still very much influenced by our traditional thinking on this matter. I also enjoyed the concerts and can remember standing on a platform singing songs in my mother's language. Pretty tunes to others, but a tremendous private joke to myself, because I was abusing everybody in the audience... The biggest thing Sogeri did to me was that it brought me together with other boys from all parts of Papua and New Guinea and I learned to know and like them. Many of them have remained my friends throughout life.[9]

In *Ten Thousand Years in a Lifetime,* Kiki talks about the intensity of political consciousness during the late 1960s and early 1970s. The nationalist ferment intensified with the formation of the first indigenous political party. Kiki recounts how he became part of that early nationalist group: "The idea of a political party came to me very slowly and to most of my colleagues. In a sense the actual formation of the party took place rather suddenly in June 1967, but to me the real beginnings go back to early 1964, when we started the Bully Beef Club at Administrative College."[10] The club provided the opportunity for the young leaders to develop "a platform for serious political discussion." The interest in politics intensified in their informal discussions after their "political science class" at the Administrative College. Kiki recounts that their "political consciousness developed" in those occasions. The unhappiness and dissatisfaction towards the administration translated into a political action movement. A group feeling of subjugation and ill treatment began to surface among the Bully Beef Club members. The young students realized that even though they "came from all parts of the country" they had a common cause to stand up against:

> There were eight of us, seven men and one woman, who started the Bully Beef Club. It was a kind of contribution club. From our rather scanty pocket money we contributed each week to buy bully beef in order to augment our ration at the college. The bully beef was always kept in a classroom…But soon the club also became a platform for serious political discussion. Many of the subjects brought up in the political science class were heatedly discussed by us in the evenings. The following year the club revived. Its numbers grew to twelve and we now had some very dramatic fellows in it, like Joseph Nombri and Michael Somare. It is in this club that our political consciousness developed."[11]

They challenged the ruling regime's policy on the future of Papua New Guinea. In a submission to the Select Committee on the future of Papua New Guinea, the members of the Bully Beef Club (by then it was not yet a political party) "pointed out that the present system of administration was 'out of date, autocratic, unrealistic and inflexible. The domination of the Federal Government in the affairs of Papua New-Guinea was unfair, paternalistic, and excluded the leaders of Papua New Guinea opportunities in the decision making process. The Bully Beef Club's submission argued that "the domination and exclusion was already resulting in disillusion, friction, and steadily deteriorating race relations". The transition to self-government was only possible if these obstacles were removed.[12] The Bully Beef Club could not "visualize a change over to self-government at any time in the future except under greatly worsened conditions and with a strong possibility of a complete break-down of amity and goodwill."[13]

The submission was high powered. The colonial situation was described as a 'master-servant' relationship, enforced by the Australian administration. The Australians had to step down from power and let the nationals run their own country. Ironic as it may seem, the pressure was not for immediate independence. It was envisaged that the Australian government work closely with Papua New Guinean leaders, but not as a basis for continued colonial control or domination. This enraged the conservative members of the House. The House was made up of mostly Australian entrepreneurs who were patriotic about continued Australian control of the Territory of Papua and New Guinea.

The general public reacted with mixed feelings about the effect of the radical new ideas introduced by the young Papua New Guinean parliamentarians.

Comments and criticisms appeared in the *South Pacific Post* (*Post-Courier*) and Australian newspapers (*The Australian, The Age*).[13] In the Second House of Assembly sitting Pangu Pati had fourteen elected representatives in the House of Assembly. Despite his loss in election, Kiki remained as Pangu Pati's Secretary. The political victory encouraged the elected members to unite and press for issues of home rule and political victory. In his participation as a founding member of the Pangu Pati, Kiki was proud to see that the Pangu Pati was a symbol of unity of the Papuans and New Guineans, highlanders and coastlanders, working together to get their independence. Kiki writes: "At this moment in our history I can see my country's future mapped out. We know where we want to go and I think we know how to get there."[14] The Pangu Pati platform became the basis of nationalism and collective bargaining for political independence. The members of Pangu Pati were young, bold, and visionary.

Kiki's energy and inspiration were also motivated by his experiences in Fiji as a medical student. In Fiji he observed and participated in the labour union movements. Reflecting on his work experiences under the administration in Papua New Guinea Kiki saw that under the colonial administration Australians mistreated his people in ways that were denigrating: "I have come a very long way. And yet the long way I have traveled has not separated me from my people. The support and understanding I get from these allegedly 'primitive' and 'backward' people gives me much strength."[15] Kiki's public stature and his extraordinary personality were influenced by his early childhood years in the Orokolo society.

A NARRATIVE DISCOURSE

Ten Thousand Years in a Lifetime ignited the literary flames in Papua New Guinea. Kiki's autobiography played an important role in the evolution of the literary culture in Papua New Guinea. Just as autobiographical writings have played an important role in the literary traditions of the Western civilization, Kiki's autobiography has provided a model for literary creation in Papua New Guinea. The book proclaims itself as a narrative text in the literary sense of the word and opens up new possibilities that give voice to the unspoken, unwritten text. As a narrative text, the book enables the writing of an unfolding historical process through the eyes of the narrator. In doing so the oral and the written culture are transformed into meaningful discourses. The narrative text epitomizes the fact/fiction polarities, wrestling to establish and constitute absolute categories of feeling and perceiving reality, but usually ends up "splitting the subject of the discourse into a narrating self and an experiencing self, which can never coincide exactly."[16] According to this logic we have Albert Maori Kiki, the author as the creator of a narrative discourse in the form of his autobiography: *Ten Thousand Years in a Lifetime*.

On the other hand we have Albert Maori Kiki the subject of the book, *Ten Thousand Years in a Lifetime.* This subject splits and becomes the narrating self and an experiencing self. The narrating self is the one whose voice is heard right across the book. The experiencing self is the one we picture in the voice of the narrating self. Kiki has therefore placed himself in the center of his narrative discourse. He attempts to find a resolution to the tension of the split. Without doing so the book would have become irrelevant and perhaps "reflect a sentimental indulgence in his private memories; it speaks only of what in his early childhood presages his later development, the truth may easily be distorted by his polemical bias."[17]

For instance, on several occasions, he reprints letters, official documents, election pamphlets and newspaper articles, which have relevance or are about him. He defends or offers explanations, reasons, and justifications of his participation. In this case we have Kiki's narrating self-taking dominance over the experiencing self, a self that participated in the activities linked to these letters and articles.

Kiki is engaged in a process of revision and reflection of the past. He provokes a radical insight into the present conditions affecting him and his people. He handles his subject with great honesty, in the same manner as he approached his people. He writes with a deep felt compassion, personal honesty, and gives a cogent interpretation of his people's myths and legends that remain an integral part of his character and mode of feelings.

This is similar to Jean-Jacques Rousseau's *The Confessions.* According to Stull, an autobiography like Rousseau's "present[s] the reader with a totally new concept of man, modern man, conscious of his uniqueness and therefore, of this alienation from society. And this man is not afraid to show his shortcomings as well as his virtues in all sincerity."[18] Sincerity and truthfulness to the story of man is, according to Rousseau, "the singly most important aspect" of autobiography, where the narrator tries "to show everything, without dissimulation, without falsification, and above all, without omissions."[19] Thus in Kiki's autobiography we see the author taking the ordinary village experiences and his modern experience as the focus. He allows readers to perceive in it any familiarity to or difference to their own experiences. Kiki wrote as an insider, as someone who was able to bridge the two worlds; the ancient mysteries revealed to him by his mother existing in fruitful conjunction with the modern pathologist, welfare officer, politician, and leader of his people. Kiki's book is the first important written statement of self-expression borne out of the space created by colonialism, but delivered at the right moment in history.

Ten Thousand Years in a Lifetime remains the most inspiring text for Papua New Guinean writers. As literature, autobiography, and as a social, political statement produced by a Papua New Guinean, *Ten Thousand Years in a Lifetime* impresses the readers easily. It is a story (in the loose sense of the word) about a passionate man, with great personality, and concerned about the problems of his country. Kiki is "ruthlessly outspoken and perhaps too honest for a politician."[20] It is a story also of the Orokolo culture, described as "stone age culture," but with daily practice of art and its symbolic interpretations of customs, rituals, and initiation practices.[21] Kiki is both the teller of his story and reteller of the stories of his people heard and learned in his childhood and upbringing. As the first important book written by a Papua New Guinean "it tells the story of a man, who in his own lifetime spanned thousands of years of human development."[22]

Kiki's book set the stage for the Papua New Guineans to express themselves in writing. Papua New Guineans have stories to tell and share among themselves and others. Opportunities to use written expressions opened up literary opportunities (literary magazine, journals, newspapers, etc), workshops, conferences, and performances for young Papua New Guineans. The sudden urge to express themselves came from within their inner selves and from experiencing decades of colonialism under various European powers. The publication of *Ten Thousand Years in a Lifetime* challenged the dominating image of Europeans, long fashioned in the colonial process.

Papua New Guinean writings denounced the sterile gestures and boundaries of western discourses of New Guinea, resulting in the critical interrogation of negative knowledge of power and political boundaries between whites and blacks, New Guineans and Papuans, highlanders and coastlanders, administrators and villagers, Christianity and paganism. *Ten Thousand Years in a Lifetime* symbolically announces the unification of Papua and New Guinea as one country. It destroyed some of the worst fears and cynicisms of the colonial legacy:

> Those who wish to deny us independence keep telling us about a number of problems we shall not be able to deal with as an independent nation. They say there is tension between Papua and New Guinea, tension between highlanders and coastal people, and that we shall never be able to unite. They say we shall abandon democratic procedure, which is being taught to us so carefully now, and we shall introduce one party government. Some think we shall become communists. Some say the army will stage a coup and introduce military dictatorship. Some say we have trouble with our Chinese minority or mixed-race people. Others fear we will kick out the Australian planters. Most of them feel the country will collapse economically because Australian aid will dry up after independence.[23]

Kiki's book brought together a force transformed by its powerful images and symbolism, its determined character and personality, the truth and honesty of a man who is not ashamed of the humble traditions of his people or of the changes taking place in Papua New Guinea. The book viewed as an intertextual object simplifies "the power of the dominating force (administration, church) and allowing it to be contested on the same level as that common to the subordinate cultures (village, customs, rituals)."[24] In other words, *Ten Thousand Years in a Lifetime*, chooses to cross time and space to wrestle with the truth. It is through techniques of recollection and explanation that Kiki is able to evoke the past with such ease and comfort. He describes the various social classes and practices as well as revises the old chants and fables entwined symbolically in the mythology and artistic rituals and traditions of his people. A lot of the oral tradition that Kiki grew up with is represented in his autobiography.

As an autobiographical work, *Ten Thousand Years in a Lifetime* has to maintain a truthful interpretation of the author's life and the many mysteries, practices, and experiences of his people. It is directed towards the specific truth of the self "which transforms the conception of the psyche, particularly in the realization of the complexity."[25] It develops "along with the awareness of the impact of historical change."[26] The realization of the individual's development as part of the general social process focuses on the individual as the historical force to give the sum total of a whole social trend and political development of a generation.[27] The inner experience or the burden of a weighty experience "cannot be borne until it is composed in autobiography."[28]

Ten Thousand Years in a Lifetime is read as a classical or conventional autobiography. According to a working definition of a classical or conventional autobiography, "the author's sole purpose is to present the story of his life as factually and 'objectively' as possible."[29] What we have in *Ten Thousand Years in a Lifetime* is the fusion of factual experiences of the author, the mythological heritage (from which the author finds inspiration), and the prophetic vision of early nationalistic leaders. It is a book about the divide between the village and the modern world. The author has attempted to bridge "the gaps in a single lifetime and survived the experience as a whole man, not nervously divided between two ways of life, two moral cultural loyalties."[30] Perhaps this might explain the feature of the Papua New Guinean novels that succeeded this publication. Beier was pleased that his collaboration with Kiki had ignited immediate interest in writing and raised serious objections from the colonials regarding the first book ever written by a Papua New Guinea:

> Kiki's book was translated into Swedish and Japanese and there were paperback editions in Germany and New Zealand. There were over 40 reviews and reports appearing in Australia and Germany alone, I have not been able to collect reviews from any other country. The success may owe something to the fact that it was an absolute first: a book from a country that had produced no written literature in English so far, and an author who had a range of experiences that no other author could match. But it certainly could not have had

such a lasting success without the quality of the storytelling that has all the liveliness, warmth and directness of oral literature .[31]

It is through techniques of recollection and explanation that Kiki is able to evoke the past with such ease and comfort. He describes the various social classes and practices while revising the old chants and fables entwined symbolically in the mythology and artistic rituals and traditions of his people. Much of the oral traditions that Kiki grew up with were written in his autobiography. Most of the oral traditions remain unwritten in Orokolo, but the task is to present the society as it has accommodated the author:

> Our people are not really aware of the causes that made them abandon their ways of life. Nowadays they lay some blame on people like myself. You have adopted the white man's way of life' the old men could tell me, "Look at you! You are getting fat. Should an Orokolo man look like that?" They think with the sadness of the old days when the young girls "marked" their trees. And I too regret the passing of those days. Thinking back now, it seems to me that we are healthier then, and happier. I remember very little sickness in Orokolo we wore next to no clothes, but our bodies were strong and shiny.

> Of course no customs continues forever, anywhere in the world. Orokolo can hardly be an exception and yet I feel cheated somehow, when I remember that I never sat in the *hehe eravo*, and that no Orokolo girl ever marked me as her tree."[32]

Maori Kiki's generation accepted the social and cultural changes as an inevitable. The older people left behind in the villages lamented the lost of tradition, blaming the younger generation of betraying their cultures and societies by following the white man's ways. Maori Kiki knew that as an educated member of the tribe the responsibility now felt on his generation to do something about taking control of the change. The onus now is on the young leaders of Papua New Guinea to develop strategic plans and visions to reclaim some of the lost traditions and knowledge systems of their people. Challenges are now far more demanding than before.

CONCLUSION

Writers in any new nation are usually the proto-elites whose immediate preoccupation is with political independence. Often the proto-elites go through experiences as a divided person, with concerns for the age-old traditions and the inherited values of the western coloniser. In their divided selves the proto-elites wrestle with political nationalism and subject positions created in the process of colonization. This dilemma is, however, subjected to forces of internal pressure and consciousness as in Paulias Matane's *Aimbe, the Pastor* (1979) and Jim Baital's *Tali* (1976) or results in a personal choice to remain outside of it as in Russell Soaba's *Wanpis* (1977).

Kiki's book is comparable with Sir Michael Somare's autobiography published in the year of the country's first independence celebrations.[33] The life stories of Kiki and Somare are similar in many ways. Both autobiographies reveal the extraordinary experiences of the first national leaders: their early childhood, initiation, struggle through the colonial education, their frustrations with the job they were given as junior officers in the administrative hierarchy, and their concerns for a fair representation of people's wishes and political achievements. The publication of these two autobiographies represents two important phases of political development in the country. Kiki's autobiography represents the phase leading up to 1968 (the time of the Second House of Assembly) and self-government in 1973. Sir Michael Somare's *Sana* (1975) covers the political development leading from self-government to independence, from 1968 to 1975. Both autobiographies reveal the problems, challenges, and the roads each leader took to arrive at the critical juncture in the national history of their country.

10

COLONIALISM TO CULTURE FRAGMENTATION

T*he Crocodile* (1971) by Vincent Eri is the first Papua New Guinean novel.[1] *The Crocodile* is the signature success story of the Ulli Beier literary era. It is the most concrete result of the "prophets" at the University of Papua New Guinea's creative writing class. It is an expression of indigenous authorship that soared in the late 1960s and 1970s. Most students in educational institutions in the 1970s have read *The Crocodile,* a novel written by their own local writer. *The Crocodile* is the most significant work to have come out of the colonial Papua New Guinea and the South Pacific Islands. It established itself as a classic post-colonial novel. The novel is a success in every sense of the word. Its first publication sold out immediately. It quickly soared into the critical attention of the literary scholars and critics.

Part of Eri's success as a post-colonial novelist is the simple and lucid prose of his work. The publication of *The Crocodile* functioned in two significant ways. First, it informs the non-Moveave, non-Papua New Guinean viewer of the rich heritage of the oral traditions in the author's society. Second, Eri writes about what he knows of his people and his experiences as a child of his people. As a teacher, Eri wanted to teach the world about his people. He does so successfully. He allows the indigenous perspectives to take dominance in his novel by emphasizing its structural form and re-describing images, once sketched by expatriate writers. Writing years later Ulli Beier describes the experience with Eri in a poignant way:

> I took to Vincent Eri at once and enjoyed working with him. I looked forward to his further installments of his novel *The Crocodile*. He was not exactly hardworking, but each chapter, when it finally came, made extremely entertaining reading and we often spent long, open-ended sessions discussing his writing. By the time he was to take his degree in 1970, however, he had not written the final chapter of the novel and I had to twist his arm, threatening to withhold his degree if he didn't complete it. Vincent Eri never wrote anything again in his life, but he went on to make a brilliant career as Ambassador of Papua New Guinea to Australia and eventually as Governor General of Papua New Guinea. Writing the novel, however, helped him to find himself and to acquire

that urbane sense of humour and the easy self-assurance that made a better ambassador and a better governor.[2]

As the first novel by a local author *The Crocodile* faced a horde of cynical criticisms from non Papua New Guinean readers. At times, the worst exaggerations of western thought served as the basis of bias and prejudiced judgments. Ulli Beier recounts some of these critical readings of Eri's novel:

Not surprisingly, the first novel by a Papuan attracted a great deal of attention. Betty Collins, in the *Sunday Australian* (28 February, 1971), said that 'Vincent Eri writes English with lyrical simplicity' and that 'his novel, *The Crocodile*, needs no paternal pat on the head. Lucid, sometimes beautiful, sometimes horrible, it tells with direct simplicity the life of Hoiri (pronounced Ho-erri), a boy from a hill village, who grows up, marries and become a carrier for the Australians during the war against the Japanese.'

Harry Jackman, in *The Australian* (6 February, 1971), says: 'It is a work of power, clarity and integrity.' But many Australians felt upset about what they considered to be the unfair ridiculing of Australian government officers and, in particular, offices of ANGAU (Australia New Guinea Administrative Unit). Maslyn Williams, writing in the *Sydney Morning Herald* (20 February, 1971), said that the pictures Vincent Eri drew of Australian administrative officers were 'cut out caricatures' and that if that was what he really believed, the suggestion that this book was a worthy contribution to New Guinea literature 'could be dismissed as ridiculous.' This highly sensitive reaction to a Papua New Guinean who dared to lampoon Australians was somewhat absurd in a Australian colony where many Australians still referred to New Guineans as 'boys', 'bush kanakas' or 'rock apes'. After a century of being pictured as 'cut out caricatures', one could surely forgive Papua New Guineans for having a bit of fun at the expense of their oppressors. Harry Jackman, however, took a very different view. Having been an ANGAU officer himself and having lived among the people of the Papuan Gulf as a co-op officer, he said that he could vouch for the integrity of the book. And Betty Collins said in *The Australian*: 'For the rest of us, expatriates who live in New Guinea…*The Crocodile* is a gentle but salutary lesson in understanding and loving another people."[3]

On the other hand, confusion and reluctance to accept the Papua New Guinean author is a healthy reaction to the emerging indigenous literary tradition. Krauth in his study of the literature of Papua New Guinea highlights the evocation of negative critical attitudes to the emergence of the new literature. In his support of Eri's novel Krauth writes that while "Eri's subject matter (as with that of other Papua New Guinean writers) correlated with the areas of sociological, historical and political study, … the main point is that Eri's book is a novel, not an autobiography, not a history, thesis, not a sociological treatise, not a piece of journalism."[4] As a work of fiction *The Crocodile* invites its own terms of critical reading.

A number of questions guide us to understand Eri's novel. Has Eri achieved what he has set out to do? Has he undermined his didactical approach by allowing Hoiri, the protagonist, to be disillusioned by becoming the unfulfilled quester and defeated hero at the end of the novel? Is Hoiri a symbolic betrayer of his cultural upbringing? Is his tragic defeat fated by a kind of prenatal destiny? The critical features of Eri's novel need explication. Relegating *The Crocodile* into categories of metafiction, metaethnology, or autobiography is difficult. Do we read the novel from an outside perspective (i.e. anthropological or literary criticism) or from within the structure and cultural contexts of the novel?

Eri's novel is a work of fiction with an array of historical, political, psychological, and cultural knowledge textualised in the structures of the novel. As a structure of experience, the novel captures the varied and het erogenous experiences of Eri's people under Australian colonial control. From the perspective of postcolonial reading, Eri had produced a text that will remain important in our analysis of Papua New Guinean societies fragmented through the process of colonialism.

Eri assumes the role of the artist as a teacher. He is an artist with a teacher's background. The role is pedagogical.[5] Eri portrays the disturbed psychological condition of the Moveave people and the uneasy acceptance of the negative influences of the colonizer. Eri's Moveave society, like most colonized societies, undergoes external invasion and conquest, cultural confrontation, and conflicts during the early years of colonization. Eri represents this critical moment in history of the Moveave society:

> No one was more troubled than Sevese. He wished Hoiri had never come into this world. He cursed the government and blamed Tamate [Toaripi name for the Reverend James Chalmers, the London Missionary Society pioneer who was murdered at Goaribari Island in 1901] for carrying the Word of God to the village, opening up the way for the patrol officers to be ordering his people around. If only the Government officers were like Tamate and other missionaries, who understood people and cared for their feelings, it would not be so bad. Maybe, when people die and change their skins, their feelings and ideas also change.[6]

The colonialising force was invasive and intrusive. The colonizers created a new psychology that undermined the people's views of themselves as a proud and powerful people. The colonisers gave the invaded Moveaves a new image characterized as inferior and submissive. Sevese curses the missionaries and the colonial government for invading the cohesive and harmonious Moveave society. Eri represents the pervasiveness of the colonizer's control and manipulation. It also reveals the colonized man's exposure to the worst realities of the colonial environment. In the passage that follows Sevese accepts this colonial domination:

> "Hoiri, my son, the truth of what I had always told you about keeping on with schooling is beginning to show itself now. If you were a teacher or a clerk you wouldn't be recruited for a carrier. This is only the beginning. By the time you are as old as I am, there will be a slot in your shoulders where the round end of a long stick will rest comfortably. Your hip joints will be loose from swinging in time with the movements of the patrol box."[7]

Sevese's statement of truth to his son Hoiri reflects the negative knowledge and the false imagery reinforced through the colonial education. The implantation of the pervasive and negative knowledge on the invaded people's consciousness is internalized. It severs the indigenous perspective by marginalizing it. Eri reveals the stubborn, hypocritical, and intolerant attitudes of the white colonial man. Of Mr. Smith, the young patrol officer, Eri writes:

> Mr. Smith had been long in the district. He would have been no older than Hoiri, but tall and fair. A healthy ripe pawpaw was the nearest shape and colour to his face; the cheeks were slightly red, either from the heat of the sun or the quantities of the rum he consumed. The flies seemed to have a particular liking for the white skin. He was stationed at Kerema, the district headquarters, where he had carried out a few minor patrols accompanied by a more experienced patrol officer, at least one in which he was on his own. Once on board, he removed his boots and relaxed in a deck chair and began reading a newspaper. The sergeant and the cook shared the shade of the canvas. At intervals Mr. Smith swiped at the flies and said, "The blasted flies — they won't leave me alone! Why don't you buzz around the smelly kanakas on board?"[8]

In this scathing description, Eri paints Mr. Smith as a caricature of the young, inexperienced patrol officers, often controlled by their white superior superman image and general arrogance towards the native conditions in Papua New Guinea. Eri's portraiture of the young Mr. Smith is satiric in many ways, but also speculative. In most colonized societies the mysteries and phenomena inherent in the physical features, the general attitude, and the material possessions of the white men are a common experience. In another passage Eri brings home this point:

Hera was not alone in his wish to learn the secret of easy access to lots and lots of money. It was common knowledge among his people that all white men who came to work in their country knew the secret of where all the money came from, but they dared not reveal it to the black men. The last thing the white men wanted was the black men become their equals. But if the white men had any sense of shame at all, they would admit openly that the wealth they proudly enjoyed didn't really belong to them. It was all confusing, to say the least. If they had easy access to all that stolen wealth, why did they come up to this country which some of them regarded as a bastard of a place to work in?[9]

Eri focuses on the indigenous characters more than the European characters. The protagonist alone, for instance, is well described. Eri describes the elements that shaped Hoiri's character. On their first trade expedition Hoiri learnt valuable lessons from his father:

The evening was calm and the sea was almost flat. On the seaward side, a short distance away, tiny waves lapped on the sand. The lakatoi was tied up in an inlet, just inside the junction where the river met the sea. Hoiri found it difficult to sleep. He listened to his father talk about the constant raids that the Toaripis used to make on their men, women and children on fishing trips.[10]

The lessons from his father Sevese, his aunt Suaea, and other villagers shaped the character of Hoiri. Krauth argues that Hoiri's character is shaped by the social and cultural contexts of the novel: "from social unity in the novel's first half to social fragmentation in the later half."[11] Eri has characterized the village people with deep and detailed compassion. The success of this technique is that the author claims the authority to describe his own people, their customs, and way of life. Growing up in his own society Eri feels connected to his people and owes it to them for the person he became. Eri's description of Hoiri's life is a reflection of the author's own life as a Moveave man.

Eri allows the village people around Hoiri to show their emotions and relationships to one another. The Moveave people have deep kinship relations to one another. Their understanding of one another is the social and culture glue that hold them together.

Eri paints Hoiri's childhood life as profoundly innocent. The childhood society of Hoiri is a closely-knit society, bound by its close kinships and harmony. The bond that Hoiri has to his aunt and cousin is incorrigible. In his matured life Hoiri experiences a frustrating and alienating experience. He realizes that "people are essentially isolated from the other and the society is a mass of fragments rather than a close-knit cooperative whole."[12] The fragmentation is caused by the influences from outside of the Moveave society through the process of colonial expansion.

The societies and eras are inseparable. The reality of the present condition of the colonized man is complicated. No one escapes. Entrapment and self-denial, however, are necessary in the crucial moments of history. The entrapment and personal sacrifices are the consequences of accepting the government's presence in their societies. Hoiri is trapped between tradition and modern cultures. Hoiri changes "his cultural framework and the fluidity of his conscious movements from a European frame of reference to a Papua New Guinea one as frequently as he could."[13] It is an ambiguous position, which Hoiri must live with.

Hoiri has to adjust to the cultural framework of thinking. Hoiri's reference to "the place above the rapids," for instance, could mean both in the Christian sense of the reference to heaven or in the traditional sense of the phrase referring to the people who live above the rapids, the unexplored territory of the fearsome warriors.[14] Such ambiguity can, however, place Hoiri intellectually above "the thinking of his own culture and that of the whites: the implication is that he has applied the evaluation that missionaries have used to denigrate his own culture's mythology (i.e., that it is mere superstition) to Christian mythology."[15]

The novel is closely tied up with the rituals, ceremonies, customs, and traditions of the Moveave people; their traditional relationships (personal, family), their trade relationships (trade partners and politics), and their mythical world. The very problem of the colonized is to break the barrier of cultural conformity. Only by transcending the subverted level can the colonized be recognized as important. This requires characters of the novel to move between the two contesting worlds. At times this movement is mimetic as in the post-colonial phase, and at other times by a complex process of assimilation.

The novel is written with a dual structure based on (i) Hoiri's childhood innocence and (ii) his grown-up adult experience. The childhood experience is centred on the early years of Hoiri in the village, his childhood dreams, fantasies, and innocence. Within this ages of innocence Hoiri's natural transition to manhood, his contact with the mysterious world of the white man, and the idyllic village traditions combine to initiate him to take on the second stage of his life.[16] The second stage is one of experience, from which he realizes the vulnerability and worst consequences that result from serious confrontations of both worlds. Hoiri is more a victim than a hero, the disillusioned man who has only to be drawn into the abyss of nothingness. Of this second stage Krauth explains Hoiri's disillusionment:

> He experiences the material ideal gone bad in the bombs and gun fire of warfare, and he suffers from the misfortune of being involved in a sorcery pay

back, the outcome of the personal relationships ideal gone bad. With the loss of his wife, Hoiri's attempt at achieving fulfillment in the traditional way is turned sour. The second half of the novel traces Hoiri's period of tragic experiences. He is forced towards disillusionment with both ways of life.[17]

Recurring themes, situations, and images unifies the two parts. The recurring devices weld the novel together by signaling the progressive stages in Hoiri's development and acting as reference points between these stages.[18] A kind of rhythm and tempo of literary aesthetics is fashioned in the novel. The first four chapters are all based on Hoiri's childhood. The rest are about contact with the outside world. The last chapter is the end result of such an experience. Here in the Bakhtinian sense we see that the structure is cyclical, in that "there is no broad or deep realistic emblematic; meaning does not exceed the sociohistorical limitations inherent in the images", that it "makes itself felt itself with particular force, therefore the beginnings of growth and the perpetual renewal of life are weakened, separated from the progressive forces of history and even opposed to them; thus growth, in this context, makes life a senseless running-in-place at one historical point, at one level of historical development."[19] Hoiri explores this world with questions at the intersection of every new experience.

The general experience is pivotal. Hoiri moves between the traditional and modern cultures. Hoiri resorts to easy speculation about the white culture, the material possession of white goods, and the white world he remembers from his journey to Port Moresby. Hoiri's predicament is more a psychological abyss than an empty void. By presenting such a condition of vacuousness Eri brings his novel to an ending without an end. We discover an abyss of disillusionment played out in the novel. Hoiri experiences disillusionment, confusion, and anxiety, in the physical and cultural environments that constitute him. All through the novel Hoiri dwells in the geographical and mental circles, which we are made aware. Notions of exclusion mark the cultural boundaries in the traditional Moveave society. Hoiri's Moveave culture has fixed structures able to contain its people before the arrival of Europeans. Soon after that destabilizing agent these structures become weak and unable to hold together the Moveave social and cultural ways.

The world of *The Crocodile* is circular in nature. This generates entrapment and destruction. In a way the circular journey and the shifting of Hoiri's mental ideas serve as a metaphysical aspect of the novel. The protagonist is straddled between the world of the real as well as that of rituals and magics. It is an intrinsic aspect of many postcolonial novels. *The Crocodile* is based on the author's own psychological, historical, and cultural background. Such a condition has deep roots in the metaphysical cosmos of Eri's people. Eri demonstrates his ability to contain both worlds, by appropriating the written word to contain the artistic, magical, mythical, and spiritual world of his unwritten culture.

Eri's role as a writer and teacher is an important responsibility. It is a privileged position. Eri textualizes his people's culture and society. Being a product of the oral society, the author is aware of its immense cultural depth by giving a scope to it in the written form. There are problems, however, with such a practice. An author conditioned by the structures, morphology, and style of the written discourse can restrict the entirety of a specific subject. This may be true, where the written word claims only to represent both worlds in the novel, and where its structure and conventional nature is inadequate to represent the unconscious, unconventional, and complicated nature of the unwritten world. Glass points out some of these problems in Eri's work. For example, Hoiri's description of Mitoro's buttocks as "two round pots" suggests pleasing physical contours, but ambiguous in interpretation. Eri's precise connotations for the pots within the Papua New Guinea context as items of high value, used in the age-old Hiri trade cycle between the Gulf people and their Motuan partners are ambiguous if the novel is read without the cultural context.[20] The question that arises is whether we read *The Crocodile* with a western precision of structure and narrative technique or style?

The world that Eri portrays is one of cultural fragmentation and chaos. The ideal village condition and the physical make-up of the traditional man fall apart into fragments of ridiculous proportions through the loss of traditions and the cultural betrayal by acts of submission. Just as Hoiri's admiration of Mitoro's beauty and qualities as characteristics of an ideal village woman is denied to him when a crocodile takes her life, Eri presents the ideal village situations and qualities destroyed by forces of change. These forces of change are symbolically presented as the destructive power of the crocodile. The crocodile operates on other levels as well. On the one hand it is the powers of evil and sorcery:

> "Yes, this is no ordinary crocodile," Hoiri said to himself when he saw the crocodile make an about-turn and head towards him. He heard a whistle, presumably in reply to his, come from the direction of the crocodile. He did not reply, fearing he might give himself away the second time. Still the crocodile kept coming straight at him. The edge of the water was no more than a foot away from where Hoiri stood. Finding itself in shallow water, the reptile raised itself on its legs and hands. The object that had seemed no more than a yard in length a few seconds ago, had suddenly transformed itself into a huge dug-out canoe. With slow steps the horrifying creature advanced; then it stopped.[21]

At another level, the crocodile as a metaphor represents the destructive powers of the colonial forces. Associated with these themes are the conscription into the patrol teams as carriers and Hoiri's marriage to Mitoro in the church, even though they were already married through the traditional marriage ceremony.

Although the establishment of European culture "on the Moveave district and the fact that power is valued in Papua New Guinea culture for its own sake makes possible the acceptance of the superior white technology."[22] Power is institutionalized and maintained through force.

The Crocodile represents the "cultural fragmentation caused by the influx of Australians during the Second World War and the profound historical changes this meant for the people of Papua New Guinea."[23] Even before the war, Moveave and many contact societies in Papua New Guinea were already experiencing cultural fragmentation. The war is only one of the dramatic forces of destruction and cultural fragmentation:

> All the way down the river, Larry Brown told the Moveave men that as long as they remained loyal to the King and the Australian Government, their lands, gardens, women and children would always be theirs. The Japanese were bad people and were after all these things for themselves. If the Japanese won the war they, the brown men, would forever become like prisoners working for nothing for the Japanese. He also told them that Australians were not running away. He forecast that very soon there would be big ships, belonging to Australia, going up that river loaded with guns, soldiers and cargo. If Australia won the war, the brown men would be treated as brothers and would sit at table with the white men.[24]

Eri explores the idea of fragmentation further, to the whole set of values that characterizes Hoiri's upbringing as a villager. This includes the test of these values as they come in confrontation with the ones outside of his childhood society. The quest for an ideal self and an ideal society is often impossible. Cultures that operate in a contact society are vulnerable. This leads to fragmentation as they attempt to accommodate or reject those aspects absent from the original culture. Eri acknowledges cultural fragmentation in his society.

Eri has created a method that provides a passage into time. His style of writing is compared to styles of other postcolonial writers. Writing from within a colonized space enables Eri to appropriate the written text, once denied to indigenous authors. The first works of fiction from colonized people often wedge their way through a very revolutionary process. The seizure of the written text often "involves an entirely different and intrusive (invasive) orientation to knowledge and interpretation" of the colonial people, but one which is essentially mimetic.[25] This feature is regarded as the seizing of the word or the written text as a way of "retaining the seed of self-regeneration and the power to create and recreate the world." Through writing authors release a dense proliferation of possibilities.[26]

The reimagining of New Guinea, the re-describing of the unwritten world is necessary, but within the colonized author's own contextual framework. *The*

TRANSITIONS AND TRANSFORMATIONS

Crocodile represents a society making a transition into a new historical phase. The seizing of the means of communication and the liberation of the postcolonial writing by appropriation of the written word is critical in the process of self-assertion and of reconstruction of the world as an unfolding historical process. [27]

CONCLUSION

Eri's method is to provide us with a journey in-ward, into the space of events, and to experience time. Time in the western sense would be inappropriate. Important cultural elements are recalled through events and happenings. Once in the sphere of Eri's world, the non-Moveave's cultural and ideological background is unable to make sense of the ritualistic world. There is nothing to facilitate the reader's critical knowledge of the world of the novel. As non-Moveave readers we are faced with the ultimate decision to share Hoiri's tragic world. Hoiri's gradual progress into the world outside of his own leads to further conflicts and confrontations. The novel is closely-knit with the fabric of the colonial and traditional societies. Just as Hoiri is accepted as a village man brought up in his traditional society and making an entry into the colonial world, the book also enters another world. *The Crocodile* has achieved what may be described as the oral word making its entry into the written word.

11

WANPIS EXISTENTIALISM

One of the most common misreadings of Soaba's *Wanpis* (1977) is that it is a racist text.[1] The prejudice is based on a certain degree of ignorance and lack of critical appreciation of two philosophical concepts in the book. In *Wanpis* (1977) Soaba explores the western existential ideas of the individual and self, in his own terms. The two terms: "lusman" and "wanpis" stem directly from the Tok Pisin language. The conventional use of the term "lusman" means a person who is unattached, an individual without roots, or place. The word "wanpis" means a person who is alone, perhaps loosely attached or detached in a temporary way from others. Soaba's concepts of "lusman" and "wanpis" go beyond the conventional meaning of these words. Soaba appropriates the Western philosophical knowledge for his own use. It also signals two points of departures in his textual practice: the departure from the literary influence of the Ulli Beier and the decision to be an artist, an existential writer committed to his work. Readers of Papua New Guinean writing may praise and exalt the works of Soaba's contemporaries, but Soaba challenges the reader's critical and preconceived notions of a Papua New Guinean novel.

Wanpis is indeed a very difficult work. Part of the difficulty has to do with the heavy adoption of existential ideas. Readers of the pastoral-village literature, concerned with the nostalgic dreams of the past find it difficult to understand the philosophical basis of Soaba's work. In *Wanpis,* Soaba explores broad ideas from existentialism to Marxism, but within his own cultural contexts. This exploration takes him beyond familiar cultural grounds and traditional writing styles of his contemporaries. He is concerned with the "modes of survival, conformity and rebellion, contrasting the confused sensibilities of its characters' inner worlds with the brutally absurd fates dictated to them by history and social pressures."[2] Soaba focuses on the highly conscious Papua New Guinean intellectuals and members of the elite class, artists, bureaucrats, school dropouts, and workers forming the postcolonial setting of Papua New Guinea.

Three broad categories are used to explore the existential conditions that enable Papua New Guineans to interaction among themselves. These categories are *"lusman"*, *"split-egg nostalgia"*, and *"wanpis"*. The three categories are interconnected to each other, forcing the boundaries between them to remain negotiable without needing to conform to the purely western definitions of existential self, humanism, and society.

Soaba discusses the notion of "lusman" as the experiences that depict the intellectual 'drop-out' from any tertiary institutions, beyond which he/she is a hero with good qualities that are absorbed into the work force or that are useful in village communities. The few bright ones who continue on to higher education are poorly educated. They are still worshipping the old mistakes and the establishments of colonial institutions. These behaviours and attitudes alienate them from their own social or cultural institutions.[3] A "lusman" as an alienated person has no sense of belonging. The irony is that suddenly a new aspiration for self-consciousness develops and takes shape out of that placelessness. Since a "lusman" cannot sustain or defend himself against a society's ignorance of his existence, he or she must become a "wanpis", maybe as a last deathbed wish. In "Split-egg nostalgia" Soaba talks about the dream of the great return to the village. The idealization of the pasts and the sudden upsurge of national pride and solidarity are featured in this section of the book.

The characters in this section, however, do not return to the village. They only recognize that feeling of being attached to some common place of identity. They thrive on a sense of belonging to their past and society. This section forms the basis of Soaba's investigation of the students' cultural and political activities in the University of Papua New Guinea in the 1970s. It also focuses on the solidarity of Papua New Guineans as they waded through the difficult transitional period to independence.[4]

Wanpis was written in the critical period prior to and at the dawn of Independence. To capture the dominant mood at that time Soaba represents the nationalist sentiments in the novel without sounding optimistic. Here is a novel, at the birth of national consciousness, which argues for and represents the reality and the aspiration for Independence and nationhood. Everyone must rely on principles of group solidarity and nationalistic goals. Such ambitions are deceptive. To achieve nationhood a binding force is needed. The binding force surfaces as a struggle rather than as a smooth transition. Soaba prefers the truth unveiled rather than being withheld by deception. He foresees that the truth of this struggle, this experience of being liberated from the colonized space, is at the cost of self-expression and individual sacrifices.

It is difficult to pinpoint who in the novel represents the "lusman" and who represents the "wanpis" characters. All characters are represented in the "split-egg nostalgia" category. The "split-egg nostalgia" category is the overlapping point. In this category Soaba portrays Papua New Guinea societies split between the traditional past and present postcolonial conditions, between the villages and towns, and between traditional cultures and modern cultures. The nostalgic return to the original order, the idyllic cultural order, is possible, but at a cost. Within this liminality individual characters realize the dichotomy of their existence. It is critical that they declare their allegiances, their sense of belonging, cohesion, and unity in a new social, cultural, and religious order.

In later interviews Soaba makes clear the critical process of the novel and the concept of "lusman" and "wanpis". In an article he published about Albert Wendt as the Pacific's existentialist writer, Soaba attempts a definition of the concept of "lusman" and "wanpis", but with reference to his own works.[5] The "lusman" according to Soaba is born free with unlimited freedom and is responsible for the nature of his own self. This kind of individual is someone who acknowledges the self as the entirety of his existence, but refuses to acknowledge the rules, cultural boundaries, ethical, or moral rules of the society. He lacks conformity. He refuses to acknowledge the existence of a society. This is demonstrated more profoundly in the poet figure James St. Nativeson, the real lusman, who is damned and trapped. The "lusman" figure is the most complicated character in the novel. This character is the real outsider. This character is motivated by "habitual orientation towards hatred and self-hatred born of his incapacity to meet life and society in self-respecting terms, the unreconstructed individualist, the man or person that no ameliorate, let alone utopian, society can tolerate or assimilate, because his very existence undermines its rationale for or claims to excellence." This kind of individual is someone who "exemplifies human nature inaccessible to national social planning." Such an individual is capable of suffering or causing suffering irrespective "of any asocial or theoretical assumption that suffering and perversity can be legislated out of existence. His very spitefulness is, ultimately, part of the essence of his (and our) humanity, if humanity is regarded as what is left in the viscera of rebellious subjectivity against any totalitarian polity of repressive control."[6]

Soaba's existential ideas developed in his earlier works, investigated the ideas of self and society.[7] He is aware of the external conflict, but also of something missing, the internal conflict of the self, its relation to the society or the society's relation to the self. Soaba's purpose in *Wanpis* is to express the inner strengths and weaknesses of the individual characters. In so doing the "essential self" of the characters are identified and asserted in the novel. The characters are swayed into believing in an individual's indifference to society as a consequence of social and cultural conflict.[8]

On the other hand, Soaba realizes that self-acceptance, self-definition, and discovery are essential qualities of consciousness, which are powerful justifications for being part of a split society. This society has difficulties with maintaining nationhood as a result of the diversity of cultures, languages, and histories. Thus *Wanpis* opens up with different characters with different views, ideas, influences, and backgrounds. The characters eventually work towards building a new society; "each attempting to weave the fabric of a better future from the shreds of a tattered past."[9]

The "lusman" idea, explored extensively in the first two parts of the novel, is based on Abel Willborough's narration and reminiscence. Towards the end of the book a new emphasis on James St. Nativeson is constructed. The strategy is important for the exposition of the "wanpis" notion in the book. The narrator, Abel Willborough, for instance, realizes this shift of identity, from his own "lusman" identity to that of a "wanpis" as a necessary condition of survival:

> I was born at dusk. True. I spent the first moments of my life in the darkness, waiting for the next dawn. True again. Symbolically, that is. I never did, and perhaps I never will, know what that next dawn was. Still, I arrived to find it one day, somewhere.[10]

Soaba's idea of a "lusman" is similar to Dostoeyevsky's narrator in *Notes from Underground*, where "the narrator [is] irrevocably self-divided, and acutely aware of his division; he is continually doing things that he does and does not want to do. Indeed, any one so deeply motivated as he is by spite and perversity (key words in the story), and who has his intelligence, is bound to possess a strong sense of his own dividedness."[11] The basic condition of such perversity or existential self has to do with alienation and loneliness. Abel Willborough is a lonely and alienated child from his mixed-race blood. His mother died while he was away in school. He took on a shadowy character in his school days. The indifference of his half-sister upon his graduation from high school forces him to live away from home. He is the intellectual hiding behind the facades of indifference. Unlike James St. Nativeson, Abel Willborough is willing to conform to the society. The society becomes his shelter for his own weaknesses. He becomes a "wanpis" according to Soaba's definition. This alienated, self-denying character suddenly shifts identity, from being a "lusman" to being a "wanpis" by assuming the role of a husband, would-be-father, and responsible citizen:

> I have no choice. Can't flee the city; can't abandon myself. Ha! What frail pre-emptions! Nope. Can't abandon myself. Having a wife and family is no excuse, I know; but one day in the life of a man there is this, this business of belonging, a moment of decision, a desire to battle it all out, until he discovers that he is not totally alone. No, not even just be the fatherless native.[12]

A "lusman" is free to abandon himself. He is even happy to take his own life when and wherever he wishes. A "lusman" is more at home with his intellectual and artistic creations. In *Wanpis* the poet is isolated and alienated. The society is unable to sustain him. The emphasis is to show that the "lusman" is a poet and artist, who is more an intellectual outsider than most, seeking solitude as inspiration to live through the dreadful human conditions. He is content with writing poetry and random notes for a novel. A "lusman" is essentially a truth seeker who lives by principles, which are based on the conduct of the self. James St. Nativeson as a true artist refuses to die in bureaucracy, an institution of self-deception and political mimicry. On the other hand he is prepared to undergo martyrdom for believing in the self and the virtues of self. The "lusman's" death is the most forceful expression of this martyrdom:

> He lay flat on his stomach, legs spread, arms outstretched, teeth clenched, chin tightly pressed onto the concrete pavement, ready to bloat in [Port] Moresby's thick humidity. A pair of dead eyes stared ahead of him, each socket displaying suffering, discontent, but more of a dead hero whose photographer had striven in vain to make the corpse smile again. The body was butchered by broken bottles on this hot, drunken Saturday, a gash in his bloody mess of hair, several cuts on each forearm,and a slit lower lip forming a second mouth. Constant exudations of red soaked his clothes: a dead frog in a pool of human blood.[13]

Soaba's vivid description of James St. Nativeson's death is disturbing, but presents a powerful expression of violence and death during crucial moments of transition in a newly independent country. Such expressions explain the uncertainties, the betrayal fever of a new bourgeoisie, and the cultural death of the previous generation. The overall aim is to infuse these two ideas into a coherent unity. James St. Nativeson is an inspiring and binding force as well as a symbolic figure of human sacrifice. This binding factor is represented by James St. Nativeson's death.

Soaba is suggesting that while a "lusman" is forced to live on his own, it is horrifying to imagine the dreadful condition of such a living without human contacts. James St. Nativeson is the most alienated individual. His existence in the novel is on the edge of the normal society's experience. He suffers from what the society calls a rebellious, unconventional human experience, yet he insists on being left alone, to write in the solitary confinement of his flat, however absurd it may be:

> No one else but James St. Nativeson, that All Saints' graduate, who could never afford a University degree nor any similar academic qualification but to shape and mould his own talents and creativity whilst shut in a room among piles of Western Existentialist novels and essays; whilst he'd spent all his youth wasting away in the narrow confinement of bureaucratic clerkship; and whilst dreaming only but never becoming the country's poet and hero, its historical figure, its forerunner of free thought and honesty in the self, would choose to

die like this; a battered face, squandered youth; artistic insight squashed under the weight of human underdevelopment, deaf national harmony and political dreams of pot-bellied independence.[14]

As for the "wanpis" it is the contrary. According to Soaba, a "wanpis" takes Sartre's idea of existentialism based on broad ideas of humanism. In this case a "wanpis" is someone who is "condemned to be free", but is part of humanity. He or she continues to live responsibly, as he or she is no longer free like a "lusman".

The "wanpis" is attached to the society either temporarily or permanently. He or she questions his or her sense of freedom a lot, but realizes that "the society is part of him [her]" and the "society constitutes him[her]."[15] A "wanpis" character is the perfect opposite of a "lusman" figure. He or she is someone who is prepared to change his or her identity, assume a new responsibility, and welcome all ideas of assimilation. In many ways the "wanpis" character recognizes the hopeless condition of his or her entrapment. He or she tries to improve it. He or she is trapped in by his or her birth and nature of being part of a larger constitutive whole. A "wanpis" is prepared to live through it. At birth he or she is a "lusman", but in later adult years he or she develops into a "wanpis" figure:

> I discovered, after moving among the crowd. Fears of complete insecurity and self-betrayal began to stalk my conscience.... yet I felt at the same time that I needed some kind of release. As such I moved at ease amid the din of the gathering, with some difficulty at first but tactically afterwards, no longer afraid of the dangers of self-exposure, thinking I had no choice but to pretend to live with the crowd.[16]

Wanpis is a semi-autobiographical work based on Soaba's association with people who went through school with him and have moved to occupy important places in society. Soaba indicates in his interview with Chris Tiffin that the last part of the novel, especially James St. Nativeson's poetry and notes, is his favourite.[17] The notes made by James St. Nativeson in his "Random Notes of a Novel" also reflects Soaba's background in writing *Wanpis*:

> The characters in this novel are not just literary inventions; they are based on the friends I currently treasure, and without whose personal sacrifice in terms of intellectual contribution to the content of this book, I would never attempt an effort as ambitious as this. Where necessary the reader should not fear the liberty of assuming that any of these characters can be an autobiographical representation.[18]

In *Wanpis* there is a great deal of physical and psychological loss. The idea of loss is a shared experience of Abel Willborough, Just Call Me Joe, Nathaniel, Vera Nondasiri, Sheila Jivi La and Mr. Goldsworth. The loss is both experienced at personal as well as the societal level. The characters' loss of their family, culture, and original beliefs is weighed against society's loss, at the expense of independence. This loss is very much a positive thing. In experiencing loss characters achieve personal freedom and liberty beyond the doors of the past. This is well illustrated in the symbolic death of James St. Nativeson and the comical celebration of the other Anuki companions during the time James St. Nativeson lies dying in the hospital bed.

Soaba is engaged with the cultural transformation in the postcolonial era. Soaba envisions a society that is multicultural, multilingual, and ordinary. Such a society must encompass every human experience. The cost of such a society is dearer than envisioned. By virtue of an individual's commitment, as in the case of the writer martyr, whose sacrificial death unifies individuals of a society as a cohesive unit, Papuans and New Guineans unite to form a nation called Papua New Guinea. Soaba is not pretending he is right in prophesying, but at least he is honest in uncovering the realities of the postcolonial Papua New Guinea.

Alienation is a necessary step to freedom. Soaba's characters are people who have enough sense of their alienated pasts and the dark blind background of their early innocent years. They recognize themselves as living in the present: to live, is to conform and to make the best of everything, even out of the most abhorrently chaotic or violent experiences. At least that is what Soaba is suggesting:

> I think there is no denying that we are all lusman. To a certain extent I would agree with the western Existentialist. Do I feel out of place in this country? Yes, well I'm a poet in one way or another so most of my characters are those who can't conform easily to the society they constitute. Some of the lusman and wanpis images are brave enough to declare that it is not I who must constitute the society. The society must constitute me.[19]

Soaba uses personal experiences and philosophical ideas in his fiction in a politically conscious way. The use of philosophical ideas is basic to works of literature, as noted in Wordsworth's autobiographical works where poetry and truth precedes textuality to contribute to the greater understanding of man and society. Thus existentialism was relevant for Soaba to pursue values of individuals, man, and society in the Melanesian context. Soaba pursued this objective, only in as much as is possible in the character of James St. Nativeson, who seems to be the only thinking person in the whole book. One can feel for James St. Nativeson as a tragic creation.

Soaba's characters are created with great beauty and force. Each one of them is a self-contained archetype, an individual spread across the entire society. Soaba is working towards the alienated individual in modern society. The individual is not someone who is disillusioned and confused as in Eri's *The Crocodile* (1971), but one who is certain about himself, his inner strengths and weaknesses.

The significance of Soaba's ideas of "lusman" and "wanpis" is that they form the basis of Soaba's textual practice in *Wanpis* and in his other works. Soaba probes into the intellectual, cultural, and psychological life of a colonized people. He uses the character of the poet figure and artist. James St. Nativeson's ideas, philosophies, writings, and life seem to have formed the core of the Anuki folk's life outside of their village. Soaba's adoption of a biblical theme, and the naming of Jimi Damebo as James St. Nativeson, after James Baldwin, work as a hybridization of powerful forms of textuality. This is a significant aspect of Soaba's work.

Wanpis is a book about writing from the colonized, the subverted, and the non-western writers' perspectives. This is emphasized in the novel:

"One day he'd decided to read the dictionary out of some curiosity which he had forgotten immediately after he had picked up the volume. He chucked it into the fire. Simply because the dictionary was like everyone else. Obsolete… If he accepted things as they were, he told himself, he would be what James St. Nativeson called 'a lusman without principles.'"[21]

Simply, the act of refusal of the common, conventional, or popular requires the act of formulating one's own principles and rules of textuality. Soaba is advocating the reconstruction of thought by rejecting the western sense of pleasure and power, and the search for an inner soul's meaning. In so doing, Soaba has provided an entirely fresh and unique perspective of the indigene's psyche and self-consciousness in the literature of Papua New Guinea. Soaba uses text as a political weapon to dismiss commonly held opinions about the art of writing as belonging to the western world, and to reverse possible textual description of the invaded world. Spivak argues that the supposedly "inscribed" and "textualised" from the "uninscribed" or the "unworlded" world by the imperial empire is yet to be reworlded.[21] In other words, Soaba is seen here as simply attempting a "reworlding" of world textualised in the western imperialists' discourses.

In the years after the publication of this novel Soaba became more absorbed in the ideas he explored in *Wanpis*, making his critics unsure about their evaluation of the work or even of the author's life as a writer. The novel was not reprinted even though a new wave of students appreciated the deep literary and philosophical value of the work. The book has its level of difficulty inherent in the novelistic discourses constructed in the work, but with incisive unmasking of the complexity in the layers of discourses inherent in such existentialist work, the novel fit alongside western classics and even some of the best works of Oceanic literary imagination.

CONCLUSION

There is a radical challenge of the accepted norms, namely those that have to do with inheritance based on male line of descent. Dominating forces of power in the Pacific can also be those are already structured within the indigenous cultures. The dominating power could be patriarchal male dominated system of authority — the patriarchy of or the Western influenced systems of power and control, which includes the state and its apparatus. Soaba is making the point that cultural metaphors provide the lenses from which to look through ourselves. Finding the source of our authority as Pacific peoples requires that we reclaim our rights to our destiny. Life is full of parables, metaphors, history, and narratives that we can draw from to reaffirm our place in the wider world.

Constructing Double Consciousness

The study of literature and writers often concentrate on writers associated with the University of Papua New Guinea, the Institute of Papua New Guinea Studies, and the literary forums operated by these institutions. The problem with this emphasis is that anything produced outside of institutional (UPNG) influence was regarded as trivial and unworthy of literary analysis. One of the writers outside of the UPNG group is Paulias Matane, a prolific writer whose work ranges from autobiography to non fiction and fiction. His most notable literary achievement is the Aimbe series of books. Matane's fiction is meant for the popular readership outside of the academic classrooms.

In 1979 Matane published *Aimbe, the Pastor*.[1] It was reprinted as *Ripples in the South Pacific Ocean: A Historical Novel Portraying the Dawn of Civilization in Papua New Guinea* (2003). Matane's *Aimbe, the Pastor* (1979) is a literary work with a popular outlook and a touch of realism. The novel makes full use of the story-telling features of PNG oral traditions. Matane combines these techniques with the recollections of historical events and the fascinating accounts of people who lived through the colonial history.

The novel makes use of the storytelling culture in Papua New Guinea oral societies. Matane's narrative pattern is similar to the narrative tradition that developed with other PNG writers such as Kiki, Eri, Umba, Kituai, Baital, and Soaba. Matane's novels are a brilliant series of narratives based on Aimbe, a fictional hero from the East New Britain Province. The theme of contact, the world wars, the influence of the missions, as well as the conflict of traditions and individual decisions are explored in all three novels: *Aimbe, the Challenger*, *Aimbe, the School Drop-out*, and *Aimbe, the Villager*.[2]

Matane's writings meet the need for a writing that is both popular and readable. His work employs the art of good storytelling and telling of a yarn with social, political, and cultural significance. Matane's primary aim is to provide something that could reach non-sophisticated readers such as school children and other ordinary Papua New Guineans. All his novels have similar qualities. His novels are popular in schools during the 1970s and 1980s. The need for popular novels was a step away from Kiki's autobiography, Eri's serious fiction and Soaba's sophisticated existential novel. Matane's writing had a wide readership within the country because of its simplicity and realistic quality employed in the writing of the novels. The Education Department and churches found Matane's books useful for their purposes. In all fairness his works played an important role in the developing literature of Papua New Guinea.

THE WORLD OF AIMBE

The world of Aimbe is the colonized world. Matane writes about the conditions in which the dominant takes control of power and forms of knowledge, and subverting the invaded people into a level of inferiority. Matane aims at bringing these worlds together as an imagined community. Through the fictionalized world Matane is also sharing his experiences in the colonial world. The narratives of Aimbe comes close to the author's own experiences as a village boy moving into the modern world and taking up positions of authority in the country.

Matane's *Ripple*s is a work of fiction based on aspects of the author's own life and that of his people during the colonial period. The text is a fictional creation based on actual events occurring in the author's time or in the colonial history of Papua New Guinea.[3] *Ripples* is about the experiences of colonization in New Guinea where planters and missionaries were instrumental in creating cultural fusion and economic exploitations. The book is about colonial control and the negative influences of that control and order.

The book has a didactive value in educating Papua New Guineans about themselves and their history. In this passage, for example, Aimbe's early oratory suggests the forced participation of Papua New Guineans in the labour and plantation economy of the German colonization in German New Guinea. The expansion of foreign ideas and exploitation of New Guineans, their land and rights were rampant at the height of German colonial expansion in the Pacific. Aimbe resists the colonial planters, but he also makes allowance for new ideas:

"Though your attitude towards us was harsh, we learned a great deal from you and your friends in the nearby plantations. The things we learned are both good and bad...We learned how to look after the plantation...the bad points... First, your arrogant attitudes to us are not welcome. Second your belief that we are not intelligent is absolutely without foundation. Third, when your coconuts are ready, you will sell their meat (copra) to other countries. The money will be sent to your country. In other words, we are working hard for you and your relatives, who sit on their rocking chairs in your country doing nothing. Fourth, there is a degree of dependence on you. This destroys our independence and our pride. As independent proud people, we survive, but the other groups here and at the neighbouring plantations fall into this degrading trap. Most of them do not want to go back to their villages. They have lost their self-esteem, their dignity, and above all, their worth. They are nothing if and when they return to their villages."[4]

This passage demonstrates Matane's authorial intrusion in the text (declaring his personal views) instead of drawing on the simple and often submissive attitudes of New Guineans during the colonial period. It appears Aimbe could speak in as clear language as the plantation owners. It appears also that in making his points of argument Aimbe is very well versed in the international economic and political systems. Given the environment that most of the colonized in their early history had no idea what existed outside, this authorial intrusion suggest that Matane is bringing the colonizers or European colonizers as readers into the text of native subjected voices. It is unclear whether Matane has completely distorted this to make a point, but it is obvious that reactions to the colonial planters were strong in those days. Mobilization of people from different areas, languages, and cultures was also evident.

The colonized formed into social, political, and cultural units to react against one powerful figure, represented in the form of colonizers. Overt reactions and protests during the colonial period were rare, but violent, and at times they received harsh and punitive treatments from their colonial masters. If there were reactions and disagreements the New Guineans were normally passive, rather than respond to them in violent manners.

During the period when New Guinea was under the responsibility of Germany as a protectorate, the plantation economy boomed. New Guineans were reluctant to challenge the Germans, but justified their presence with far less resistance. Yet there was a degree of intelligence and self-consciousness exercised during the period of plantation experience that developed out of the alienating conditions.

New Guineans were regarded by the colonials and missionaries as "mendacious, rude and willful children; full of arrogance and darkness, who only want what to them was beloved and cannot bring themselves under any order or authority," according to one missionary in his report.[5] The missionaries and the planters, however, played an important role in colonizing New Guinea. One study of colonialism and missionary influence in New Guinean shows: "They helped to introduce the capitalist order in patriarchal and religious forms, creating new economic relationships, political structures and systems of cultural symbols."[6] New Guinea labour was used in Church-oriented business, thereby fusing "secular forms of development" with secular state responsibilities.[7] For example "the infrastructure created by the mission society developed into an alternative state in which New Guineans owed primary allegiance to church-centred social and political structures."[8]

The opposition in the character of a New Guinean during colonization is imminent. This dilemma is one that creates a lot of problems. The perils of survival and necessary leadership were important elements in the cohesion of the society in times of invasion and destruction. Aimbe as the chosen leader is unable to fulfill the expectations of him in the traditional Tolai society. He inherits the title from his father Luluiai, who preceded him as the traditional leader. In a vision from the spirits' world, his father counsels him to be courageous and compassionate, to be a spokesman for his people.

In another vision the spirit of his wily uncle offers an alternative role to be more powerful and brave. Luaina Aimbe in the end takes his father's counsel. He is taken to work on a coconut plantation. There he uses his role as a village leader to speak for the condition of labourers and the general treatment of labourers by planters. He challenges the plantation authorities and defies some of their rules.

CONFLICTING ROLES

Aimbe, the protagonist of *Ripples*, occupies two different conflicting roles. He is a village leader and a pastor of the Christian religion. These roles often disagree with each other, thus resulting in rejection of one and consolidation of the other. This leads to a very problematic area of consciousness and representation.

The book is intended as a cultural, historical, or political representation of the Papua New Guinea in the colonial period. The protagonist of the novel is a problematic representative of his Papua New Guinean culture, values, and ideas. He feigns representation in most cases to match the two different values and traditions. Does Aimbe represent his people or the colonial world? Could Aimbe's early resistance to the planters be a fake resistance? Could Aimbe's fake resistance be motivated by self-esteem or status? It seems that he speaks for his people, as a villager, but maintains a dominant role as an agent of the colonial power. Such conflicting roles of the protagonist affect the over-all impact and seriousness of the novel.

Matane chooses the work of the ministry to demonstrate the reactions and conflicts pertinent to such roles. His interest in the book is in the examination of these reactions and conflicts in the contact Tolai society. Aimbe chooses to achieve power and authority by using the introduced ideas and processes of leadership. He also undermines the traditional power of Tolai leadership inherited from his father.

Aimbe loses the traditional authority by choosing the role of a pastor within the introduced religious work. Without realizing the decision to embrace the coloniser's introduced religion makes him exploit his own people. He strengthens and consolidates this exploitative role by what he preaches. Aimbe knows that as a preacher he must work against traditional religious practices and ways of life. He also knows that within him, a degree of guilt of exploitation, reside deep within the subconscious of the Tolai self. He feels guilty for seducing Kanai — a moment suggestive of the double consciousness by which a sense of power leads one to exploit another less powerful. Aimbe's guilt remains troubling until he retired from the ministry. This type of double consciousness characterized many people divided by the introduced ideas, ideology, and manners of behavior brought with the arrival of colonialism. Aimbe's position is one of cultural betrayal as well as unconscious submission to the new forces of power. He has to submit to the mission influence by betraying his cultures and traditions.

Matane's work is set against the colonial backdrop of cultural invasion, rejection, and forceful submission. These conditions of cultural invasion and subversion work as a disintegrative force. Colonizers established institutions that maintain their power and authority. The same institutions destabilized existing structures of the power and authority. It is a fact of colonialism that forces the invaded to see themselves as having inferiority complexes.[9] Colonised people more often are led to believe that they are inferior and their subjugation is determined by God that any questions raised regarding its validity must not emerge. The master slave relationship evident in the colonial environment reinforced a false sense of ideology as we witness in the life of Aimbe, the pastor. Colonization in many ways takes further strength and power from the submission of the colonized. The colonizers celebrate their role in so-called pacification rites and civilizing projects where the imperial power has its flags flying.

Many colonized societies in Africa, Asia, Caribbean and the Pacific began to resist colonialism by asserting their cultural values, traditions and seeking political freedom from their colonizers. The colonized people became aware of the rate at which their cultures and traditions disappeared. Matane sets *Ripples* in this period of cultural imperialism and invasion of the local customs and lives. The massive denigration of cultures and people by missions and the infliction of European tradition on the minds of the local people are highlighted in the book.

COLONIZATION IN NEW GUINEA

The book is an alphabet of colonization in New Guinea. First, there is the traditional non-contact society, which is contacted by, explorers, missionaries, gold prospectors, or the plantation labour recruiters. The first missionaries establish their presence by spreading the word of God, introduced the Bible, and later reaffirming new forms of order and ideas based on the Christian religion. Once this is established colonial officers move into to exploit the labour of the colonized and acquire land for the plantation economy of the empire.

More land acquisition for the colonial plantation economy took place during the colonial period. More labourers are recruited. World War I comes to New Guinea. Schools and churches are opened and pastors give elementary classes. There are further interactions between villagers and missionaries, other villagers and the outside world. The Second World War is fought in New Guinea. The post-war activities of rehabilitation and strengthening of colonial work in New Guinea take place. This leads on to the time of self-government.

Papuan New Guineans are colonized and transformed in the image of the colonizers. This development is evident in Aimbe's own life. He grows up in the village, takes up a traditional leadership, faces a new threat to his leadership from the first white man, he becomes an outsider, and is further exposed to new ideas brought by missionaries. He is taken away from his people to work on the plantation, which helps weakens the basis of a strong cultural attachment to his people.

The missionaries and the colonial officers influence him in a profound way. Aimbe's traditional leadership is held to task. The missions Christianized him and called him Aimbe, instead of Luaina as his people named him. He is sent to Nagunan elementary school, Wailik High School, and the missionary training school at Vunavartovo. As a brilliant and outspoken student of the Christian ministry school he becomes the leader of the students. After graduating from that school he becomes a pastor in another village. Aimbe works as a devout pastor to bring Christianity to his people. This process of removing Aimbe from his village transforms Aimbe's way of looking at things as a village leader. The mission education makes him speak and behave the way they want him to.

PROBLEMATIC CONSCIOUSNESS

The creation of a character with double consciousness is problematic. The consciousness of the colonized is suppressed further with the collective power of individuals in a society is disintegrated and won over to the side of the colonizer. Aimbe in the mental frame of the missionary pastor is at odds with his personality as a village person, traditional leader, and spokesman for his people against intrusive forces of colonialism. Practical problems and serious challenges take a new significance in Aimbe's life. He is often split between the two roles or denies one for the other. Often his traditional side is denied for the missionary work. Perhaps Matane wants to show a political reason for such split characteristics of Aimbe.

By giving him the role of a pastor, Matane gives him new powers and authority that goes beyond the traditional powers and authority. Aimbe's position seems to go beyond the colonized position to one that asserts power based on economic and political realities. The plantation life, for instance, changes Aimbe's ways of looking at things and approaches to life. He acquires new knowledge of planting coconuts, the cash economy, and self-reliance. The new knowledge proves useful. On his return to his own village, Aimbe starts a similar plantation.

Melting two cultures and systems is a difficult task. Aimbe struggles to bridge two cultures during his year at Ralokor. In public he says that the traditional dances, craftwork, and practicing magic are part of their lives. This is contradictory. Aimbe also tells people that he still believes in some of the traditional practices. He goes out of his way to participate in one of the dances. On the other hand, he discourages immoral cultural practices such as payback killings, adultery, stealing, and bearing false witness against another. Aimbe is a man with a double conscience. He becomes a victim of these contradictory and opposing forces. In one of his preachings he says:

> If I am to be effective in my work, I must move closer to you than ever before. It seems to me that there is a big gap between you and me. The gap is our main problem. It's no wonder that you do not tell me what you plan to do in the villages and the men's houses, because you feel that you would be doing things against the teachings of the church. We must try to remove the problems and narrow the gap. I call on you to assist me as much as you can. If you do, there is no longer misunderstanding between us. We will work together for the betterment of our village.[10]

The villagers accept this appeal. In reality, the gap between the church views and the villagers is hard to bridge. Aimbe recognizes this gap and attempts to bridge it. This is also Matane's offer to bridge the gap created by the different forces of colonialism. This is an important aspect of post-colonial texts, where the mediator of the gap is often someone split between the two extremes.

Aimbe as an individual recognizes the need to answer for the alienated voice and to lead them. As the chosen leader of his people Aimbe recognizes the masks of difference. He attempts to bridge this difference of cultures and ideas. Through his status as a village leader he challenges the new order. Through his mission travels he acquires new knowledge and unites different tribes and people. In the process he encounters many difficulties for such decisions. In his role as the pastor of the church, he dismisses his traditions and customs to allow the work of the mission to progress. This works against him. Aimbe is unable to progress. With the wisdom of his traditional training, however, he is able to pursue further knowledge of his people, who seem to distrust him because he is an agent of destruction. Aimbe recognizes this and accommodates the traditional aspects of his people with the rules of the church.

Matane's fiction is intertextual as well as operating as a popular realist novel. He has taken every care in describing the village rituals such as mourning and praying for the lost ones. Matane also considers the ritual of praying and blessing the upcoming young generation to uphold their identity, protect themselves from the enemy, and to be prosperous.

The intertextual practice is one that Matane uses in an effective way. Intertextuality goes beyond the surface of a reading text to include those things implied by an author as well, but which are readily available to the reader's mind, such as church belief and implications, traditional myths, legends and their implications to men, bible teachings, classroom conversations, and rules of conduct.

The written and the unwritten texts negotiate with each other in this book. Aimbe is a product of both the oral culture and the written culture. He is a villager as well as a pastor. Matane is attempting to be as realistic as possible. He uses religious beliefs to an artistic end. In the life story of Aimbe, the pastor, he introduces emotions and psychological drama. The different personalities presented in this way provide effective circumstances of conflict and resolution. Matane attempts to present the self-delusion faced by Aimbe, and the vulnerability of his religious pilgrimage as a pastor embarked on a false track. Matane mixes rich emotional conflicts as a source of irony. These conflicts, however, are characteristic of an author at odds with his own artistic intentions.[11]

Matane's novel is work of imaginative fiction. He draws materials from tangible, real, and historical experiences. It is a serious statement with political overtones about his people during the time of colonialism. Matane has provided an important insight into time and space, allowing history to be read between them. This is a kind of revision, taking on those things of the past and recreating them into a memorable sequence, with an elevated significance. In the process of revision the author explores and describes his people's condition of survival during the critical moments of colonialism. It is fictional reality. It is history re-examined and rewritten. By doing so, Matane as an author (with the capacity to dream or imagine), reconstructs the fragmented world affected by colonial conquest and exploitation. His very act of writing a story drawn from the past experiences gives him the status of a historian. The visions and series of questions at the end of the book ask for critical answers. We are shocked to find Aimbe, the old man, turning away from the church and the life he has been living all these years. The future of the country and the attitudes of the younger generation to the church are given prominence at the end of the book:

> Although the church was still strong, it appeared that it was for the older people only. One could observe that those in attendance at the church services were mostly old men and women. There were normally fewer men than women. The number of young people was even smaller. As the years went by, there were fewer young people in the church than before.

People did not appear to be critical about going to church anymore. Many men looked forward to Sundays so that they could rest from their busy lives. But, of course, they did not rest at home with their wives and children. Apart from taking active parts in sports, they used Sundays either in town or on the beaches with cartons of beer. When Mondays came, they would still have hangovers, so that Mondays were considered unproductive days.

Aimbe forecast that, within the next two to three generations, there would be fewer people following any church teachings, so that the natural death of the most important teachings was expected. This would be unfortunate, but it was going to come. There was no question about that.[12]

The type of knowledge forced on to the colonized people is negative. Often people end up in disillusionment, confusion, and total negation of their own cultures. The above passages sum up the attitude of the younger generation, and its confused mentality.

Matane's overall emphasis is on Aimbe's progress into the ministry, his work with the church, and his reactions to white prejudices and ignorance. Aimbe is more reactionary as a village leader under the colonial administration, but is passive as a participant in the very mechanism, which denigrates his people and culture. One weakness of the book, however, is that Matane has not given much thought and respect to Aimbe's wife who remains nameless throughout the book. The wife seems to occupy a trivial, less significant aspect in Aimbe's life. The development of the wife's character could have given a balance of human values, parental responsibilities, men and women, love and marriage conflicts in such societies. The deep resentment by the people against colonial rule is covered in the work of Aimbe so that other issues become further neglected. We are forced to see through the eyes of Aimbe as the pastor. This is an ambivalent position because Aimbe is a villager at heart and on the surface a pastor. Aimbe is someone who is trapped by his allegiance to his people, tradition, and society. He is also someone who has been the product of the colonial education and the mission system. Aimbe in a way is trapped by his own inability to maintain his traditions. He is a fully ordained pastor in the church. Aimbe works as a missionary, but in his heart he is a Tolai villager. He is presented with the choice either to completely reject one side of his life for another or maintain both aspects of his life. If he rejects the mission work, he feels guilty and fears retribution. When he rejects the work of his people he feels guilty of neglecting and exploiting them. This creates a double conscience for Aimbe.

The shortfall in the book is poor character development. Aimbe seems trapped in time. We see him progress and develop in an environment in which he only has to adjust. One of the reasons for this shortfall is that Matane's construction of the narrative pays more attention to events, Aimbe's work and activities as a pastor. This is a compressed narrative development, but one which must fall into the intertextual play. An aspect of the intertextual play is that the authorial intrusion (his own ideas and reactions) to things in his fictional creation is of vital importance in the development of the characters. Thus the author's own views and reactions to social, political, economical, cultural, and religious forces replace lack of character development. *Ripples,* is, perhaps, Matane's most ambitious work, which considers the traditional, colonial, and the Christian experience.

CONCLUSION

Matane reprinted this particular book 25 years later under a new title. The interest the book generated as a recommended text in literature courses indicated the currency in the treatment of political and historical issues that Matane had fictionalized. Reading *Ripples* as a work historical fiction opens up the fertile ground for Papua New Guineans to engage with some of the issues they are dealing with as a result of the colonized history. The notion of double consciousness strikes home the awareness that a radical shift in thinking is necessary.

FICTIONALIZING THE CONTACT EXPERIENCE

The inaccessible and rugged terrains of the Highlands made it a challenging area for colonization. Many early explorers, patrol officers, missionaries, and gold prospectors trekked the mountains in the early 1930s. Some of the tribes contacted, for the first time, resisted the outsiders. Others received the first missionaries and gold prospectors with confusion. Most of these societies believed that their ancestors and dead relatives were returning to them. Missionaries and government officials took advantage of friendly receptions and introduced their establishments. Three important groups of Europeans penetrated the Highlands in the 1930s: the Australian government officials, gold prospectors, and the missionaries. Accompanying these groups were coastal policemen and carriers. The white missionaries and Australian gold prospectors were regarded as people from the realm above. The coastal policemen and carriers were regarded as those from the world beneath the earth's surface: "As for the carriers, because it was believed that, when lightning fell to the earth, damaged to trees and objects was consequently affected by forces from under the ground, these foreigners were connected with blackness (*Koko*) of the earth and were considered as the 'ground moving' men who caused earthquakes" Many communities considered the people living in the clouds (Konekupa) as powerful people lived in the clouds (*Konekupa*): "these sky beings were nowhere near as prominent in Middle Wahgi traditions as they were in Mal Enga and other highland mythology, at least the appearance of the whites could be placed in the time honoured beliefs, whereas notions about the underground origins of the carriers was generated by the simple white/black division in that first band of patrollers, as well as by the manner in which the carriers laughed off intimacies and women's emotional asseverations that they were departed ones returned."[1]

Contact with the Highlanders opened up a new chapter in the history of Papua New Guinea. Missionaries and government officers moved in and established their permanent places in the Highlands. Contact also provided opportunities for curious young Highlanders to move out to see the world outside of their enclosed societies. Just going down to the coast, see the sea, work on the plantations, being inside of a plane, moving to other areas of Highlands, or just to move into the main administrative centres was considered the outside world for the young Highlanders. First contact made it possible for the Highlanders to venture beyond their tribal boundaries into unknown territories. They began to communicate with the outsiders with the language introduced to them. On their return to their villages they brought with them new modern items to aid them in their day-to-day living.

Ignatius Kilage's *My Mother Calls Me Yaltep* (1980) is exactly about this experience.[2] Kilage, following the footsteps of earlier Highlands writers like Benjamin Umba, August Kituai, and Peter Kama Kerpi, fictionalizes this important contact experience. Although his predecessors portray the Highlands experience in short fictions and plays, Kilage is the first to use the novel. Kilage portrays a contact society caught up in the rapid transition from the enclosed world into a modern changing environment. New ideas, new people, and even some of the illusory beliefs of their ancestors were put to test by their eagerness to change and understand the outside world. *My Mother Calls Me Yaltep* comes closer to explaining some of the claims concerning land alienation, cultural disorientation, and rural urban migration.

The book is about the Kuman speakers of the Simbu Province, occupying the gorges of the upper Simbu country. The story is about a Kuman man called Yaltep, who was born and raised in Womatne in the Simbu province. The first missionary who arrived in the area baptised Yaltep as Joseph, though he uses Joseph less than expected. The book opens up with Yaltep introducing himself as a Simbu man from the Kuman speaking group of people. He says he "was born a bit too early to see and try to understand and keep up with the tremendous changes" occurring all over the land, including the Simbu province:

> You may not be able to understand the confused state of my mind as you may have been spared the painful experience of trying to understand two diametrically opposed cultures at once. Since I had the privilege of a peculiar and unique experience I wish to tell the story of my life in my own way. I can only hope that you will get a glimpse of, and experience my bewilderment at such stupendous progress in a lifetime.[3]

The book is about characters forced into living diametrically divided lives. The book is also about a society that is diametrically divided. The book is a thinly sketched autobiography of Ignatius Kilage. The story is narrated in the first person by Joseph Yaltep. The first person narration is forceful, direct, and provides vivid observational qualities, which bring to the present moment the peculiar experiences of a Kuman man.

Kilage uses Tennyson's poem "Ulysses" to describe Yaltep's whole experience as a pioneer Kuman to experience the arrival of modernity and the confusion that came with it. Towards the end of the book Yaltep remembers the poem read to him by his teacher friend:

Tho' much is taken, much abides; and tho'
We are not now that strength which in old days
Moved earth and heaven; that which we are, we are;
One equal temper of heroic hearts,
Made weak by time and fate, but strong in will
To strive, to seek, to find and not to yield.[4]

Kilage's use of the poem suggests another form of knowledge acquired from the outside world's art and culture. The use of "Ulysses" is a form of authorial intrusion. The author is perhaps conscious of his own fictional creation, as an Odyssean journey of quest. It is more likely that Kilage intended Tennyson's poem as a summarizing aspect of his fiction, drawing parallels between the traditional knowledge and the new knowledge introduced into the Highlands, between the oral and the written word, and between fiction and the real world.

Written poetry is absent in the Highlands society. The use of Tennyson's poetry is another outside intrusion into the oral poetics of Simbu society. The introduction of Tok Pisin language to the Highlanders is also problematic. The use of Tok Pisin is more elaborate. The conflict between the coastal teacher's use of Tok Pisin (the introduced language) and Yaltep's imitation of it to convince Kauna's mother is a deception on Yaltep's part. Yaltep believes that by using the introduced language Yaltep's status is raised to the level of the coastal teacher. On the other hand it demerits the power of the Kuman language to bargain for wealth and social status. Nonetheless these are Kilage's attempts to bring out the mimetic aspects of the contact experiences.

Yaltep's descriptions of the stupendous Highlands landscapes are remarkable. The Highlands is pictured with a striking beauty and colour. This is a unique aspect of the novel. The landscape is an aesthetic symbol in fiction. It is also part of the traditional myths and legends of the people. The quality of myth and the way the cosmos is interconnected to a whole is explained in many ways through the land. Yaltep grows up to understand and feel deep connection to his land. Kilage compares upper Simbu with thel lower Simbu, their different climatic aspects and their different cultural practices. Yaltep is a product of both societies. He grew up in both of them.

Kilage also goes further to contrast the Highlands landscape with the coastal landscape. The Highlands landscape is more real, concrete, and ever present. The coastal scenery is, however, a landscape of the mind. This imagined world exists outside of the Highlands society. This is an important distinction. The whole book operates on the level of consciousness activated by real experiences and those that are imagined. Yaltep experiences both worlds. This is an important position as it describes a society's efforts to locate meaning within the landscape, its cosmology, and the cultural contexts. For example, Yaltep makes this observation of the lower Simbu; "In marked contrast to the Gowe valley, the lower Simbu was warmer... and at times the sun becoming very hot or has heavy rainfall." The rain brought with it great destruction and havoc to the landscape, gardens, and people living in a Simbu valley. Many left their houses on the slopes to other areas: "Masses of earth and water went screaming down the slopes into the turbulent Simbu, and the Simbu in turn, with its new strength, moved huge boulders and ancient mossy trees standing in its banks. So great was the force of the elements that the trees went crashing down like reeds."[5] The description reflects the author's love of his homeland.

The land and its cruel beauty is a fearsome enough phenomenon requiring explanation in both the traditional and modern senses. This also signals Kilage's own preoccupation with the humble beauty of his land and the pride he has for it. It is also a phenomenon that arouses the imagination. Kilage plays with the landscape of the mind for contrast. For example, Yaltep begs the coastal friend to tell him about the coastal society:

The man was a true patriot who painted life on the coast with vivid and striking colours. All in all, after he had finished, I had an idea that the coast was a paradise, where you just have to look around to pick the fruit that was plentiful and live a carefree life. His vivid pictures of a huge body of water, which he called *sol wara,* which was much bigger than the Piunde Aunde Lake at the foot of Mt. Wilhelm, stirred my imagination with all sorts of fantastic ideas, which were, as I found out later on, out of all proportions. This imagination filled me with an anxious desire to see the coast, at all costs.[6]

The landscape of the imagination is constructed here as fantastic, exotic, and unreal. It is presented in a dream form, mixed with fantasy and mythical explanations. Yaltep's life in the Simbu valley is the only real world that he can relate to without hesitation. He could give on the spot explanations to any unusual formation or shape of the land, without resorting to a dream-like mental search. He could relate his surroundings, in a meaningful way, with the mythical inheritance of his people.

In *My Mother Calls Me Yaltep* place is constructed with full imagination. Kilage's privileged position as a writer is one that allows both passionate and archetypal ethnographical descriptions to dominate his discourse. This creates a nationalistic feeling as well as a feeling of a cultural and physical attachment to the land. The author is, therefore, the first interpreter to give accurate descriptions of his own surroundings and culture. Instead of being an observer without any intimate spiritual, cultural, and meaningful attachment to the land, Kilage expresses his feelings and spiritual attachment to his land and people.

Kilage, like his contemporaries, is lodged in a space of poetically evoked landscape, the reality of his imagination, and the imaginative mental construction of a subject, which has its bases both in the oral language and in the written culture. His preoccupation with landscape resonates that of V. S. Naipaul in *A Bend in the River* where the author is "concerned with man's ancient harmony with the land and man's new efforts to placate to subdue the land. An important aspect of this new struggle is the relationship between place and reality, ultimately leading back to questions of personal perceptions of the world."[7] Kilage's perception is influenced by his personal and nationalistic views expressed at the time of writing.

Yaltep's people associate anything that does not belong to the ground as "something that belonged to the above" or that which is part of the mythical universe or to the world below the earth's surface, very much the kind of explanation given to the first Europeans who arrived in their valley. The introduced goods and animals were strange to the Highlanders. The novel is a dual manifestation of the beliefs and cosmogony of this Highlands society. Making sense of the things they heard about and saw introduced by outsiders takes up most of their time. The first aeroplane introduced in the Highlands, for example, was awe-inspiring. The curious Highlanders invented new stories about these strange objects. It is not surprising that Kilage introduces the story of the aeroplane in his book. Long before Yaltep was born, the people spoke about this mysterious object, which they saw as an "extraordinary white bird making thunderous and booming sounds". This account is made known to Yaltep:

> After a little while they heard the noise again. They stood on the hillside watching it disappear in the eastern horizon whence it came. That strange bird was the first aeroplane that flew over the Highlands. Tradition also has it, that for months after that strange bird came and went, there were rumours that the Gende people of Bundi were about to perform one of their famous magic spells (known as *Kimagl*) on the Mitnandi people. The fearsome Gerigl or Gende people over the other side of Mondi were notorious for their Kimagl. The rumours were spreading everywhere. The people did not venture far from their home, for it was also said that the predicted catastrophe would fall on them in the form of floods or slides.[8]

This is a unique aspect of the Papua New Guinean novel. After introducing the incident in history, the author goes on further to explain how the people who were present during an event relate to it or how the events had affected them. In *My Mother Calls Me Yaltep*, Kilage takes pain in explaining the unique events in the early days of outside presence in the Simbu valley. Soon after the sighting of the aeroplane and the rumours about the *nigl kande* or *gigl yomba* (the peculiar ghost) seen in the lower Simbu, the people took every precaution to defend themselves against any malady this ghost might bring. The peculiar ghost was the arrival of the first Europeans in the Highlands. To avoid this peculiar spirit's spell and power, the people prepared themselves by "casting counter spells, putting up strong posts in front of their houses to ensure that those strange beings would not follow the river up to its source."[9]

Despite this preparation, called the "*Endi Yombuglo* and the *Binga* ceremony (literally, post ferns) cast as "signs of powerful spells...at the main gates of men's houses, to ward off evil influences and protect those who were within the fence," the first Europeans arrived. The arrival began from Kangrie and crossed the Mondi pass to Gowe Kualke river junction. The Simbu people were well prepared for the arrival of the Europeans. They took every measure of safety to defend against any physical challenge or against the evil spell that might be brought by the ghosts. To their dismay, the arrival was disruptive and one of irreversible misunderstanding. They explained that these were "the spirits of their ancestors" returning to them. Two types of white men arrived in the Highlands: the *batres* (fathers or priest) and *Kiaps* (patrol officers). Each of them was representative of different forces of change. The missionaries, patrol officers, and the coastlanders accompanying them had tremendous influence with their powers over the people of the Highlands.

The narrative of Yaltep concerns itself with the acquaintance of both Europeans and the coastlanders with the Simbus. It also demonstrates the good-natured spirit and the willingness of Yaltep's people to get to know the people outside of their tribal units. Yaltep is often confronted with questions that do not have simple answers, but which serve as motivating factors in his quest for the truth.

The problem of unanswered questions remains the most enigmatic aspect of the book. They are immersed in the world of magic, dream, fantasy, imagination, and the supernatural world. This world counter exists with the world of reality, facts, and with concrete objects such as mountains, landforms, landscapes, floods, and rain. Within these two worlds are humans. In these worlds, humans seek both protection and inspiration. They understand their environment and make it possible to perceive the supernatural forces within it. To make sense of a place where one lives one must have both spiritual and physical attachment to it. As part of the business of making sense, the priest in the Catholic Church baptizes Yaltep as Joseph. A ritualistic ceremony is performed. These names were held high as spiritual names even though there was a sense of fantasy about them. The acceptance of the Christian ritual of baptism was very much attached to a supernatural belief that having a Christianized name and a rosary around the neck would ward off evil spirits. Yaltep's mother took the initiative to baptize Yaltep because she "was convinced that the batres were the good spirits."[10] Yaltep felt this was a sign of goodwill and protection. This is ironic in many ways. The baptism and rosary hardly served as icons of the new religious power, but as extensions of an old belief that of warding off evil spirits.

Yaltep's confusion is resolved through two voyages. He makes one voyage through the mythical world of his people. In the second voyage he makes it through a mental absorption of these happenings through the passage of education and physical removal from the environment associated with the mythical inheritance of his people. Yaltep's confusion is more profound in the first of these voyages. There are limits to his quest for answers. He is more confused, resists these new ideas and people, and still participates in other events associated with the foreigners. He is unable to understand fully the new forces at work. His own culture has marked cultural boundaries and fixed mental boundaries to cogitate in. We see this clearly when Yaltep courts Kauna, his childhood friend, before their marriage. He does all he can, but finds that another force more powerful and influential hampers his success in winning Kauna's heart. The school teacher (*shule yagl*) from the coast represents the other force. He shows interest in Kauna, bribing her and her mother with new items from outside. This pleases the girl and her parents. Yaltep is unable to offer the equivalent. There is fear that he could lose Kauna to the school teacher.

This is the normal custom of courting among the Kumans, allowing suitable men to court a young woman as long as she is still living in her mother's home. Yaltep loses hope of marrying his sweet heart. He contemplates violence. He decides to burn the school teacher's house. This does not eventuate. Yaltep is advised by his grandfather to take Kauna to the upper Simbu before the patrol officer arrives for the first census. This allows Yaltep to secure Kauna as his future wife. Kauna and Yaltep, however, are not counted in the census. After the census Yaltep becomes more furious about the affair between Kauna and the school teacher. One group of villagers favour the school teacher (*shule yagl*) while the other group favours Yaltep. Yaltep decides to break the Kuman custom of courtship. He beats up the teacher one night in Kauna's mother's house. The mother protests this against Yaltep. The school teacher, however, "was just following the conventions; as it is not forbidden to visit girls when they are still at their own houses."[11] After Yaltep attacks the school teacher, he attempts a brilliant imitation of the coastlander's language:

> *Yu harim tok bilong mi, yu save Kauna i meri bilong mi. Tasol givim em planti samting, na yu laik kisim em. Em i no stret, nau yu finis long dispela haus, sapos mi lukim yu kam hia gen bai mi kilim yu...yu save?*[11]

The teacher may have observed the conventions of the Kuman society, but he still represents a force of corruption and bribery that undermines the Kuman men's way of courting. Yaltep too follows the customs, but the new forces overshadow his measure of pride for his customs. Yaltep resorts to violence and challenges the forces of power with new aggression and force.

His eloquence in the school teacher's language taught to him by a friend, however, appears as a symbol of deception and negativity. Yaltep does not have to speak the school teacher's language to be on equal footing with the teacher. Yaltep's bride could be anybody's where suitors from within the same society can compete for her hand in marriage. We see this clearly before Kauna is fully married to Yaltep. She is allowed to court other men in the society. Yaltep is also allowed to court other women before he finally marries Kauna. Kauna, however, ends up being held by the Kombri tribe to be married to one of their men. According to the Kuman courting custom word is sent to the tribe to send Kauna back to their tribe. This custom is called *ambu kugl angua*. This courting custom of the Highlands can be confusing to outsiders. This is a strong presentation of one of the most important customs of the people. Kilage attempts to show here that the courting customs have their own significance and importance in the Highlands societies.

JOURNEYS OF DISCOVERY

Yaltep's quest is illuminated through the passage of education and learning of the introduced culture. At first Yaltep refuses to go to school. Later he realizes that it was a silly mistake. As time goes by he depends more on it. This is displayed in the use of Tok Pisin, the language of education and the outside world, to impress Kauna's mother. Yaltep later learns to speak and write Tok Pisin to survive the plantation life. Yaltep travels first to Goroka and Madang as a plantation labourer:

> Our hearts were left behind in the cool mountains and Womatne. With mixed feelings and bitter anguish at leaving the dearest place on earth and with the excitement of seeing the wonderland, we accompanied the kiap and his train to Kundiawa. There we were given documents to take overland to Goroka. In those days, there were no roads and we had to go overland. Sometimes through hostile regions whose people spoke different languages and had different ways of dressing.[12]

The journey described here begins in the wilderness and ends up in the world of wonder. This is a new and exciting experience. The experience of flying out in an aeroplane is itself spellbinding. It shatters the images of the supernatural long held by the Kuman people. Yaltep experiences what he would not have experienced if he had remained confined to his own cultural boundaries and limited geographical experience marked by tribal lands. He is not only participating in a self-seeking knowledge schema, but that he is elevated from the world of his grandfathers and parents to one that comes closer to the people from the sky. He travels into the world of the spirits. The travel promises him newfound knowledge and a sense of self-pride.

Journeys from the village into the modern world are significant ones. Similar connections are made by the spread of outside items brought by missionaries, carriers, policemen, and teachers. With the Highlands Labour Scheme firmly established by 1951, more and more Highlanders moved out into plantations on the coast. Those returning from plantation work brought with them new metal items and shell money. By the 1960s mission education took an important place in the Highlands. Modern currency circulation saw popular beliefs about the supernatural origins of white wealth and cargo undermined and weakened. The logical conclusion to this change of attitude is that "the strangers could not have had wealth except through the kinds of reciprocal relationship which religious activity made possible."[13] Around the 1940s and 1950s, more Highlanders were recruited on the labour recruitment list. The opportunity to acquire new knowledge and material possessions had by then become competitive in the highlands. To the Highlanders, the journeying out was more important than remaining in the cultural enclosures.

Yaltep makes subsequent journeys to other centers. As he moves further away from the Highlands society he learns new knowledge and gains new experiences, though at times confusing and frustrating. In these journeys Yaltep becomes familiar with the outside world. He readily adjusts to the new unfamiliar surroundings. Yaltep learns to read and write. He goes away to work on a plantation in Rabaul. There his ability to speak Tok Pisin gets him a comfortable job in the mistress's kitchen. One day he misunderstands the white mistress's instruction. He over bakes the bread with the clock shut in the oven. He runs away, ashamed of his mistake, hangs out with a policeman from his own area, and later moves to work on a plantation at Wakunai in the North Solomons Province. Yaltep returns to the Simbu province again, after someone tricked him with the news that his mother had died. This was a cunning trick by one of his clansmen who was jealous of Yaltep's achievement. In Simbu he learns more about reading and writing from a sympathetic schoolteacher, who later helps him travel to Port Moresby. Yaltep visits the national parliament in session. He dislikes Port Moresby. He pleads with his friend to return to Simbu, where he belongs. He is sent home.

Ignatius Kilage's novel is a literary enactment of the colonial activities and the political events in the Highlands since the time of their first contact in the 1930s. *My Mother Calls Me Yaltep* is about the Highlanders quest outside in search of this new knowledge and participation in the unfolding historical events in the highlands of Papua New Guinea. The last chapters of the novel concentrate on the political events around the 1960s and 1970s.

Kilage combines ethnographical details, actual historical accounts, events, and incidents to fictionalize the Highlands experience: "Fictionalizing is the enactment of humankind's creativity and as there is no limit to what can be staged, the creative process itself bears the inscription of fictionality: the structure of double meaning… Thus fictionalizing enacts our being in the middle of things by turning the very involvement into a mirror for itself."[14]

CONCLUSION

Yaltep's character is fictionalized into a kind of duality. By fictionalizing actual incidents, often autobiographical or real events, Kilage brings his people's experiences into the world of fiction and written culture. This duality is mediated to form a system of interpretation of myths, the beliefs of the people, social cultural and ethical values, as well as their history. This is the artistic beauty of Kilage's fiction. Kilage brings his peoples's experience into a totality that is made possible through fiction.

ORAL HISTORY TO FOLK OPERA

The influence of oral tradition on the modern Papua New Guinean plays is a stable source of creativity. The historical development of drama, theatre, and playwrights in the early period of writing in Papua New Guinea has received critical attention.[1] The emergence of a unique Papua New Guinea stage drama tradition is evidence of the vast reservoir of creativity in Papua New Guinea. The first PNG playwrights adopted the western forms of drama and infused it with traditional performance art. Early plays such *Manki Masta* by Kumalau Tawali, *Cargo* by Arthur Jawodimbari, *The Unexpected Hawk* by John Waiko, *The Ungrateful Daughter* by Leo Hannet and *Alive* by M. Lovori set the stage for a full evolution of modern drama and folk opera to emerge in Papua New Guinea.[2] These plays written before Independence in Papua New Guinea focused on the colonized environment. The performances of these plays were often the stage for political protests and resistance to Australian colonization of Papua New Guinea. These plays were "performed with astonishing success by the Arts and Drama Society of the University of Papua New Guinea in November 1967."[3] The real beginning of Papua New Guinea modern drama began with these plays, most notably with Leo Hannet's *Em Rod Bilong Kago*, followed by others: "The style of plays was dictated by the shape of the space. Everything was performed in the round, and that's how the writers perceived a theatre space."[4]

The tradition of theatre performances continued into the period after Independence. Two important theatre companies were formed to serve as the vehicle of Papua New Guinean plays. The National Theatre Company and the Raun Raun Theatre Company were formed under the umbrella of the National Cultural Commission. The existence of these two theatre companies saw the production of a number of plays. The National Theatre Company occupied itself with themes of social change and national dream in the post-independence era. The Raun Raun Theatre, on the other hand, took a different route to theatre performances.

The Raun Raun Theatre began in 1975 with the aim to produce plays about the problems and challenges faced by Papua New Guineans in their villages. The mission was "to invent a new kind of theatre, which would capture the atmosphere and the spirit of Papua New Guinea traditional culture but express it in a contemporary way."[5] Unlike the plays performed a decade earlier, the Raun Raun Theatre began a new stage, one which adopted traditional folklore, dance, legends, and myths to represent the contemporary experience.

Greg Murphy founded the Raun Raun Theatre. He became its first director. Murphy recognized the need for a theatre that does not adhere to conventional Western theatre. Folk operas provide a model to take in traditional drama forms, oral expressions, and the cultural life of the people that are presented in a realistic way on stage. Murphy believed most audience would identify with this new theatre.[6] To capture the moods and interests of the audience a satisfactory presentation was necessary.

The Raun Raun Theatre adopted the writings of John Kasaipwalova for experimentation on stage as folk opera. Murphy, the then director of Raun Raun Theatre felt "a form of Theatrical expression" from within the traditions of Papua New Guinea was emerging. The new theatre … would evoke the culture, music, dance and the traditional celebrations. Kasaipwalova submitted an epic poem "Sail The Midnight Sun," in 1979. The production of a major trilogy as folk opera began that year.[7] A new era for folk opera started when "Sail The Midnight Sun" was performed right across the country. The audience was delighted to find something they could truly call their own.[8] This form of theatre appealed very well to the taste of new emerging theatre groups throughout the country. Folk opera is a kind of "synthesis of different cultural expressions wherein a kind of national expression is created" (see Stella, BA Honours subthesis).[9] This type of theatre occurs elsewhere in Africa and other parts of the world. "The remnants of what used to be the National Theatre Company," writes William Takaku, one of the pioneer actors on stage, "and the Raun Raun, were slotted together into a thing called the National Performing Arts Troupe. It has two sections, one in Goroka and the other one in Port Moresby."[10]

Since then, new theatre groups have adopted the Raun Raun Theatre model. Theatre groups began performing plays, featuring traditional legends of culture heroes and mythical figures. Duadua Theatre of Lae came out with "The Boy from the Sea". The National Theatre Company's "Eberia" was a very successful musical play (1980). "Ba Oro" was staged in Port Moresby in 1984. North Solomons Traveling Theatre performed "Matanasil" across the country in 1985. Aiyura National High School adopted a traditional legend from North Solomons Province called "Bananga" for the school production.[11]

NORA VAGI BRASH

One of the outstanding playwrights to emerge in Papua New Guinea is Nora Vagi Brash. She remains the foremost and the only Papua New Guinean female playwright. Nora Brash was involved with acting in amateur theatre, radio plays, and street theatre in early 1970s. Her exposure to the world of theatre in England inspired her to write her own plays on her return to Papua New Guinea. The National Arts School employed Nora Brash as an assistant lecturer in puppetry, dance, and drama. She then moved on to become one of the two artistic directors with the National Theatre Company. Nora Brash wrote her own scripts for the puppets using traditional stories of Papua New Guinea.

The National Theatre Company toured local villages and performed in the streets. They went to the Pacific Arts Festival in Rotorua and Wellington, New Zealand. They also danced in Point Venus in Tahiti and a small group went to the Black Arts Festival in Nigeria. In 1978 Nora Brash resigned from the National Theatre Company to take up studies for her BA degree at the University of Papua New Guinea. She maintained her interests in theatre and wrote several of plays. Nora Brash joined the National Broadcasting Commission in 1980. She also became the deputy chairperson of the National Cultural Council and a member of the board of the Institute of Papua New Guinea Studies. In this chapter we consider Nora Vagi Brash's stage play *Taurama*.[12] She wrote *Taurama* in Singapore.

Taurama is Nora Brash's most important play depicting the independence of Papua New Guinea. *Taurama* is based on an actual historical event that occurred in a Motuan society about five centuries ago.[13] The cultural hero is Kevau Dagora, the only survivor of the terrible Taurama Massacre revenges on the Lakwaharus (Tubuserea) who caused the massacre. Kevau Dagora grows up in exile at Badihagwa, under the protection of an old couple. He is treated as an outsider, but through courage and the process of reconciliation gains confidence of the Motu people. He marries the daughter of the woman who caused the massacre. In a twist of fate he releases the haunting spirits of Taurama to establish peace among the Motu people through a marriage feast. The play gave Nora Brash the opportunity to use oral history of her own people to tell a contemporary history unfolding in the postcolonial Papua New Guinea.

MODERN MOTU HISTORY

The Motuans are divided into two distinct groups: The Eastern Motu and the Western Motu. The Western Motu settled in early settlements of Vabukori, Boera, and Tatana. In Eastern Motu group the early settlements of Motu speakers concentrated in the villages of Taurama, Boera, and Lakwaharu (now called Tubuserea): "The Western Motu lived in seven villages situated between Bootless Inlet and Galley Reach: Pari, Poreporena, and Elevala, which form part of the village cluster known as Hanuabada; Porebada; Rea Rea; and Manumanu. Western Motu *Iduhu* are also found in Boera."[14] *Iduhu* is defined as the "corporate descend groups or clans of which villages are composed" and are patrilineal in descend. Early European accounts record the most distant origins of the Western Motu. The two villages of Motu Hanua and Taurama were once situated in Bootless Inlet: "Motu Hanua, now usually known as Motupore, means 'island village' or possibly 'Motu village'…According to one version, Eastern Motu living at Loloata made war on Motu Hanua and the inhabitants moved to Taurama where they built a village, or rather a series of hamlets. Tubumaga Idibana (right) *iduhu* settled at the foot of Taurama hill at Hanua Lalona while half Tubumaga Laurina (left) *iduhu* were located in the next bay at Avakeikei and half Laurina were at Tutu. Kahanamona Idibana and Kahanamona Rea Rea *iduhu* were at Dagolata while Kahanamona Idaro *iduhu* were staying at Idarobada."[15]

Constant warfare forced the Western Motuans to split further. Bootless Inlet was abandoned by the Western Motu as a result of consistent warfare with Lakwaharu (Tubuserea):

> Warfare continued and the following account, with variations, of the destruc-tion of Taurama by the Lakwaharu and the refounding of the village at Pari is well-known throughout the Motu-speaking area. Some youths laughed at an old woman, who became angry. She told some visitors from the Koita village of Baruni that the youths were going to attack them and the Baruni people stealthily crept away. To revenge themselves the Baruni planted magic poisons in the village and the Taurama people became too weak to resist the Lakwaharu who surrounded and burned the village.
>
> Only one woman, Konio Daroa, who was the wife of a Taurama leader, escaped through the floor of her house and made her way to her brother, Puka [Oala] Daroa, of Laurina *iduhu*, who was living at Badihagwa. Konio was pregnant when she escaped from Taurama and she bore a son, Kevau Dagora. When he grew up he assembled a fleet of Western Motu war canoes and at-tacked the Lakwaharu in several battles until their chief, Magani Baru, sued for peace.
> With the help of a Vabukori leader, Mase Gaudi, peace was made and Magani Baru helped Kevau build a new village at Tauata. The village is known by the nickname, Pari, because fish were so plentiful that they slipped down people's throat ('Pari means 'wet' in Motu). Kevau Dagora lived six genera-tions ascending from a man born in 1923."[16]

The account of the Taurama massacre introduced here through the historian Nigel Oram serves the purpose of contextualizing the play "Taurama", written for stage by Nora Vagi Brash. There are different versions of the oral history of this Motuan society. For our purpose we follow the account documented in Oram's study of Motuan history.

The history of Taurama is reenacted in modern dramatic form through the pen of Nora Vagi Brash. Retelling the story using modern theatre invigorates the oral history among the Motuans. Drama introduced an important part of the Motuan history to other Papua New Guineans occupying the traditional land of the Motu Koitabuans.

Nora Vagi Brash's aim is to conserve the oral traditions of the Motuan society. The publication and performance of *Taurama* is a landmark in modern history of drama in Papua New Guinea. Through stage art and careful usage of written historical records and oral versions of the Taurama massacre, Nora Brash reconstructed a local history of her society.

The Taurama massacre in Motuan history remains important to its people. Nora Brash assumes the traditional role of individual storyteller she tells the story of Taurama using the genre of drama. As a result of her western knowledge and her inheritance of the finest oratory skills learned from her traditional culture Nora Brash has re-enacted the story of Taurama in a medium many people saw and appreciated. She is an artist with remarkable artistic skills, able to fuse two cultures — her own culture and the written Western culture to create a new perspective and vision of the society she inhabits as well.

HISTORY THROUGH DRAMA

Taurama epitomizes the art of retelling historical accounts in a new way. The play was intended at the time of its performance for the celebration of Papua New Guinea's Ten Anniversary of Independence. The play was a success in many ways. It carried the message of peace, reconciliation, and unity among tribes and different groups of people in Papua New Guinea. Its performance was the highlight of the Independence week. Several performances were held. The play contributed in a significant way to the written culture of Papua New Guinea.

In writing the play Nora Brash documented and interpreted oral history in her Motuan society. As an artist she had two main objectives: 1) to entertain her audience and (ii) to teach her audience about the history of her people. Nora Brash constructs dialogue and controls the performance of the play. Dialogues like the one between the spirits: Biriabada, Laurabada, and Bogebada demonstrate the complexity of the world. It is also the demonstration of the Papua New Guinean playwright's pivotal experience between the spoken and the written word. In *Taurama*, Nora Brash creates a world where spirits and the people's inter-relationships seem to be more real than fiction. The spirits in the story play an important role in bringing the two tribes together:

'It was an ambitious production. I wrote in the sorcerer's part for myself. The play has magic and songs and poetry and although it is fictitious I sought the advice of my uncle, the herbalist, concerning the rituals. He told me that the rituals were too real and he was concerned that I was delving into something that might bring harm to me. On the first night the sky opened up and it rained and rained and the small children in the cast were so disappointed. When they complained, my aunt said, "Well, all Nora's mother's people are rain people and that's why they are blessing us with rain. The next nine days will be fine and we'll be performing to full houses from tomorrow." My aunt is a *babalau*, spiritual medium who can contact the spirits of the dead. She was right. The remaining nine days were fine and we performed to full houses each night."[17]

The special relationships between spiritual and living world is captured in the play. The spirits' voices in the background were intended to show the supernatural and spiritual presence in the lives of Papua New Guineans. The belief in the invisibleness of the spirit world and its obvious communication with the people through chants, invocations, dreams, and rituals, suggests a close relationship between the real world and the spirit world. Kevau Dagora's initiation is very ritualistic. The dialogue with the spirit world signifies the ritualistic performance in many Melanesian societies. Rituals are often associated with the supernatural world. Kevau's initiation and his first contact with the spirits of his people is the moment of Kevau's realization of his manhood, his sense of belonging, and his reason to exist in the world as someone with a past.

The play brings out another feature of the traditional and oral culture. There is a special relationship between the spirits of Taurama and the living descendents of Taurama in the persons of Rakatania and Kevau Dagora. Dagora, the ghost father wails as his son goes through the initiation at the burnt out site:

There is no place here in the land of the living. We are thirsty and hungry. Our eyes are tired from the want of sleep. The food and water here are but mere shadows. Only you, our living relative will take us, poor wretched souls to some rest. There are two roads, to drop blood would mean more unavenged spirits to roam, or bring our enemies together and honour us with a feast.[18]

Such spirit and human relationships are found in many Melanesian societies. The Motuans have access to the supernatural world through chants, prayers, incantations, ritual utterances, and dreams. In *Taurama,* the living descendents have access to the dead world through a dream, via Kevau, at the burnt-out site. The spirits of the massacred people living around the site direct Kevau to take necessary actions to restore their avenging spirit.

Kevau is confronted with two choices: Either to avenge the Lakwaharu'a through bloodshed or to make peace. Through the advice of his elders, he decides against avenging the Lakwaharu. Making peace is the best decision to make for the sake of the future of Kevau's clan. The dream interpreter, Babalau advises Chief Badi to take the second task as seen in Kevau's dream. The chief says:

> After much consultation with the Babalau I have decided to agree with our enemies and make peace. We cannot live safely in our own village peacefully if the spirits of our dead and of Taurama have not been pacified. They are tormented and increased in number by our constant fighting.[19]

Taurama has one unique feature that is worth discussing. The play evolves around performance in an orally expressed society. In *Taurama*, Nora Brash uses Motu and English interchangeably. In its actual performance form the Taurama massacre is brought to reality in a dramatic way by balancing its liveliness with materials that are purely spoken and oral in nature, especially those spoken in Motu without translation. The meaning, rhythms, and patterns of the oral poetry or chant were recited without any translation. Brash tries to keep her dialogues centered in the village community and their perceptions of the world. As is the example in the advice of Ade Tua:

> Flowers bloom to be picked. Every woman is born to marry, and after the sweetness come the suffering. The day by day toil-the do this and do that.[20]

Another angry Goada shouts in anger:

> I'll kill him. I'll drag his body naked through the village in pig shit. Why does he think he is dragging my sister's decency through filth and mud?... Shah! lau o-p. I'll squash him like an ant...Who he have married at all? It was I Goada who say you to him to marry Dobi. My sister don't worry. I'll split his throat and feed the rest of him to the sharks. *Sisia kuhi natuna oi diaka.*[21]

Nora Brash's understanding of her society's history and the dilemma it faces in the changing times of Papua New Guinea are transmitted through her plays. All her plays address a particular dilemma in contemporary Papua New Guinea. Nora Brash satirizes Papua New Guinea in her other plays, but in *Taurama* she veers from the hilarious, comical, and satirical tone. Her plays: *Which Way Big Man, High Cost of Living Differently,* and *Black Market Buai* reflect Brash's preoccupation with poking fun at, rebuking, or shaming Papua New Guineans steering off the course in their lives in contemporary times.[22] The characters in these plays are modern educated Papua New Guineans with manners that are at odds with traditional values and ways of doing things. Nora Brash picks on their attitudes, behaviours, mannerisms, and affluent styles that are pretentious and hypocritical. In Nora Brash's views the clash of traditional cultures against introduced cultures is inevitable. There are Papua New Guineans who maintain their traditional lifestyles and values. Then there are those who have abandoned their traditional cultures for the new Western cultures.

The message Nora Brash wants to covey to Papua New Guineans is that a conscious re-evaluation of the new values inherited through the process of change is needed. Without doing so, as Nora Brash thinks, Papua New Guinea is on the road to abandonment of important traditional values for false masquerade of postmodern superficial values.

NEGOTIATING PEOPLE'S RIGHTS

Nora Brash negotiates her people's rights to their land on which Papua New Guinea inserted its capital city. The voice of the Motu Koita people is marginalized in modern day Papua New Guinea. Migrants from other parts of Papua New Guinea have completely swamped Port Moresby city, overpopulating it and creating squatter settlements on Motu Koita land. Unemployed semi-literate people to literate public servants from other parts of Papua New Guinea are the main pushers of emerging settlements in Port Moresby. The land on which the Motu Koita once held as hunting, gardening, and ceremonial grounds are no longer theirs. The demand for spaces to make gardens for vegetables and settlements to cater for the expanding population of the city, the accelerated movement of rural urban drift, and the increasing neglect in the planning of the city has pushed off the Motu Koita from resisting what is happening to them and their land.

Educating non-Motu Koitabuans about the history and stories of the place is important, but when no one listens or respects such histories and stories, then the sense of ignorance permeates the discourse of development and civil justice in Papua New Guinea's capital city. Ignoring the plight and rights of the traditional landowners in the National Capital District invites formation of negative consciousness that invites violent resistance. Disassembly, disintegration, and ambivalent sentiments are distilled in such a way that it becomes possible to see it used against nationalistic imaginings.

The lessons Nora Brash wants us to consider are that the Motu and Koitabuans lived side-by-side to each other, though there were infighting and differences among the different *Iduhu* that make up the Motuan villages along the coast, from east to west. Peace is always mediated. Splitting of *iduhu* groups and new formations of Motuan groups never extended beyond the existing traditional settlements on the present day location of the villages. *Iduhu* rivalries and warfare existed side by side with gift exchange, wealth distribution, and customary recognition of mutual networking. One reason Motuans had a strong mutual relationship with the Koitabuans was the trade network

179

of goods and items of value each could produce based on either the geography of their concentration or the magico-religious preoccupations. The Motuans are sea people and the Koitabuans are land people, resulting in exchange of food items and exchange of cultural knowledge, passed through a mutually beneficial relationship. Intermarriages amongst these two groups of people often worked at cementing their relationships. Over thousands of year before the arrival of Europeans the Motuans and Koitabuans maintained their mutual respect for each other; they respected land and used specific spaces for ceremonies and trade.

WESTERN MOTU

The Western Motu lived in two original settlements, Motu Hanua (Tubuserea) and Taurama. Motu Hanua appears to have been abandoned first, followed by small settlements along the northern shores of Bootless Inlet. Finally, some seven generations ago, Taurama was destroyed by the Lakwaharu. A new village was founded at Badihagwa. Later the inhabitants of Badihagwa moved to the shore and, joined by others already settled in the mangroves, formed the villages of Tanobada, Poreporena and Elevala. From these villages Pari was founded to the east and Rea Rea, Manumanu, and Porebada to the northwest.

> The Lakwaharu, joined by Koiari speakers from the Sogeri area, settled at Tubusereia. Migrants from their village then joined inland people to form Gaba Gaba and Gaire. Barakau was largely derived from Tubusereia. These four villages constituted the Eastern Motu tribe.
>
> A separate migration of Motu-speakers settled near the boundary of the present Gulf and Central provinces. They moved to the south-east, leaving settlements at Tarova and Delena where they now speak Roro. One section moved to Boera where they are said to have begun the *hiri* expeditions.
>
> The Koita and Koiari, whose languages belong to the same family, separated somewhere in the Sogeri area. The Koita came down the Laloki and settled in the Nebira-Gubinimu area. From there, they dispersed. Isumata, including Namura and Arauwa, went west. Arauwa made a village at Buria and Namura at Darebo. The others reached Galley Reach where some elements stayed behind at Gorohu and Kido. The remainder returned to the east and settled at Taurama, Gobina, and Aemakara.
>
> The eastern Koita moved towards the sea and became the ancestors of the people of Kila Kila and Korobosea villages and of Gorobe *iduhu* at Pari. A number of *iduhu* moving from the Nebira area combined to form Baruni village.
>
> As a result of Koiari attacks and disease some time before the first Europeans came in the 1870s, the Koita were forced either to settle in their own villages on the coast or to join Motu villages. Hohodae and Kuriu form

distinct Koita sections in Hanuabada and Koita *iduhu* are found in all villages in the Western Motu area except Manumanu.[23]

METAPHOR OF NATION

Nora Vagi Brash used the play *Taurama* as a metaphor to strengthen the nation-hood of Papua New Guinea ten years after gaining Independence from Australia in 1975. The theme of national unity was highlighted. Brash used the play as a way of reinventing the nation in its most fragile stage, suggesting of course that maturity of a nation is a long road yet to travel. Using the play Brash imagines the nation made up differences of views, histories, backgrounds, and perspectives. In Anderson's words all nations are imagined:

> In fact, all communities larger than primordial villages of face-to-face contact (and perhaps even these) are imagined. Communities are to be distinguished, not by their falsity/genuineness, but by the style in which they are imagined.[24]

Motuan villagers "have always known that they are connected to people they have never seen, but these ties were once imagined particularistically — as indefinitely stretchable nets of kinship and clientship."[25] In imagining their interconnectedness and evoking the rebuilding of a severed relationship of the past, the Motu Koita also imagined themselves as part of a larger nation, consisting of other tribes, cultures, and people. In so doing the Motu Koitabuans understood that new relationships have to emerge in their relationship to other communities. Anderson makes the point that every nation is imagined as *limited* and *sovereign* "because even the largest of them, encompassing perhaps a billion living human beings, has finite, if elastic, boundaries, beyond which lie other nations. No nation imagines itself coterminous with mankind."[26] The nation is imagined as sovereign because "nations dream of being free, and if under God, directly so. The gage and emblem of this freedom is the sovereign state."[27] Finally, Anderson argues that a nation is imagined as a "*community*, because, regardless of the actual inequality and exploitation that may prevail in each, the nation is always conceived as a deep, horizontal comradeship." [28]

In the case of Papua New Guinea, its history as an independent nation was disrupted by the performance of a locally specific history in order to reinvent the nation without needing to lose sight of the allegorical cultural map created from it. The allegorical cultural map helped to reshape, reinvent, and reconceptualize the nation. Brash's *Taurama* asks us to rethink the nation of Papua New Guinea in a different way to that which we first began to think of before Independence. The actual Taurama massacre and the peace made to restore the severed relationships among the living descendants of Lakwaharu and Taurama serves as the allegory of the modern Papua New Guinea imagined by those who first instigated its political independence. It was one imagined in spite of the push for a split to occur at the insistence of the early Papua Besena movement: "Papua Besena would have only one objective: the freedom of Papua to determine its own future and control the land, welfare and development of its own people. In doing this we will oppose all forms of colonialism in Papua and work towards informing the people of their rights and freeing them from the slave mentality of subject people."[29]

The central themes of the Papuan separatist movement are twofold: "a belief that Papua was being neglected in the area of economic development and a reaction against migration from New Guinea to Port Moresby."[30] The Papua Besena movement dissipated into thin air after Papua and New Guinea conjoined to form the Independent State of Papua New Guinea in 16th September 1975. Independence and sovereignty disrupted the Papuan separatist's narratives of difference.

An affirmation of interruption to the flow of different narratives of what a nation constitutes is witnessed in the staging of *Taurama* at the time of the country's Tenth Anniversary Independence celebration. One senses Nora Brash making the point that without solving the internal social and historical conflicts Papua New Guinea is heading towards a bleak future with many different unresolved issues and conflicts. The occurrence therefore threatens the stability of the sovereign state of Papua New Guinea. In *Taurama*, Brash links the past with the present, history with the possible narrative of the future. In her other plays, Nora Brash concerns herself with making the narrative or play work to change the way people have created a false sense of identity in post-independence Papua New Guinea. Nora Brash is telling us to return to the traditions of our communities to discover the ways in which different communities formed, fragmented, and reinvented themselves by observing ways in which peace, amity, and cooperation were maintained in society:

> Nora believes that much of the imposed European law, inherited from Australia at Independence in 1975 and accepted by the educated national elite, is not suited to Melanesian society. "If we are going to use the Anglo-Saxon imported law we must try and blend it with some of our own so that it means something to us.' In Nora's society people obeyed rules handed down from their ancestors and enforced by the elders through taboos and social pressure such as public ridicule. In her play *Taurama* she attempted to portray 'the vigorous pre-colonial village life. In *Taurama* the unwritten laws are there. Two feuding tribes break their spears to appease the ancestral spirits and live in harmony through arranged marriages and by respecting the customs of each other's societies. In *Taurama* days we did not need the imported written laws to put society right'."[31]

Taurama fulfils the collective desires of Motu Koitabuans to remain united, but also to observe the fragility of such desires tested by others outside of that society. Motu Koitabu societies too have to watch the changes around them. These changes are shared with other Papua New Guineans choosing to live in Port Moresby. The constant ruffle and tussle for access to resources and opportunities in the post-independence Papua New Guinea must surely affect the relationships of Motuan Koitabuans among themselves and to others occupying their land in the National Capital District of Papua New Guinea.

CONCLUSION

Through the play *Taurama* Brash brings together both the imaginings of the Motu Koita community and the imaginings of other communities in forming what is known as Papua New Guinea, a collective of entities unknown to each other or related to each other, yet recognizing the limited sense of what the nation can offer to them and within a defined sovereign boundary. In a way the performance of *Taurama* during the time of reimagining the nation serves as an allegory of the postcolonial history and its narratives in Papua New Guinea. The story of Motu Koita is no longer about the history of Motu Koita, but about the larger collective of groups of people in a postcolonial nation. In other words the story of Taurama as a stage play is performed to a wider community of others imagining themselves as one people — one nation. By doing so the story of *Taurama* is overlaid with the postcolonial history of Papua New Guinea: "We can think of it as the overlaying of an allegorical cultural map upon the narrative of official history to effectively 'reshape' it."[32] Without Nora Vagi Brash's efforts in bringing this history out to the public, the history would have remained buried in the dying traditions of the Motu villages under the pressures of modern change and influence of other Papua New Guinean cultures in the capital city of Port Moresby.

Contemporary Undercurrents

The connection between literary and contemporary events provides the fertile ground for literary constructions to take place. Works of literature published at the turn of the century focus on the experiences of Papua New Guineans in their participation in the global market economy, regional political discussions, and in representation of the traditional way of life and knowledge systems. The contemporary writers are concerned over the difficult and often conflicting transitions Papua New Guineans are making in their lives after Independence in September 16th 1975. The experience of the Post-Independence generation is captured in the writings of the second and third generation of writers in Papua New Guinea. In this chapter the discussion focuses on how writers envisioned and critiqued their own cultures, social way of life, manners of behavior, and how the writers redefined themselves within the problematic space that is imbued with false pretense, empty promises, and social, political, and economic difficulties. The unresolved conflicts often lead to violence, bloodshed, and threat to break away.

Post-Independence Generation

A new middle class, a growing urban poor, and the stagnant reality of most rural communities shape the post-independence society in Papua New Guinea. The period between 1975 and 1985, ten years after Indepedence an air of disillusionment, dissatisfaction, and ambivalence settled in to claim the hopes, aspirations, and future of the young nation. The general feeling was that the government had distanced itself from the people and access to social, economic, and political services were denied to many people. A culture of self-seeking, glorifying elites, and weakened bureaucracy emerge as the barrier to the fulfillment of the Independence dream to be a free and happy people as declared in the Preamble of the Constitution of Papua New Guinea. The arrival of the second generation of PNG writers announced the change of temper from protest and fury to social criticism and self-appraisal in terms of the preoccupation of this generation. Gorle, whose study of the second generation, argued that the forum for such activities was not limited to the literary representations, but also to newspaper, radio, and television: "In discussing this periods literary production I would like to juxtapose the dwindling creative output against other forms of serious writing from the 1980s: essays, unpublished drama scripts, and letters to the editor of the *Times of Papua New Guinea*."[1]

The central argument pursued in Gorle's discussion is "that the practice of Papua New Guinea's writers was both dynamic and mimetic" to the extend that such productions gave rise to the emergence of public political opinions and perspectives on the changing social attitudes of Papua New Guineans: "My discussion of these various texts points to social change as a common concern in the writing of the decade: while a range of ideas and possible solutions are explored, the writers generally agree on the problems needing attention."[2] In her interviews with writers in Port Moresby Gorle reveals that serious writers were conscious of the kind of writing they were publishing in the period described as the second wave of writers with the social and political conscience of the nation at the core of their literary texts. Most the first wave of writers had ceased their literary life, except for a few of them such as Russell Soaba, Nora Vagi Brash, Paulias Matane, and Kumalau Tawali. The second generation writers are the younger generation influenced by their reading of the first generation of writers in Papua New Guinea. The literary production was driven by the will of individual writers to survive and articulate their experiences.

Since 1980s a number of anthologies, journals, and literary activities continued to support the continuity of the literary tradition started in the late 1960s. The concerns of the second wave of writers from 1980 onwards were on the political undercurrents and social change shaping Papua New Guinea as a nation. Papua New Guinea celebrated its first ten years as a nation in 1985, which also signaled a time of evaluation of its existence as a nation forged on heterogeneous identities. It was also a time of renewal of the spirit of progress and reconsideration of strategies and approaches to achieving the Constitutional goals Papua New Guineans have set themselves to achieve as a people. In the next ten years after 1985 Papua New Guinea sailed into rough seas with changing of captains of politics in the form of different prime ministers, through votes of no confidence and general elections. By 1990 a major internal conflict erupted into a full-scale civil war on Bougainville resulting in a bloody crisis that claimed lives of mainland Papua New Guineans and Bougainvilleans:

The combination of two decades of social disruption and massive environmental destruction came to a head in the late 1980s when Bougainvillean claims for massive compensation and part ownership of the mine were dismissed by the mining company and the Papua New Guinea government. Some islanders, led by a one-time mine surveyor named Francis Ona, obtained some explosives and sabotaged the power line to the mine, closing it. The Papua New Guinean government called out its riot police and army to restore order, and out of the bloody ensuing turmoil emerged the Bougainvilleans Revolutionary Army

(BRA) and its associated political wind the Bougainville Interim Government (BIG). The BRA drove the Papua New Guinean forces, covertly assisted by the Australian military, from much of the island. A blockade and conflict followed. The details are unclear with Bougainville effectively shut off from the rest of the world, but stories regularly emerged of barbarity on both sides—of captives hurled from helicopters or bound at the low tide mark to drown or savagely beaten with riffle butts."[3]

The threat of international intervention and involvement of Sandline mercenaries was sabotaged by a military faction. On the economic front the Papua New Guinea Kina was devalued, government's external reserve was depleted, and a slow decline in economic growth began. Social conditions and lifestyles of people changes: increased rural urban drift, overcrowding and overpopulation in urban centres, increased law and order challenges, uneven development between major centres and districts, and the increased number of young people out of school without formal employment. The poverty that gripped much of the country sound became a driving force behind people flooding into urban environments. The next decade the country went through a period of instability amid the explosion of the pandemic HIV/AIDs problem in Papua New Guinea. The unpredictable social and political landscapes gave rise to the Papua New Guineans asking themselves where they went wrong. Politicians and bureaucrats looked for answers in their boardrooms; intellectuals went silent, and writers took on a new urgency to question their leaders and those in charge about their sense of nationalism. In that questioning people became aware of another problem: corruption, poor governance, and lack of transparency had settled in firmly within the vault of societies seed of power.

SAILING THE ROUGH SEAS

Stella has published mostly short stories, poetry and critical literary articles over the years. With this new book Stella adds on to his list of publication. His earlier works include an ethnomusicological study: *Forms and Styles of Banoni Music* (1990) and *Moments in Melanesia* (1994), an anthology of writings from Melanesia.[4] If this book has anything to offer, I think it is in the precise moment of its publication, which I read as an intervention into the quiet moments of Papua New Guinean literature. Observers of Papua New Guinean literature may wish to note that *Gutsini Posa*'s publication marks the direction in which the Papua New Guinean novel is taking: a movement toward social criticism and critical evaluation of the contemporary society. Likely perhaps is the movement towards making sense of modernity and its dominant presence in the lives of many Pacific peoples.[5]

Regis Stella first wrote *Gutsini Posa* or *Rough Seas* (1999) for the National Literature Competition.[6] He won a consolation prize in that year. Since then
186

he has reworked the manuscript through a writer's fellowship at the famous University of Iowa writing school. The Institute of Pacific Studies at the University of the South Pacific, Fiji published the book in 1999. Since its publication few people in PNG have access to this wonderful novel.

Gutsini Posa in Banoni language of Bougainville means *rough seas*. Far from its existential value, *Gutsini Posa* is a novel that has two achievements: First, *Gutsini Posa* is an important literary representation of the struggle of the Bougainville people to come to terms with the crisis that has completely devastated their moral and physical strength. The backdrop of the book is the Bougainville conflict between the state of Papua New Guinea and one of its provinces, the then North Solomons province. Many lives were sacrificed on both sides of the conflict. Though, with some form of peace achieved the conflict continues to haunt everyone involved, directly or indirectly, with the conflict. The crippling condition of a society is a sadness that cannot be washed away by tears or with organized guerrilla resistance, but with strategic negotiations. Rape, senseless killing, and torture are not only violence on human rights but mark the wounds of conflict in the lives of those who have to live through crisis.

The reminder that, with divine intervention, hope comes after a people prove that collectively their spirit has not been broken, but is consolidated. Stella represents precisely this experience by the use of a volcano metaphor, a force mightier and devastating to both the oppressed and the oppressor. The relationship between human's ability to destroy themselves and yet can also be destroyed by a force greater, in the form of natural disasters, is an inevitable reality that Stella impresses upon the reader of *Gutsini Posa.*

Second, despite the differences in the characters of the book, they all have ideological strengths, which keep them intact from fragmentation. As the colonel of the Southern Command on Torogegai reminds Jamila and her response indicates, there is a deep-rooted sense of belonging to place that is seen as an ideology.

An important inference made by Stella in *Gutsini Posa* is to highlight the novelistic discourse enabling the author to address a number of issues. First, the heterogeneity in which the lives of Papua New Guineans are constructed allows dialogics to feature as a prominent factor in recognizing a common destiny. The destiny is freedom from all kinds of oppressive conditions, be it state sponsored or epistemologically instituted. Second, in the fight to liberate oneself from the onslaught of negative influences one must be willing to insert oneself in the mental construct and structures of the oppressor. In *Gutsini Posa* we see this clearly represented by Captain Gawi and Jamila, who are willing to fight for a cause that they believe in, no matter where and how it is staged. Captain Gawi, together with a few loyal soldiers plot a coup code named "Operation Electric Shock" against the government. In his support for the resistance he recruits Jamila, a native daughter of Torogegai. Jamila in her own right is boldly radical but through a misunderstood personal relationship with Penagi to playing a leading role in the struggle of liberation on Torogegai she earns her reputation of being a "Tsinara". These two characters are willing to forgo even the personal relationships for the sake of a collective struggle. Jamila becomes the heroine of the resistance and Captain Gawi becomes the sacrificial lamp — an interplay of the onto-theological conclusions, realized only in the climax of the crisis. Perhaps also in that expression peace comes at a price, attained through both strategic negotiations and consensus. *Gutsini Posa* is a novel of hope within a society bend on destabilizing itself: "Fine, people can be defeated but not conquered."[7]

Stella's exploration of the theme of journey is consistent with other Papua New Guinean writing. The journeys out and of return to the village, old ways and customs are in both spiritual and physical terms. The factors that drive such peregrination have to do with cultures and roots — the birthplace always remains the point of return. In *Gutsini Posa* both Penagi and Jamila must return in order for them to find each other, a strategic ploy suggested by the author. Strategic it is since the reclaiming of what is lost is only possible when individuals pursue such commitments. Stella is perhaps suggesting that the only way to secure lost identity is to retrace the journey to the beginning where it all began.

I read *Gutsini Posa* as a metaphor of a society fragmented by its own internal conflicts, torn by its own differences in the use of economic resources, democratic governance and social equality and on which is a need of ideological repair since nationalism has demised itself as exaggerated sentiments and political fleecing by its constitutionally elected representatives. The metaphor of the rough seas is to me a representation of the times of turmoil, conflict and contradictions in a Pacific nation's status where full-blown conflicts are the result of lack of consultation, consensus and negotiations. Stella observes: "Greed, dishonesty and hypocrisy by leaders are suffocating the nation."[8]

Stella's voice is stunning, yet controlled by the demands of the book to be as readable and provocative. Though a first novel for Stella, he secures a new place in the literary culture of Papua New Guinea. Unlike the Papua New Guinean novels that preceded *Gutsini Posa*, this one, in my opinion, is remarkable in its creative as well as critical characteristics.

CULTURE AND MATERIALISM

CBS Publishers & Distributors of India published Arnold Mundua's *The Bride's Price*.[9] Mundua had never studied literature or participated in any writing courses, but what he wrote was pure inspiration. Out of the need to express himself and write down his own experiences, he approached Sir Paulias Matane in 2001 and 2002 to assist him with the publication of his first novel.

So began Arnold Mundua's literary life, following the footsteps of his Simbu predecessors such as Peter Kama Kerpie, Ignatius Kilage, Benjamin Umba, and Toby Kagl Waim. Arnold sees writing fiction as a game of filling in the missing puzzles by piecing together various stories that make up a whole experience. He writes: "A fiction writer has essentially to piece together various stories to come to his objective of presenting his views, which he has in mind. It is like painting on a canvas to make it captivating. His task is rather more arduous. He is required to conceptualise the various strands of the story. They need to be skillfully woven against a background to look more credible. Above all it has to be entertaining, inspiring the reader to concentrate. Writing has been an obsession to me to express some of my views about the unrequited love and the ideal partners in conjugal life."[10]

Indeed Mundua's novel is about the love between the narrator Joseph Tamgo and Cathy Gior, which turns out to be unfulfilled in later life as both went separate ways. Joseph marries Anna, a cousin of Cathy, and a hard working village girl while Cathy flirts with other men, before marrying Peter Kuppal, a Hagen millionaire. Joseph's life went from his first meeting Cathy Grior, the ten year old when she was in Grade 4, with Joseph himself a thirteen year old in grade seven at Rosary High School. Joseph went on to Forestry College in Bulolo and Cathy completed her primary school and high school before entering the Balob Teacher's College.

As the narrative line goes after their respective vocational training in those institutions the two meet again in the village and found themselves enjoying each other's company. This led them to discover a secret love they have for each other since the first time they met so many years ago. Joseph returns to his job as a Forest Surveyor with the Bunning Brothers, a logging company in Vanimo, Sandaun Province. Cathy lands her first job as a teacher in Hobe Community School in the Karamui District of the Simbu Province. They contacted each other by letters until one day Joseph could not hold back any longer. He finds himself lying to his boss. He took a leave to visit his love back in the Simbu Province. At first this adventure turns out exciting, but quickly turns into a nightmare with Cathy becoming possessed by evil spirits of a mountain they trespassed near the school. Joseph afraid of the repercussions this might bring departs quickly to his village before leaving for Vanimo, but finds the wrath of Cathy's mother Kumo, very humiliating.

Joseph returns to Vanimo again, expecting Cathy to join up with him during the Christmas vacation that year. To his bewilderment Cathy never made the trip. Instead Cathy elopes with John Mitna, a salesman from the Coca -Cola company based in Hagen. This began Cathy's move away from Joseph, even though Joseph gave her a second chance to be with him again. Joseph, on the other hand affected by Cathy's lack of commitment to their relationship decides to enrol as a mature student at the University of Technology's Forestry program. A year before completing his studies, his father suggested that Joseph get married to a village girl quickly, to which Joseph decided that since Anna Thortia, the daughter of the Councillor of the Siako clan, was the preferred choice, the marriage was immediately arranged. The marriage turns out to be the best in the village for a long time. The arranged marriage turns out to be a blessing for both Peter and Anna., They respected each other and made many people envious of the pair.

Cathy, on the other hand marries Peter Kuppal, a millionaire who offers an attractive bride's price to Cathy's parents and relatives. Peter is an old man, who ropes in 15 wives, but deserted them, retaining two at the time of his marriage with Cathy. He also has a daughter of Cathy's age. Peter's other wives and his daughter are jealous of Cathy when they find that she has become his favourite due to her physical charms and intelligence. Because of this, Cathy sees dark days, including her physical torture and murder by Peter's second wife.

The novel is written in the first person narration with 23 chapters including a forward by his Excellency the Governor General of Papua New Guinea, Sir Paulias Matane, an author's note and a glossary. Arnold Mundua writes naturally with a unique sense for minute details that make great writers. The plot of the narrative is clear and the author brings out the flesh of the story in very descriptive and powerful ways of writing. Mundua has written a novel that is both entertaining and very anthropogenic of the Gembogl society. This is one aspect of the Papua New Guinea novel that makes it more than a novel since the reader is introduced to the language, cultures, lifestyles, social behaviours and attitudes of the writer to his society. The novel, written in a delectable style, interspersed with romance, suspense, and adventure, brings to focus the picturesque ambience of Papua New Guinea, and its distinct marriage systems involving the payment of bride's price to make it legal. The reader is made aware of the life-style of people in PNG's villages, their belief in exorcism, and the marriage and funeral rites as well as rituals prevalent among Melanesians. The various strands of the novel, woven dexterously by the novelist, keep the reader fully engrossed right from the beginning to the end.

TABU: UNWRITING THE COLONIAL LEGACY

Two things intriguing things are captured in *Tabu* (2003), a first novel by Moses Maladina, politician, former PNG Ambassador to New Zealand and former managing director of Air Niugini.[11] What is intriguing for my generation is the story of the first victim of the White Women's Protection Ordinance in Governor Murray's era and of course the Sandline Crisis during the days of

Bougainville civil conflict. Both events took place at the time when I was not around to witness them.

It is good, however, to read about them in the form of fiction as covered in Maladina's *Tabu*. The subtitle indicates that this is a historical fiction centred around the legacy of a love affair in colonial Papua New Guinea. The novel opens up with the execution of Sitiveni (Stephen) Goramambu, the first indigenous man tried and hanged in Port Moresby on the 29th of January 1934 under the racially prejudiced law famously known as the White Women's Protection Ordinance.[12] A law that was created, not to protect white women in the colonies, but to protect the interest of the white men, and his prejudice against the black men in the colonies.

The hanging of Sitiveni turns out to be a miscarriage of justice since he was falsely accused of carnal knowledge with the daughter of the senior sergeant Philip Sinclair and wife Majorie, when in fact it was Mr. Sinclair who should have been hanged for child molestation and incest. Chief Inspector Robert Logan, the man instrumental in wrongfully hanging Sitiveni, has so much spite for 'natives', but more specifically he hated Sitiveni because a smart 'native' was beyond his comprehension, a good friend of Governor Murray, and most of Sitiveni's love affair with Murray's niece Elizabeth Castleton Murray. Elizabeth was born in Melbourne, Australia in 1909 and died peaceful at her home in February 3rd, 1997. Elizabeth's death brought together her daughter Stephanie, grandson Edward, and great grandchildren, Rachael and Stephen.

The story line picks up with Edward Murray travelling to Papua New Guinea as the representative of Murray Holdings, together with Colonel Tom Spencer, a Timeline (Sandline) military contractor. The purpose: to crush the Bougainville Crisis with the support of the Prime Minister and a number of high level military and government ministers in Papua New Guinea and Australia.

On this journey Edward has the opportunity to read through the private dairies of his grandmother, Elizabeth. The dairies were handed to him by his mother Stephanie, before his departure to Papua New Guinea. It is through the dairies that Edward uncovers the deeply embedded mystery surrounding his grandfather Sitiveni Goramambu, who fathered Stephanie in a racially outlawed relationship with Elizabeth Murray.

In this discovery Edward realizes for the first time that his grandfather was the victim of the racially divided colonial Papua and a legal instrument applied with an unbalanced legal instrument. Edward too, begins to make sense of the larger problem Papua New Guinea face as a former colony of Australia and a country troubled by internal ethnic conflicts, corruption, bribery, exploitation by transnational companies, and unable to free itself from the neocolonial exploitations of its resources and exploitation by its own people.

The novel is written with a temporal juxtaposition of events in the 1930s and in 1997. For a first time novelist Maladina writes without too much haste, but with much more fluidity that gives readers the pleasure of reading a fictionalised history. *Tabu*, is a novel written around actual events with which Maladina, has given the reader a new sense of understanding of the historical moments that could have been forgotten by many Papua New Guineans.

In this well-wrought novel, Maladina demonstrates his excellent ability to write a story that moves the reader and without the trouble of fussing around uncontrolled narratives and vocabulary. Maladina has succeeded in his effort to reconstruct two different events in Papua New Guinea's history through very effortless prose, vivid description, and straight-forward dialogue. *Tabu*, is no doubt one of the best book written by a Papua New Guinean to have come out in the beginning of this new millennium, and I must say lucidity of the prose reminds me of the styles of world-class writers such as Toni Morrison, John Updike, J. M. Coetzee, and Trevor Shearston. Maladina sets a different style and level of writing for Papua New Guineans to emulate. Good writing sets the reader to vividly visualize the plot unfold as if watching a movie, and indeed if this book is converted into a movie it will be a success.

The book has one powerful message for Papua New Guineans: if the truth of history must be told let it be told and be corrected when we can. As is clear in Amirah Inglis' book *Not a White Woman Safe: Sexual Anxiety and Politics in Port Moresby 1920-1934*, published in 1974 by the ANU press, her chapters on Miaro and Stephen Gorumambu raises a lot of questions that need answers.[13] Indeed that would demand more research to ascertain the facts, but with a reading of Moses Maladina's historical novel we are able to see clearly the division there was in the colonial Papua under Murray's administration. Inglis has done much research on this subject and has written extensively, on this. I would have thought Maladina would have done well by acknowledging the influence that Inglis' work might have had on the construction of his novel.

Nevertheless both seem to address the same issue of the relations between black and whites in the colony of Papua. Inglis writes that Sir Hubert Murray passed the White Women's Protection Ordinance in 1926: "It was a piece of legislation discriminating in its provisions, harsh in its penalties, and startlingly out of character with Murray's rule and its effect on Papuans, not history of colonial Papua, can be complete without an explanation of it. The White Women's Protection Ordinance was the most significant expression of one aspect of the relations between black and white in the colony, the fear of sexual attack by black men on white women and girls: the "Black Peril". The extent of this fear is perhaps hard to believe today, but any reading of the papers of the day will uncover it."[14]

And Maladina's *Tabu* is exactly that: a rereading of the "Black Peril" in colonial Papua. I recommend this book to anyone interested in revisiting history and learning something from it. It is a book readers will not put down once they start reading.

Postcolonial texts embody culture, history, and truth. The power of allegory manifested in the oral language appears more important in post-colonial texts as it expresses truth about conditions created as a result of colonialism. The truth, however, is wrapped in the word and its symbolic characteristics. These symbolic characteristics are viewed through allegory and parables present in the text. Allegorical texts reveal a society's symbolic characteristics in many ways.[15]

The Anuki tribe in the Milne Bay area of Papua New Guinea, for instance, use "maiba", a form of communication, to express truth only through parables and riddles.[16] In modern day literature, Russell Soaba, an Anuki author uses, the "Maiba" to see contemporary Papua New Guinea in change. The truth is that change brings about drastic effects on culture. Old customs disappear and new cultures are introduced. The challenge of allegorical work is to embody reality in all its form. *Maiba,* the second Soaba novel is woven around the word `maiba' to present the truth about the emerging nation of Papua New Guinea.[17] The novel captures the changes Anuki, and for that matter Papua New Guinea, experience after the old guard is no longer in power. In the case of Anuki, we see the sudden upsurge of new and dangerous forces of power taking the center stage without needing authorization from anyone. In the absence of traditional power structures the new power is forcefully enforced through manipulation, violence, and subjugation of people through undemocratic processes of control.[18] Soaba brings to light the postcolonial anxiety and fear of neocolonial masters, elitism, and inappropriate forms of authority at the expanse of subjected peoples in formerly colonized societies.

The story Maiba evolves around the Anuki oral form of communication to reveal truth about something or someone through the use of parables. Soaba uses this form in his novel "to encompass the complexity of the force prevalent in the construction of modern PNG society."[19] Soaba uses the Anuki parable to highlight "the problems of cultural change and colonial encroachment" whereby the author approaches social change as "conceived within a framework of open possibilities which are neither closed non limited by the text."[20] Soaba makes use of allegory to resist closure, and thereby also resists "history, and thus abrogates the structure of power in which history is constituted."[21]

Yawasa Maibina Wawaya, the protagonists of the novel *Maiba*, comes from the traditional ruling family in Makawana village. Fate has it that she grows up condemned and forced to live in orphanage. She is deprived of her privileges as the next heir to the Magura dynasty. The deceitful, unfaithful, and selfish aunt, Mrs. Veronica Wawaya, denies Yawasa Maibina of all privileges and access to the crown. The whole village of Makawana is immersed in confusion, leading them to debate the issue of having a chief continue in their village, after the last of the Magura dynasty dies. Maiba is the last person they want to serve under as her subjects. They see in Maiba the very symbol of an evil omen. Maiba's father, the late Chief Komeroana Magura, had chosen that name; probably out of the necessity of concealing his fears and guilt from something he did in his past.

Maiba is rebuked and condemned to live in obscurity. Makawana's misfortunes seem to have something to do with the birth of Yawasa Maibina. The people of Makawana refuse to recognize her; they even consider her dirty, irresponsible, and unworthy of ruling the village after her father's death. Maiba has also failed to lead her people out of their pasts to link up with the rest of the world. Her failure at completing university studies meant she is unfit to lead her people. Her antagonists use the excuses to begin a whole string of events that ruffled and undermined the traditional authority and power structures under the Magura dynasty.

Maiba grows up in a matured way under negating circumstances. Through problems, hardships, and the negative attitudes to her, she learns to maintain her own dignity and strengthen as a leader. Her stern and mere presence arouses fear in the hearts of Makawana challengers. The challenge to Maiba's authority is often projected at a distance, yet those who are responsible for such actions, know that Maiba would contest them anytime she chooses.

Soaba's Makawana village is a microcosm of Papua New Guinea. Since Independence the concentration of power shifted from the traditional authority to the new educated and powerful elites in the new nation. Traditional indigenous forms of power shifted to the new introduced Western system of power. Followers of traditional forms of authority found themselves pushed off the road of political, social and cultural change. Disrespect for tradition and undermining of traditional ways of knowledge began to set in. Since Independence more Papua New Guinean villages have undergone tremendous change that left them struggling to maintain a balance between the traditional world and the modern worlds.

The new world is also a world that has different degrees of challenges. The new leaders found the new power a way to access wealth and build their own empires. In *Maiba* Doboro Thomas represents the opportunists and those who seize power to rule a society. The village orator, Elder Yaraga, succumbs to bribery and barbaric influences of Doboro Thomas. The village is shrouded with fear and insecurity. The old orator's trade store falls into the hand of Koboni, the rape of Christine and the threat of the gun that Koboni employs as his power of authority over Makawana are all the result of a lawless chaotic society Makawana is controlled by a few corrupt people. Maiba in her matured age becomes aware of her responsibility to take action to regain the traditional authority. Since her father's death:

Life, thought Maiba, whether it may become, is basically ugly, neglected, for owned upon and mocked even murdered: it is in the heart of man, the Wawaya of us all, who is so busy wishing to be complete as a human being that he cannot communicate with us. Soon, our brother, the royal Rabobo in all mankind, who is disguised as a teachers' college student, will come home, and the doors of our present myths and mysteries in truth the Maiba of our existences will be unlocked, and out funeral days won't be as sadly solemn as they seem.[22]

The modern day Papua New Guinea, at least for Soaba, is a strange society ripe with corruption, bribery, and all kinds of social disorder. Every day in the media we hear of high-level corruptions of respected members of the community. *Maiba*, was published 10 years after the country's Independence. Soaba's reflection on the path taken by Papua New Guinea in the decade after its birth seems to correspond to Maiba path since her birth. She is neglected, abused, and is pushed off from making important decisions to shape her own destiny. Maiba's life seems dependent on the estranged aunt Veronica Wawaya, whose interest is not in Maiba, but on her own exploitation of the relationships that she had constructed after she had married into the Wawaya family.

IDENTITY STRUGGLES

Soaba brings out the importance of names and what they signify in the novel. Anuki names have meanings that are embedded in the culture. Yawasa Maibina is shortened to Maiba, to mean the truth only through parables. Koboni is a label used in urban Port Moresby to refer to a evil person, evil spirit, or a notorious criminal with no respect for people. Royal Bob Rabobob is a reference to a royal decent in the Magura dynasty. In this case Royal Bob Rabobo is the biological child of Chief Magura in his illicit relationship with Veronica Wawaya. Naming as a strategy in the construction of the novel has given Soaba an intertextual perspective in locating his perspectives from within Anuki and outside of it. In *Maiba*, we note the author making use of the Anuki form of communication as well as the parables from the Christian Bible as is exemplified through the sacrificial death of Christine and Timothy Wawaya. Makawana is a society already infused with introduced ideas from the world. Soaba introduces Russian names, African folklore, and Christianity's influences. Makawana is a society flooded with new ideas, names, labels, and ways of doing things. It is a society faced with the challenge to remain true to its traditional ways or to change with the introduced way of life.

Soaba represents the traditions of the Anuki both as an insider and an outsider. As in his other novel *Wanpis* (1978) he uses the philosophy of existentialism to explore the mysteries of self, answer questions of independence, and observe his society.[23] In *Maiba* Soaba assesses and commits himself to the literature of the society where the protagonist is a female fighting the social, personal, political, and gender differentiation in the society. Soaba says his writing is a work of art: "A work of art is read and praised for its quality "to represent that state of self-consciousness as consciously and existentially as possible to include and treat" the novel art as bringing out a simple truth."[24] Through writing, Soaba is able to capture his views and observations of the society. Art must reflect society and reality in the way Soaba perceives his own work.

Apart from his philosophical conviction Soaba sees the society as changing and experiencing tremendous alteration to the traditionally structured society. Soaba is consciously writing about the changes to Papua New Guineans Between 1970 and 1980 so much happened within a short period of time that as an artist Soaba felt compelled to capture the changes happening in the lives of Papua New Guinea. He argues that the events of the 1970s precipitated into a national stalemate or better still created a situation where it no longer matters who made up Papua New Guinea. The imagined nation of Papua New Guinea, in Soaba's vision, is a constitution of a diversity of cultures, views, perspectives, and a perfect site for the struggle for identity.[25]

ALLEGORY OF CHANGE

Maiba is an allegory of change and contestations of ideologies in postcolonial Papua New Guinea. *Maiba* makes good use of various strategies of appropriation. The use of Anuki names and mythological names such as "Koboni", establish a certain mediation between two cultures, that of the modern and traditional. There is a "peculiar link between language and the world, and textuality, with its emphasis on reference and objectivity, in a heightened capacity to encapsulate difference."[26] The difference would either be between what is truly Papua New Guinean literate culture and the introduced imperialist culture. Such differences force the writer to place him between the two cultures by entering his consciousness in the text and viewing from both perspectives. The narrator and to an extent the protagonist speak the author's views.

This is exactly the performance of Soaba in *Maiba*, particularly in characterizing the village orator as the more learned and well-educated member of Makawana, whom the people entrusted the seal of power and authority, instead of acknowledging the chiefly rule of the Magura family. The author's views of how power is corrupted are explained through the village orator. The village orator in *Maiba* secures power through a manipulative, but clever way of controlling and maintaining influence. Doboro Thomas uses language as a process of securing power. His oratory and immense knowledge of outside societies stunt the villagers.

The base on which myth is found upon by the society, is transformed and trivialized by the language which assumes control in new order, the discourse of power with which Doboro Thomas is gradually identifying [27] People come to believe and accept Doboro Thomas as an authority, because he introduced English words when he could, the source of new power introduced into the society: "Those who surrounded Doboro Thomas agreed with him, seeing that he was using words that they had never heard before, and if anyone similarly used big English words for the first time in Makawana, he was automatically believed."[28] This exemplifies the relationship between the nexus of power and language. In postcolonial texts, the appropriation of language signifies the text as very important element of literature that cannot be dismissed.

Soaba's novels are rooted in the contemporary life. His novels draw both within a changing society and one struggling to maintain the traditional way of life and cultures. The consequences are seemingly real, as the characters become confused and dislocated, just as the traditional society does when confronted with modern influences. Like Maiba, many Papua New Guineans continue to struggle in their plights to hold on to tradition, but also to accept the transformations of their consciousness — one that is not purely traditional and yet modern. It is one that is an acknowledgment of the past and present sacrifices for a future that is true to its ideals and core values of a shared identity. Regis Stella also views *Maiba* as a postcolonial allegory of the changing Papua New Guinea: "Soaba's depiction of Maiba as alienated and displaced alludes to a number of significant contentions, including the fact that all cultures and sociopolitical systems have flaws, whether they are inherent in the system, in personalities, or in quality of leadership. Thus, *Maiba*, as an allegory of the country, is presented in such a way as to mirror and capture the broader politics of PNG postcoloniality."[28]

Soaba's point is that Papua New Guinea is only independent after it has recognized the process of securing that identity as a nation is only possible through mediation and negotiation of strategic defining elements. First it must accept the fact that change has affected traditional systems of authority and power. There is a shift in political and social situations in every society in Papua New Guinea. Confusion and negative sentiments are expressed in every corner of the country. A sense of hopelessness is the general mood in the lives of many people. The conditions of negativity and hopeless in Maiba represents the experiences of other Papua New Guineans: "Maiba's sense of helplessness and marginalization is concomitant with the assertion that nations are always in flux, acting alone to defend their political future."[29]

Soaba demonstrates his ability to use novel to provide a critique of the national sentiments and attitudes of his contemporaries. He sees Papua New Guinea as a site of contestations of ideologies, political power, and cultural systems of authority. He uses Maiba to highlight the importance of political awakening. Stella considers the "shedding of old garments" as a postcolonial metaphor for political consciousness and independence."[30] "Maiba is depicted as awakening from recovering of her sensibility, as it is redolent of becoming aware of her isolation and alienation" writes Stella in his study of Soaba's novel. "However, she alone cannot endanger profound change; her strength is with the Makawana villagers, who stand by her when she finally challenged Doboro Thomas," as is obvious in the final chapter of the novel.[31] The last chapter brings the novel to a close, depicting the resolution to the conflict, tensions, and anxieties faced under the new conditions of society created out of the change of regimes so to speak where the old order is replaced by the new order.

CONTINUITY AND HOPE

The publication of *Maiba* in mid 1980s offered a sense of hope for the struggling literary scene in Papua New Guinea. Soaba began his literary career as a young writer in the pioneer school of PNG writers. Known to be the outsider, an intellectual, and artist who refused to bow out of the scene, Soaba gave Papua New Guinea the novel *Maiba*, which immediately challenged his critics for their narrowly focused attention on his earlier works. *Maiba*'s appearance on the scene strengthened in some way the sprouting of new literary voices, a generation of new writers associated with the Ondobondo Club and the PNG Writers Union. At Waigani where most of the literary activities were taking place the arrival of *Maiba* in the literary scene meant there was a continuity of literary production from the earlier period. Soaba became the role model for the young writers of the second generation.

The 1980s was a period of transition from Independence to a developing nationhood. The euphoria of the Independence had quickly dissipated and a national assessment of self and nation was at work. *Maiba* appeared in 1985, a decade after Independence that it affirmed the need for re-evaluation of the state of affairs in the country. Many communities in Papua New Guinea changed. The simple village societies with traditional authorities have now succumbed to the modern western forms of government. Many young children born in the colonial period are making their way into the bureaucracies and employment sector in urban areas. Educated Papua New Guineans are now at the helm of government systems promoting various developmental policies and activities to improve the lives of people. The question now is whether the new systems promoted by the elites are relevant and appropriate to the people. Are the new ways of equal participation really working for the people? How much of the old system of authority and power should be changed to suit the people? How has the introduction of new ideas and way of life affected the people? These are questions that needed answers. *Maiba* reminds us that we need to reassess ourselves and the conditions created since Independence. Soaba is critical of the changes sweeping through the many communities in Papua New Guinea. Accepting the changes without raising any questions about it seems a good recipe for disaster.

Maiba is a portrayal of the traditional PNG society "trying to redefine itself within a matrix of rapid change and shifting global politics and relationships."[32] Doboro Thomas a character in the novel embodies this imagery. The moral and political corruption in the postcolonial state is alluded to in the character of Doboro Thomas: "In the end the corrupt leadership is overturned by people's power. Maiba openly and ironically challenges Thomas to kill the people, given all the evil he and his henchman have done."[33] In doing so *Maiba* highlights the anxiety resulting from the national betrayal and confusion in postcolonial Papua New Guinea. The question of national harmony and unblemished leadership is what a nation needs most after it has decided to stand on its own feet. In the case of Papua New Guinea, the new nation after Independence was no longer heading in the right direction. It quickly became embroiled in issues of political corruption and inefficient bureaucracy that the fear was that Papua New Guineans have become their own exploiters rather than liberators of their people out of colonized mentality, illiteracy, social inequality, and economic independence. A situation described as "the farce of national independence."[34] Soaba's concern is that Papua New Guinea is stronger when a sense of unity is created from the recognition of its traditional system of authority that is balanced with the new system of governance. The national vision has to be a construct of both systems rather than one forged out of the need to replace the existing order. Too much emphasis on the new introduced system can lead to complex chaos and anarchy and disunity among the people of the Papua New Guinea.

In *Maiba*, there is a sense of caution issued to young leaders of the country. Juvenile politicking, access greed, and nepotism can lead to complete fragmentation. Leadership and decision makers must abandon their self-interests and work for a collective good. Without doing so, the nation will suffer the indignities of being labeled a failed state inviting outside intervention, especially from its former colonizer. And indeed since the publication of *Maiba*, Papua New Guinea had traveled down that road, especially when few in positions of leadership had bothered to read, understand, and digest the lessons in Soaba's *Maiba*: "The novel charts a theme prevalent in post-independence PNG writing, which is very much concerned with where the country is heading and how the changes are affecting the people. It is highly allegorical with many open possibilities, reflecting the real complexity of a country undergoing the afterbirth pains of independence."[35]

Maiba is a novel that does no historicizing of the political realities inherited from the colonial history it does suggest the importance of community and collective authority within the Papua New Guinea society. *Maiba* stands out as a novel constructed on the basis of understanding how traditional political authority holds together a community through a system accepted as responsible and fair to its subjects. The novel also raises questions about how Papua New Guineans define themselves in relations to the community.

LOCAL VALUES AND POLITICAL DISCOURSES

It seems defining a national identity depends very much on the community that one belongs in the greater scheme of things. I am reminded of Partha Chatterjee's discussion of the community in postcolonial politics in India. To discuss that all forms of modern politics are the result of the colonial legacy only leads to ignoring the basis of modern politics that is the construction of the Indigenous politics such as the big man system or the Melanesian chieftainship system with the introduced modern Westminister system. As in India "modern disciplinary regime" in Papua New Guinea "is itself limited and conditioned by the numerous resistances to its hegemonic sway."[36] It is true there are un-resolved tensions "through which the twin constituents of political discourse within the modern domain — one, the categories of the liberal-democratic state produced theoretically in the West, and the other, the categories that made up the Orientalist construction of India — are continuously being re-created in ever more unrecognizable forms."[37] In Papua New Guinea the shaping of modern political discourses are the combination of both the introduced system and the traditional political systems. Joseph Ketan's study of the modern political systems in the Western Highlands community confirms this production of modern politics in Papua New Guinea:

> Traditional ideas, infighting, and practices thus become factors in contemporary state political institutions, just as modern economic resources and commodities have entered traditional ceremonial exchanges. The competition such as cash, and motor vehicles in *moka* exchanges, is a manifestation of cultural continuity. But the use of cash itself and being part of the world economy indicates change in society. These simple examples mimic broader changes, involving a significant merging of ideologies and cultural practices. A major case of incorporation presented in this study is the way in which Hageners have skillfully orchestrated 'traditional' local events, such as ceremonial gift exchanges and compensation payments, to coincide with, and culminate in, national and provincial government elections.[38]

There is a heavy influence of local values and political influences in the way modern politics is played out in the national scene. The political system inherited from the colonial system is no longer the same, but a system influenced and framed with the local political systems and ideologies. The Papua New Guinea political system is a construct of both the modern western system and the traditional Indigenous system of politics. It is interesting to note that as a result of this there might be the instance where the state has reached into the interiors of social life of many Papua New Guineans. This is only possible where "greater reach of the institutions and processes of the state into the interiors of social life, the state itself is being made sense of in terms of that other discourse, far removed from the conceptual terms of liberal political theory."[39]

The argument pursued here leads me to think of the popular misunderstanding inherent in current discussions of the modern political system in Papua New Guinea. The first discussion centers around the modern state as representing the uncontaminated state of reason and the local politics as drawn largely from tribal and ethnic politics with the tendency to contaminate and corrupt the 'pure' political state inherited from the West. The irony, as Chatterjee asserts: "Whether it is communalism or casteism, nepotism or power brokerage, thoughtless populism or the absence of a work ethic, the impact of the popular domain is seen as bearing the mark of an impurity." [40]

How is this related to the situation in Papua New Guinea? Take for example, the notion of *wantok* and its impact in the political domain of Papua New Guinea. The term has acquired deep political populism in Papua New Guinea. It is used as system of realignment based on language group, ethnic groups, regional groups, and other superficial groupings. In politics its use is often considered divisive to national politics, viewed as a consolidation of a dominant hegemonic groups working against the national interests, but for a sectorial interests with limited outcomes. Using the wantok system in national politics is considered divisive and allows corruption, nepotism, and backward politics. The term used in this sense carries with it undesirable forms of community and reflects a backward, tribal naivete in the functions of the state.

The same observation is made of the arguments pursued in Papua New Guinea about insertion of traditional politics into the national scene. At the turn of the century many political scientist orchestrated the failure of the modern state in Melanesia, especially in Papua New Guinea. The response to it from certain sectors of the society was that the nation state has not failed, but relied on the traditional foundations of Melanesian cultures such as the wantok systems, tribal networks of gift exchange and support, and allegiance to the authority in society. The problem with this argument, however, was that the modern state has completely immersed itself in the traditional political system that even the tribal, wantok, or ethnic politics was dependent on its legitimacy. No one wanted the system replaced with localized political institutions, processes and discourses promoting wantok system, tribal or ethnicity. The state would have failed completely had this been the case.

In this chapter we look at the work of four writers whose novels are excellent representations of the period described above. Through their writings these contemporary writers capture the uncertainties, confusions, and disruption to the progressive discourse of democracy. The writers have different backgrounds and exposure to literary influences. Stella is an academic with training in literature whereas Mundua is a forester by profession, with little academic training in writing or literary studies. Maladina is a lawyer, diplomat, and politician. Their novels have distinctive features that differentiate one from the other. Stella had read all the works of literature published by Papua New Guinea making him more knowledgeable in the art of writing than Mundua, who wrote out of the unstoppable urge to write novels based on personal experience. Maladina wrote the novel while serving as a diplomat in New Zealand. Russell Soaba is one pioneer writer who continues to write to this day. He has contributed to the emergence and sustenance of the literary culture of Papua New Guinea. All the books were written in the period after Independence with the subject matter revolving around events occurring in contemporary times. The issues these writers dealt with a complex and varied in many respects, yet only the surface is scratched in the fictionalized representations in the books considered here.

NOTES

Introduction: Mapping Uncharted Passages

1. See Ben Scott, *Reimaging Papua New Guinea: Culture, Democracy and Australia's Role* (Sydney: Lowy Institute for International Policy, 2005).
2. Steven Edmund Winduo, "Papua New Guinean Writing Today: The Growth of a Literary Culture," *Manoa* 2:1 (1990): 37-41; Gillian Gorle, "The Second Decade: The Theme of Social Change in the Papua New Guinean Literature, 1979-1989," *Pacific Studies* 19:1 (March 1996): 53-90; Gillian Gorle, "The Theme of Social Change in the Literature of Papua New Guinea, 1969-1979," *Pacific Studies* 18: 2 (1995): 79-113.
3. See Vilsoni Hereniko, "Representation of Cultural Identities," in *Inside Out: Literature, Cultural Politics, and Identity in the New Pacific*, ed. Vilsoni Hereniko and Rob Wilson (Lanham, Boulder, New York, Oxford: Rowman & Littlefield Publishing, Inc., 1998), 137-166; Regis Stella, "Reluctant Voyages into Otherness: Practice and Appraisal in Papua New Guinean Literature," in *Inside Out: Literature, Cultural Politics, and Identity in the New Pacific*, ed. Vilsoni Hereniko and Rob Wilson (Lanham, Boulder, New York, Oxford: Rowman & Littlefield Publishing, Inc., 1998), 221-230.
4. Steven Edmund Winduo, "Papua New Guinean Writing Today: The Growth of a Literary Culture," *Manoa* 2:1 (1990): 37-41.
5. Steven Edmund Winduo, "Preface," in *Building a Nation in Papua New Guinea: Views of the Post-Independence Generation*, ed. David Kavanamur, Charles Yala, and Quinton Clements (Canberra: Research School of Asian and Pacific Studies, ANU, 2003), xi-xv; See also Ernest Gellner, *Nations and Nationalism* (Oxford: Blackwell Publishers, 1983).
6. Regis Stella, *Imagining the Other: The Representation of the Papua New Guinean Subject* (Honolulu: Center for Pacific Islands Studies, University of Hawaii, 2007).
7. See Steven Winduo, ed., *Reframing Indigenous Knowledge: Cultural Knowledge and Practice in Papua New Guinea* (Port Moresby: Melanesian and Pacific Studies, University of Papua New Guinea, 2009).
8. See Ernesto Laclau and Chantal Mouffe, *Hegemony and Socialist Strategy*, trans. W. Moore and P. Commack (London: New Left Books, 1985); also Ernesto Laclau, *New Reflections on the Revolution of Our Times* (London: Verso, 1990); and John Mowitt, *Text: The Genealogy of an Antidisciplinary Object* (Durham: Duke University Press, 1992), 15.
9. Mowitt, *Text*, 15-16; See also Ernesto Laclau, "Populist Rupture and Discourse," *Screen Education* 34 (1980): 87.
10. Mowitt, *Text*, 16; See Ernesto Laclau, "Populist Rupture," 87.
11. Raymond Williams, *Marxism and Literature* (Oxford: Oxford University Press, 1977), 128.
12. Georg Lukacs, *The Theory of the Novel: A Historico-philosophical Essay on the Forms of Great Epic* (Cambridge, Massachusetts: The MIT Press, 1994).
13. Gayatri Chakravorty Spivak, "Can the Subaltern Speak?" in *Colonial Discourse and Post-colonial Theory: A Reader*, ed. Patrick Williams and Laura Chrisman (New York: Columbia University Press, 1988), 66-111.

14. Steven Edmund Winduo, *Hembemba: Rivers of the Forest* (Suva and Port Moresby: Institute of Pacific Studies and Language and Literature Department, UPNG, 2000).
15. Steven Edmund Winduo, "The Influence of Orality in Contemporary PNG Writing," BA Honors sub-thesis (University of Papua New Guinea, 1989).
16. Steven Edmund Winduo, "Cultural Invasion, Negative Knowledge, Self-Expression and Prose Narratives of Papua New Guinea," Masters thesis (University of Canterbury, New Zealand. 1991).

Chapter 1 Unwriting the Papuan Villager

1. Epeli Hau'ofa, "Our Sea of Islands," in *We Are the Ocean: Selected Works, Epeli Hau'ofa* (Honolulu: University of Hawaii Press, 2008), 34.
2. Noenoe K. Silva, *Aloha Betrayed: Native Hawaiian Resistance to American Colonialism* (Durham and London: Duke University Press, 2004).
3. Michelle Keown, *Pacific Islands Writing: The Postcolonial Literatures of Aotearoa/ New Zealand* (Oxford & New York: Oxford University Press, 2007), 111-112.
4. Keown, *Pacific Islands Writing,* 111.
5. Keown, *Pacific Islands Writing.*
6. Keown, *Pacific Islands Writing.*
7. Keown, *Pacific Islands Writing;* Subramani, *South Pacific Literature:From Myth to Fabulation* (Suva: Institute of Pacific Studies, 1989).
8. Keown, *Pacific Islands Writing,* 111.
9. Steven Edmund Winduo, "Unwriting Oceania: The Repositioning of the Pacific Writer Scholars Within a Folk Narrative Space," *New Literary History* 31: 11 (2000): 599-613.
10. Nigel Oram, "The Western Motu Area and the European Impact, 1872-1942," in *Papua New Guinea: A Century of Colonial Impact 1884-1984*, ed. Sione Latukefu (Port Moresby: National Research Institute, 1989), 49-74.
11. See F. E. Williams, "The Reminiscence of Ahua Ova,"*Journal of the Royal Anthropological Institute*, 17 (1939): 15-36.
12. Motu or Hiri Motu is one of the lingua franga of Papua New Guinea. The other is Tok Pisin. Together with English they are regarded as the official languages of Papua New Guinea.
13. Oram, "The Western Motu Area*,* " 58.
14. Lahui Ako, *Upstream Through Endless Sands of Blessings* (New Delhi: CBS Publishers and Distributors, 2007), 68.
15. Oram, "The Western Motu Area," 68; see also C.G. Seligman, *The Melanesians of British New Guinea*, 17-30; C.S. Belshaw, "The Last Years of Ahuia Ova", *Man*, no.228-30, 131-132; Oram, "Ahuia Ova," *Australian Dictionary of Biography*, 7: 20-21.
16. Young and Clark, *Anthropologist in Papua*, 21; *The Papuan Villager,* vol. 3. no. 1. January 1931. See also H. Nelson, '*The Papuan Villager*: a national newspaper'. *Journal of the Papua and New Guinea Society*, vol. 2. no. 1. 1968.
17. Young and Clark, *Anthropologist in Papua*.
18. Young and Clark, *Anthropologist in Papua*.
19. *Papua Annual Report* (ANR), 1927: 21; PAR, 1933:15.
20. Young and Clark, *Anthropologist in Papua*, 21.

21. James Clifford, *The Predicament of Culture: Twentieth-Century Ethnography, Literature, and Art* (Cambridge, Mass., & London: Harvard University Press, 1988), 231.
22. Young and Clark, *Anthropologist in Papua*, 36.
23. Young and Clark, *Anthropologist in Papua*.
24. *The Papuan Villager,* vol. 3. no. 1. January 1931.
25. Young and Clark, *Anthropologist in Papua*, 217.
26. Young and Clark, *Anthropologist in Papua*, 22.
27. Young and Clark, *Anthropologist in Papua*.
28. Minute by J. Farish dated August 28, 1838, quoted in B. Boman-Behram, *Education Controversies of India*, 239, cited in Gauri Visnawathan, *Masks of Conquest: Literary Studies and British Rule in India* (New York: Columbia, 1989), 2.
29. Visnawathan, *Masks of Conquest*, 2.
30. Young and Clark, *Anthropologist in Papua*, 23.
31. James Michener, *Return to Paradise* (New York: Random House, 1951), 44, 64 cited in Paul Lyons, *American Pacificism: Oceania in the U.S. Imagination* (New York: London, 2006), 28. See also Barbara McClintock, *Imperial Leather: Race, Gender, and Sexuality in the Colonial Context* (New York and London: Routledge, 1995), 38; Bruce A Harvey, *American Geographics: U.S. National Narratives and the Representation of the Non-European World, 1830-1865* (Stanford, CA: Stanford University Press, 2001).
32. Regis Stella, *Imagining the Other: The Representation of the Papua New Guinean Subject* (Honolulu: University of Hawaii Press, 2007), 126; Margaret Jolly, "Ill-Natured Comparisons: Racism and Relativism in European Representations of ni-Vanuatu From Cook's Second Voyage," *History and Anthropology* 5 (3/4), (1992): 334; Bernard Smith, *European Vision and the South Pacific*, second edition (Melbourne: Oxford University Press, 1989) 5, 42.
33. Young and Clark, *Anthropologist in Papua*.
34. Silva, *Aloha Betrayed,* 54-55.
35. Silva, *Aloha Betrayed.*
36. See Steven Edmund Winduo, "Literary Culture as Intellectual Capital for Nation Building," *Savannah Flames: a Papua New Guinean Journal of Literature, Language and Culture.* 4:1 (2001): 97-109.
37. Stella, *Imagining the Other*, 08.
38. See Geoffrey Smith, "Education, History and Development," in *Encylopaedia of Papua New Guinea*, vol. 1. A-K (Melbourne: University of Papua New Guinea, 1972), 325; see also Winduo, *Cultural Invasion.*
39. Detailed discussion on this aspect of the colonial education in Winduo, *Cultural Invasion*; see also Peter Smith, "Education Policy in Australian New Guinea: a Classic Case," in *Papua New Guinea: A Century of Colonial Impact 1884-1984*, ed. Sione Latukefu (Port Moresby: National Research Institute and the University of Papua New Guinea, 1989),314; see also F. E. Williams, "The Blending of the Cultures: an Essay on Aims of Native Education," *Anthropology Report* No.16,1935 and *Papua Annual Report*, 1936-37: 20-2.
40. Winduo, *Cultural Invasion.*
41. Winduo, *Cultural Invasion.*

42. M. Kazim Bacchus, *Education Policy and Development Strategyin the ThirdWorld* (Aldershot, Hants, UK: Avebury Gower Publishing Co Ltd, 1987), 25; cited in Regis Stella, *Imagining the Other,* 09.

43. Winduo, *Cultural Invasion.*

44. Keown, *Pacific Islands Writing,* 111-112.

45. Keown, *Pacific Islands Writing,* 158.

46. M. S. Greicus, "Literature in the University of Papua New Guinea," in *Teaching Literature in Papua New Guinea,* ed. E. Brash and M. Greicus (Port Moresby: University of Papua New Guinea, 1974), 31-34.

47. Greicus, "Literature in the University of Papua New Guinea."

48. Elton Brash, "Creative Writing, Literature and Self-Expression in Papua New Guinea," in *Teaching Literature in Papua New Guinea,* ed. E. Brash and M. Greicus (Port Moresby: University of Papua New Guinea, 1974), 39.

49. The focus was on developing courses with a personal and social relevance for young Papua New Guineans. This all began with Ulli Beier's letter of interests to the foundation Professor of Literature at UPNG, Frank Johnson. Beier's proposal "was based on the principal that the literature course would have to be related in some way to their [Papua New Guineans] own traditions, that the course should be relevant to their lives and their problems and that, rather than overwhelm them with the unattainable greatness of an allegedly 'superior' culture, they should learn to regard the English language as a useful tool, which they could mould in such a way that it could express their own feelings and aspirations." Frank Johnson liked the proposal and offered Beier the position of senior lecturership, which Beier accepted and left Nigeria for Papua New Guinea to begin his mission. See Ulli Beier, *Decolonising the Mind: The Impact of the University on culture and identity in Papua New Guinea, 1971-74,* Canberra: Research School of Pacific and Asian Studies, Australian National University, 2005), 2.

50. Brash, "Creative Writing," 39.

51. Brash, "Creative Writing."

52. Apisai Enos, "Niugini Literature," in *Teaching Literature in Papua New Guinea,* ed. E. Brash and M. Greicus (Port Moresby: University of Papua New Guinea, 1974), 46. Apisai Enos translated Tolai love charms, which was published as *Warbat.* Solomon Islander John Saunana also published his book: *Dragon Tree.* Another example is Arthur Jawodimbari's *The Sun,* which uses a traditional Binandere legend as the frame of the play. These excellent examples of writing have the influence or direct translation of unwritten folklore. Through poetry, plays, and short stories, many Papua New Guineans began to transfer their oral traditions into the written form. The National Performing Troupe, later became the National Theatre, together with the Raun Raun Theatre performed plays written by Papua New Guineans such as Arthur Jawodimbari, John Wills Teloti Kaniku, John Waiko, and John Kasaipwalova.

53. Enos, "Niugini Literature," 46.

54. See Stu Dawrs, "Naked Jazz: Re-historicizing OndoBondo Poster Poems" MA Plan B Paper, University of Hawaii, 2009.

55. Donald Stokes, *Legends from Papua New Guinea: Book Two* (Melbourne: Oxford University Press, 1996).

56. Stokes, *Legends from Papua New Guinea, 1-2.* Some of these stories present moral and ethical codes in poignant and memorable ways. *Papaya,* one of the story shows that beauty is more than skin-deep. *Sun and Sago* is about disobedience and its consequences. *The Children of the Omokey Tribe* teaches the necessity to invite to

traditional functions, all the people who should be invited. *Galo and Vasiri* emphasizes the importance of showing love and respect towards family members. And the *Ant and Lizard* illustrates the destructive force that jealousy plays in a relationship.[5] These young writers heard these stories as they grew up in their villages. In the process of education they moved out of their closed societies into the wider world thereby coming in contact with others from different societies in Papua New Guinea. To negotiate with others they used stories from their own societies to legitimate their cause. They also learned from each other the importance of cultural diversity and multiple explanations of the world.

57. See Steven Edmund Winduo, "Reconstituting Indigenous Oceanic Folktales," *Scholars Space*, Department of English, University of Hawaii online publication, 2010. In this essay I discuss further developments. Outside of the University of Papua New Guinea the *Wantok* newspaper, a Tok Pisin weekly carried a column for legends of Papua New Guinea. This was a popular section of the newspaper. Papua New Guineans contributed legends from their own areas. *New Nation* was another journal that appeared in the 1980s. It also featured traditional legends from Papua New Guinea. At the University of Technology in Lae, Donald Stokes collected stories written by students for the student yearbook called *Nexus*. Between 1970 and 1971, these students contributed their stories for inclusion. Seven years later in 1978, Stokes published a representative of these stories. Barbara Ker Wilson retold these stories in *The Turtle and the Island*. In a later edition published by Oxford University Press, Stokes retitled the collection, *Legends from Papua New Guinea: Book Two* (1996). These stories were written in the years before self-government and Independence in Papua New Guinea.

58. Susan Najita, *Decolonizing Cultures in the Pacific* (New York and Oxford: Routledge, 2008), 19.

59. Silva, *Aloha Betrayed.*

60. See Epeli Hau'ofa, *We Are the Ocean*. See Paul Lyons, *American Pacificism: Oceania in the U.S. Imagination* (New York: London, 2006); see also Vilsoni Hereniko and Rob Wilson, ed., *Inside Out: Literature, Cultural Politics, and Identity in the New Pacific.* (Boulder and New York: Rowman and Littlefield 1999); Keown, *Pacific Islands Writing.* See Stella, *Imagining the Other*; Stewart, Frank, Kareva Mateata-Allain, and Alexander Dale Mawyer, eds., *Varua Tupu: New Writing from French Polynesia* (Honolulu: Manoa: A Pacific Journal of International Writing and University of Hawaii Press, 2006); Rob Wilson, *Reimagining the American Pacific: From South Pacific to Bamboo Ridge and Beyond* (Durham: Duke University Press, 2000); Najita, *Decolonizing Cultures*; Robert Nicole, *The Word, the Pen, and the Pistol: Literature and Power in Tahiti* (New York: State University of New York Press, 2001); Bernard Smith, *European Vision and the South Pacific* (New Haven and London: Yale University Press, 1985 [1960]); Vanessa Smith, *Literary Culture and the Pacific: Nineteenth-Century Textual Encounters* (Cambridge: Cambridge University Press, 1998).

Chapter 2 Literary Culture as Intellectual Capital

1. This part of the chapter was first published as "Literary Culture as Intellectual Capital" in *Savannah Flames: A Papua New Guinean Journal of Literature, Language, and Culture.* Vol.4 (2004). This version is slightly modified.

2. Ernest Gellner, *Nations and Nationalism* (Oxford: Blackwell Publishers, 1983), 8.

3. See E. D. Hirsch, Jr., *Cultural Literacy: What Every Americans Needs to Know* (New York: 1988), 91. Taking cultural traditions and national language too much for granted can lead to loss of national memory. English as a national language has its own history. In America, English was adopted without much conflict of bloodshed as in France, Spain, Britain, and Russia. In America, English grammar, spelling, and pronunciation were normalized in 1776. The American ancient charters, the Declaration of Independence and the Constitution, were written in English, a language that is current more than two hundred years later. The relevance this point has to Papua New Guinea is that English was adopted as an official language, but that it coexists with other national languages of Papua New Guinea. In defining itself as a nation, Papua New Guinea must consider its linguistic and cultural diversity as equal in value and importance.

4. Steven Edmund Winduo, "Classroom Culture and a Showboat," *Times of Papua New Guinea* (26 January 1995).

5. Raymond Williams, *Key Words: A Vocabulary of Culture and Society* (Oxford & New York: Oxford University Press, 1976), 87-93.

6. Walter J. Ong, *Orality and Literacy: The Technologizing of the Word* (London: Routledge, Chapman, and Hall, 1982); David Diringer, *The Alphabet: A Key to the History of Mankind*, 2nd. ed. rev (New York,); Ignace J. Gelb, *A Study of Writing*, rev. ed. (Chicago, 1957).

7. Jack Goody, ed., *Literacy in Traditional Societies* (Cambridge: Cambridge University Press, 1968).

8. Gellner, *Nations and Nationalism*, 8.

9. Mikhail Bakhtin, *The Dialogic Imagination: Four Essays*, ed. Michael Holquist, trans. C. Emerson and Michael Holquist (Austin: University of Texas Press, 1981); James Glifford, *The Predicament of Culture: Twentieth Century Ethnography, Literature, and Art* (Cambridge: Cambridge Universoty Press, 1988).

10. Winduo, "Cultural Invasion," 33.

11. Winduo, "Cultural Invasion," 34.

12. See John Kadiba, "Murray and Education: Some Observations on the Ambivalence of Colonial Education Policy in Papua Before World War II," in *Papua New Guinea: a Century of Colonial Impact 1884-1984*, ed. Sione Latukefu (Port Moresby: National Research Institute, 1989) cited in Winduo, "Cultural Invasion"; F. E. Williams, "The Blending of Cultures: an Essay on Aims of Native Education," *Anthropology Report* 16 (1935); John Stoltz, "The State of Literature Teaching in Papua New Guinea High Schools," in *Teaching Literature in Papua New Guinea*, ed. Elton Brash and M. Greicus (Port Moresby: UPNG, 1972).

13. Peter Smith, "The Education Policy in Australian New Guinea: A Classic Case," in *Papua New Guinea: a Century of Colonial Impact 1884-1984*, ed. Sione Latukefu (Port Moresby: National Research Institute, 1989); M. Carney, *Education and Cultural Imperialism* (New York, 1974).

14. Gerald Graff, *Professing Literature: an Institutional History* (Chicago & London: Chicago University Press, 1987).

15. Paula Gunn Allen, "'Border Studies: The Intersection of Gender and Color," in *Introduction to Scholarship in Modern Languages and Literatures*, ed. Joseph Gibaldi (New York: Modern Language Associations, 1992), 308.

16. Pam Gilbert, "Authorizing Disadvantage: Authorship and Creativity in the Language Classroom," in *Literacy in the Changing World*, ed. Frances Christie (Victoria, 1990),

59-69; R. Gilbelt, *The Impotent Image: Reflections of Ideology in Secondary School Curriculum* (Lewes, Aust., 1984); A. Luke, *Literacy Textbooks and Ideology* (Lewes, Aust., 1988); L. Christian-Smith, "Power, Knowledge and Curriculum: Constructing Femininity in Adolescent Romance Novels," in *Language, Authority and Criticism: Readings on the School Textbooks*, ed. S. DeCastell, A. Luke & C. Luke (Lewes, Aust., 1988).

17. See Slavoj Zizek, "The Specter of Ideology," in *Mapping Ideology*, ed. Salvoj Zizek (New York & London: Verso, 1994), 1.

18. Hirsch Jr., *Cultural Literacy*, 2.

19. Paulo Freire, *Letters to Cristina: Reflections on My Life and Work* (London and New York: Routledge, 1996), 159-60.

20. Freire, *Letters to Cristina*.

21. Hirsch, Jr., *Cultural Literacy*, 126.

22. Freire, *Letters to Cristina*, 159-60.

23. Bakhtin, *The Dialogic Imagination.*

24. Pierre Bourdieu, "Cultural Reproduction and Social Reproduction," in *Knowledge, Education and Cultural Change: Papers in the Sociology of Education* (London) quoted in Pam Gilbert, "Authorizing Disadvantage: Authorship and Creativity in the Language Classroom," in *Literacy in the Changing World*, ed. Frances Christie (Victoria, 1990), 56.

25. Francis Christie and Joan Rothery, "Literacy in the Curriculum: Planning and Assessment," in *Literacy for a Changing World*, ed. Francis Christie (Victoria, 1990), 187; see also G. Boomer, ed., *Negotiating the Curriculum: A Student Teacher Partnership* (Gosford, 1982); B. Gray, "Helping the Children Become Language Learner in the Classroom" in *Aboriginal Perspective on Experience and Learning: The Role of Language in Aboriginal Education* (Geelong, 1985).

26. Naihuwo Ahai and Nicholas Faraclas, *Rights and Expectation in an Age of "Debt Crisis": Literacy and Integral Human Development in Papua New Guinea* (Port Moresby: UPNG Press, 1991); Sakarepe Kamene, "Literacy With/Without Roots?" in *Critical and Developmental Literacy,* ed. Otto Nekitel, Steven Winduo and Sakarepe Kamene (Port Moresby: UPNG Press, 1995), 10-11.

27. This part of the chapter was published as "Writing Our Own Books Means Reading Ourselves," in *Critical and Developmental Literacy*, ed. Otto Nekitel, Steven Winduo, and Sakarepe Kamene (Port Moresby: UPNG Press, 1995), 102-106.

28. Winduo, "Cultural Invasion," 5.

29. Winduo, "Cultural Invasion."

30. Charles Johnson, *Being and Race: Black Writing Since 1970* (Bloomington: Indiana University Press, 1990), 4

31. Winduo, "Cultural Invasion," 70.

32. Winduo, "Cultural Invasion," 71.

33. Winduo, "Cultural Invasion," 99.

34. Winduo, "Cultural Invasion," 99.

35. Russell Soaba, "The Writer's Place in a Difficult Society," in *Critical and Developmental Literacy*, ed. Otto Nekitel, Steven Winduo, and Sakarepe Kamene (Port Moresby: University of Papua New Guinean Press, 1995), 107-112.

36. Soaba, "The Writer's Place."

37. Steven Edmund Winduo, *Lomo'ha I am, In Spirits Voice I Call* (Suva: South Pacific Creative Arts Society, 1991).

38. Regis Stella, "Steven Edmund Winduo, *Lomo'ha I am, In Spirits Voice I Call.*" *SPAN,* 34/35 (1992/93): 360-362.
39. Russell Soaba, *Maiba* (Washington: Three Continents Press, 1985).
40. My poem "Date With Destiny" was written on the wall mural leading to the UPNG Dinning Hall.

Chapter 3 Transitions and Transformations

1. Kumalau Tawali, "Bush Kanak Speaks," in *Lali: An Anthology of Pacific Writing*, ed. Albert Wendt (Auckland: Longman Books, 1980), 183-184.
2. John Kasaipwalova, "Reluctant Flames," in *Lali: An Anthology of Pacific Writing*, ed. Albert Wendt (Auckland: Longman Books, 1980), 178-179.
3. Steven Edmund Winduo, "Dancer," in *Nuanua: South Pacific Writing in English Since 1980*, ed. Albert Wendt (Auckland and Honolulu: University of Auckland and University of Hawaii, 1996), 248.
4. Steven Edmund Winduo, *Hembemba: Rivers of the Forest* (Suva and Port Moresby: Institute of Pacific Studies and the Language and Literature Department, 2000).

Chapter 4 Constructing Indigenous Poetics

1. Allan Natachee, *Aia: Mekeo Songs* (Port Moresby: Papua Pocket Poets, 1965). Natachee's collection *Aia* is the first of the Ulli Beier edited Papua Pocket Poet series. Beier talks more about his meeting with Alan Natachee, who was born as Avaisa Pinongo and brought up in a Catholic nuns' convent at the age of five. Natachee was inspired to write poetry after reading a piece by Lord Tennyson in 1935. See Ulli Beier, "'Cautiously Advance Atomic Age'—The Papuan 'Poet Laureate'," *Decolonising the Mind: The Impact of the University on Culture and Identity in Papua New Guinea, 1971-74* (Canberra: Pandanus Books: Research School of Pacific and Asian Studies, The Australian National University, 2005), 12-19.
2. Natachee. *Aia: Mekeo Songs.*
3. Natachee. *Aia: Mekeo Songs.*
4. Natachee. *Aia: Mekeo Songs.*
5. Natachee. *Aia: Mekeo Songs.*
6. Kirpal Singh, "PNG Writing in English: Problems and Prospects," *Bikmaus* (Port Moresby: Institute of Papua New Guinea Studies, 1983): 18-19.
7. Beier, *Decolonising the Mind*, 18.
8. Kumalau Tawali, *Signs in the Sky* (Port Moresby: Papua Pocket Poets, 1970).
9. Kalyan Chatterjee, "Papua New Guinean Literature: Innocence and Self-Knowledge," *Pacific Writers: A South Pacific Communication Journal*, 14:1 (1993): 31.
10. Kumalau Tawali. *Tribesman's Heart Beat* (Madang: Kristen Press, 1978).
11. Tawali, *Tribesman's Heart Beat*, 1.
12. Tawali, *Tribesman's Heart Beat.*
13. Tawali *Tribesman's Heart Beat.*
14. Tawali *Tribesman's Heart Beat.*
15. Tawali, "Busk Kanaka Speaks," in *Lali: A Pacific Anthology*, ed. Albert Wendt (Auckland: Longman Paul, 1980), 183-184.
16. Tawali *Tribesman's Heart Beat*, 2.
17. John Kasaipwalova, "Reluctant Flame," in *Lali: A Pacific Anthology*, ed. Albert Wendt (Auckland: Longman Paul, 1980), 176-182.

18. Tawali, *Tribesman's Heart Beat*, 3.
19. Tawali, *Tribesman's Heart Beat*, 5.
20. Tawali, *Tribesman's Heart Beat*, 12-13.
21. Tawali, *Tribesman's Heart Beat*, 20-22.
22. Tawali, *Tribesman's Heart Beat*, 40-41.
23. Paschal Waisi, *Weli Nimou* (Canberra: ANU, 1985).
24. Paschal Waisi, "The Laufis World View: An Attempt to Locate its Metaphysical Base" (BA. Honours, dissertation, University of Papua New Guinea, 1982).
25. Waisi, *Weli Nimou.*
26. Waisi, "The Laufis World View."
27. Waisi, "Lau'um Pingis (Epistemology)," *Reframing Indigenous Knowledge: Cultural Knowledge and Practices in Papua New Guinea.*ed. Steven Edmund Winduo (Port Moresby: Melanesian and Pacific Studies, 2009), 27-38; see also Paschal Waisi, *Looking Through Ancestors' Eye-holes* (Port Moresby: UPNG Press and Bookshop, 2010).
28. Waisi, *Weli Nimou,* 8-9.
29. Waisi, *Weli Nimou.*
30. Waisi, *Weli Nimou.*
31. Waisi, *Weli Nimou.*
32. Waisi, *Weli Nimou.*
33. Waisi, *Weli Nimou.*
34. Waisi, *Weli Nimou.*
35. Waisi, *Weli Nimou.*
36. Subramani, *South Pacific Literature: From Myth to Fabulation* (Suva: Institute of Pacific Studies, 1985).
37. Russell Soaba. *Kwamra: A Season of Harvest* (Port Moresby: Anuki Country Press, 2000).
38. Russell Soaba. *Maiba: A Papuan Novel* (Washington, DC.: Three Continents Press, 1985).
39. Soaba, *Kwamra*, vii.
40. Soaba, *Kwamra.*
41. Soaba, *Kwamra.*
42. Soaba, *Kwamra.*
43. Soaba, *Kwamra.*
44. Soaba, *Kwamra.*

Chapter 5 Creative Spirit and Political Energy

1. Antonio Gramsci, *Selections from Political Writings, 1921-1926*, trans. & ed. Quintin Hoare (Minneapolis: University of Minnesota Press, 1990).
2. Beier, *Decolonizing the Mind.*
3. Ngugi wa Thiong'o, *Decolonizing the Mind: The Politics of Language in African Literature (*London: James Currey, 1986).
4. Beier, *Decolonizing the Mind.*
5. Albert Maori Kiki, *Kiki: Ten Thousand Years in a Lifetime: A New Guinea Autobiography* (Melbourne: Cheshire, 1968).

6. Michael Somare, *Sana* (Port Moresby: Niugini Press Pty Ltd, 1975). (Somare served as PNG prime minister from Independence in 1975, until 1980; from 1982 until 1985, and from 2002 to 2011]).
7. Beier, *Decolonizing the Mind,* 12-19
8. Beier, *Decolonizing the Mind.*
9. Beier, *Decolonizing the Mind.*
10. Brash, "The Place of Literature," 36-7.
11. Brash, "The Place of Literature."
12. Brash, "The Place of Literature."
13. Beier, *Decolonizing the Mind.*
14. Subramani, "The Oceanic Imaginary," *SPAN* 48/49 (April& October 1999): 1-13.
15. Ken Goodwin, "Invective and Obliqueness in Political Poetry: Kasaipwalova, Brathwaite and Soyinka," in *Awakened Conscience: Studies in Commonwealth Literature*, ed. C. D. Narasimharah (New Delhi: Sterling Publishers, 1978), 251.
16. Albert Wendt. *Nuanua: Pacific Writing in English since 1980* (Auckland and Honolulu: Auckland University Press and University of Hawaii Press, 1995), 4.
17. Chatterjee, "Papua New Guinean Literature," 6.
18. Bernard Narokobi, "Melanesian Way," *Through Melanesian Eyes: An Anthology of Contemporary Papua New Guinean Writing*, comp. Ganga Powell (Melbourne: Macmillan, 1987), 155-156.
19. Narokobi, "Melanesian Way."
20. Bruce Knauft, "The Melanesian Warfare: a Theoretical History," *Oceania* 60, no. 4 (1990): 251.
21. Beavers (1920) quoted in Bruce Knauft, "The Melanesian Warfare: a Theoretical History," *Oceania* 60, no.4 (1990): 251.
22. Gayatri Chakravarti Spivak, "Subaltern Studies: Deconstructing Historiography," *Other Worlds: Essays in Cultural Politics* (New York: Routledge, 1988), 203.
23. Bernard Minol, "The Melanesian Way?" *Through Melanesian Eyes: An Anthology of Papua New Guinean Writing*, comp. Ganga Powell (Melbourne: Macmillan, 1987), 164.
24. Spivak, "Subaltern Studies," 203.
25. Amilal Cabral, *Revolution in Guinea: Unity and Struggle: Speeches and Writings* (London: Heineman, 1980), 62.
26. Ngugi wa Thiong'o, *Decolonising the Mind,* 16.
27. Ngugi wa Thiong'o, *Decolonising the Mind.*
28. Emmanuel Ngara, *Art and Ideology in the African Novel: a Study of the Influence of Marxism on African Writing* (London: Heineman, 1985), 26.
29. Louis Althusser, "Theory, Theoretical Practice and Theoretical Formation: Ideology and Struggle" *Althusser: The Detour of Theory*, Gregory Elliott (London: Verso, 1987), 29.
30. Ian C. Campbell, *A History of the Pacific Islands* (Christchurch: University of Canterbury, 1989).
31. Althusser, "Theory, Theoretical Practice."
32. Althusser, "Theory, Theoretical Practice."
33. Althusser, "Theory, Theoretical Practice."
34. Althusser, "Theory, Theoretical Practice."
35. Althusser, "Theory, Theoretical Practice."
36. Ngara, *Art and Ideology in the African Novel.*

37. Waiko, "The Place of Literature ," 5.
38. Waiko, "The Place of Literature."
39. Ngugi wa Thiong'o, *Decolonising the Mind.*
40. Ngugi wa Thiong'o, *Decolonising the Mind.*
41. gugi wa Thiong'o, *Decolonising the Mind.*
42. Stella, "Reluctant Voyages,"222.

Chapter 6 Double Conscience Without the Instrument to Liberate

1. Brash, "Creative Writing," 35-42.
2. Waiko, "The Place of Literature,"4-6.
3. Otto Nekitel, "What is Happening to Our Vernaculars?" *Bikmaus* 2: 2 (June 1984): 89-98.
4. Steven Edmund Winduo, "Rethinking the 'Melanesian Way' as Ideology and Nationalism: A Literary Perspective," *Yagl-Ambu*, 17: 3 (1994): 50-61.
5. Waiko, "The Place of Literature."
6. Nash Sorariba, *A Medal Without Honour* (Port Moresby: University of Papua New Guinea Press, 1997).
7. Sakarepe Kamene, "Literacy With/Without Roots," in *Critical and Developmental Literacy*, ed. Otto Nekitel, Sakarepe Kamene and Steven Winduo (Port Moresby: University of Papua New Guinea Press, 1995), 79-93.
8. Kakah Kais and Bernard Minol, *Pokop of Pohyomou* (Port Moresby: University of Papua New Guinea Press, 1996).
9. Ken Goodwin, "Is a Commonwealth Literary History Possible?" *SPAN* 21 (October 1985), 9-28.
10. Steven Edmund Winduo, "Introduction" *A Medal Without Honour* (Port Moresby: University of Papua New Guinea, 1997), vi-vii.
11. Kilage, "An Interview," 67.
12. Russell Soaba, *Wanpis* (Port Moresby: Institute of Papua New Guinea Studies, 1978); Steven Edmund Winduo, *Lomo'ha I am in Spirit's Voice I Call* (Suva: South Pacific Creative Arts Society, 1990).
13. Sorariba, *A Medal Without Honour.*
14. Sorariba, *A Medal Without Honour.*
15. Bernard S. Minol, "The Cultural and Historical Background to PNG Fiction: Mythmaking, truth Telling and Maus Wara," Ph.D Dissertation, University of Queensland, 1987.
16. Sorariba, *A Medal Without Honour.*
17. Sorariba, *A Medal Without Honour.*
18. Sorariba, *A Medal Without Honour.*
19. Sorariba, *A Medal Without Honour.*
20. Sorariba, *A Medal Without Honour.*
21. Edward Said, *Orientalism* (New York: Vintage, 1978).
22. Said, *Orientalism.*
23. Ignatius Kilage, *My Mother Calls Me Yaltep* (Melbourne: Oxford University Press, 1980); Michael Yake Mel and Toby Kagl Waim, *Two Highland Novels* (Port Moresby: Institute of Papua New Guinea Studies, 1984); Russell Soaba, *Maiba* (Washington: Three Continents Press, 1985); Joseph Aguang, *The Sorcerers* (Port Moresby: Institute

of Papua New Guinea Studies, 1992); Michael Yake Mell, *The Call of the Land* (Port Moresby: Institute of Papua New Guinea Studies, 1994).

24. See Russell Soaba, "The Writer's Place in a Difficult Society", *Critical and Developmental Literacy*, ed. Otto Nekitel, Sakarepe Kamene and Steven Edmund Winduo (Port Moresby: University of Papua New Guinea Press, 1995), 107-112; Steven Edmund Winduo, "Writing Our Own Books Means Reading Ourselves", in *Critical and Developmental Literacy*, ed. Otto Nekitel, Sakarepe Kamene and Steven Edmund Winduo (Port Moresby: University of Papua New Guinea Press, 1995), 102-106.

25. Regis Stella, comp., *Moments in Melanesia* (Melbourne: Oxford University Press, 1992).

26. Stuart Watson, ed., *Lost in Jungle Ways* (Melbourne: Dellasta Pasifika, 1994)

27. Benedict Anderson, *Imagined Community* (New York: Verso, 1983), 6.

28. Frantz Fanon, *Black Skin White Mask* (London: Penguin Book, 1967), 94.

29. Ron Crocombe, "Book Distribution in the Pacific Islands," in *The Written Word: Writing, Publishing and Information in the Pacific Islands* (Suva: Institute of Pacific Studies, 1985), 29-30.

30. See Gill Gorle, "Writing in English or Frustration? Some Views From Papua New Guinea," Kunapipi *Journal of Postcolonial Writing,* 15: 2 (1993): 128-132; Gorle, "The Theme of Social Change in the Literature of Papua New Guinea, 1969-1979," *Pacific Studies*, 18: 2 (1995): 79-113; Paul Sharrad, "A Map of PNG Stories in English," *Bikmaus*, 5: 2(1984): 1-16.

31. Chatterjee, "Papua New Guinea Literature," 6.

32. Susan Simmons, "Creating Faces of the Age." A paper presented at the 17th Waigani Seminar, University of Papua New Guinea, September 1988.

33. Chatterjee, "Papua New Guinea Literature," 6.

34. Chatterjee, "Papua New Guinea Literature."

35. Bernard Narokobi, *The Melanesian Way,* Port Moresby, IPNGS, (1980), iv.

36. Narokobi, *The Melanesian Way,* iv

37. Julian Maaka, *The Confession and Other Stories* (Suva: The University of the South Pacific, 1985); Simmons, "Creating Faces of the Age."

38. Bill Ashcroft, "The Influence of Oral Traditions on PNG Writing." A paper presented at the 17th Waigani Seminar, University of Papua New Guinea, September, 1988.

39. Ashcroft, "The Influence of Oral Traditions on PNG Writing."

Chapter 7 Listen My Country

1. Adeola James, comp., *PNG Women Writers: An Anthology* (Sydney: Pearson Educational Australia,1996), 2.

2. James, *PNG Women Writers*, 1.

3. Gayum Kuman cited in Adeola James. comp., *PNG Women Writers: An Anthology* (Sydney: Pearson Educational Australia, 1996), 1.

4. James, *PNG Women Writers,* 1.

5. Kapa Darius Kelep-Malpo, *Gender Equality at the Workplace* (Goroka: Kim Printing 2009), 22.

6. Malpo, *Gender Equality,* 5.

7. AnnTurner, *Views from Interviews: The Changing Role of Women* (Melbourne: Oxford University Press, 1993); also cited in the Malpo, *Gender Equity,*59.

8. Nora Vagi Brash, *PNG Women Writers: An Anthology*, comp. Adeola James (Sydney: Pearson Educational Australia, 1996), 18.
9. Brash. *PNG Women Writers,* 18.
10. Brash. *PNG Women Writers*, 23.
11. Brash. *PNG Women Writers.*
12. Brash. *PNG Women Writers.*
13. Brash. *PNG Women Writers.*
14. Loujaya Dunar, *PNG Women Writers: An Anthology.* Comp. Adeola James (Sydney: Pearson Educational Australia, 1996), 231.
15. Mary Toliman, *PNG Women Writers: An Anthology.* Comp. Adeola James (Sydney: Pearson Educational Australia, 1996), 282.
16. Brash, *PNG Women Writers,* 19.
17. Josephine Abaijah, *PNG Women Writers: An Anthology.* Comp. Adeola James (Sydney: Pearson Educational Australia, 1996), 2.
18. Abaijah, *PNG Women Writers,* 5.
19. Abaijah, *PNG Women Writers,* 24-25.
20. Abaijah, *PNG Women Writers,* 8.
21. Toliman, *PNG Women Writers,* 283.
22. Dunar, *PNG Women Writers,* 227.
23. Joyce Kumbeli, *PNG Women Writers: An Anthology.* comp. Adeola James (Sydney: Pearson Educational Australia, 1996), 124.
24. Brash, *PNG Women Writers,* 18.
25. Toliman, *PNG Women Writers,* 275.
26. Dunar (Kouza), *PNG Women Writers,* 221.
27. Eric Johns, *PNG History Through Stories: Book One* (Sydney: Pearson Longman, 2004).
28. Alice Wadega, *Listen My Country* (Sydney: Pacific Publications, 1981).
29. Gayatri Spivak,"Can the Subaltern Speak?" in *Colonial Discourse and Postcolonial Theory: A Reader,* ed., Patrick Williams and Laure (New York: Columbia UniversityPress, 1994), 66-111.
30. Tony Deklin, "In Search of a Home-Grown Constitution: The Constitutional Development in Papua New Guinea Between 1962 and 1975," in *Papua New Guinea: A Century of Colonial Impact 1884-1984,* ed.Sione Latukefu (Port Moresby: The National Research Institute and the University of Papua New Guinea in association with the PNG Centennial Committee, 1989), 399-417; Anne Kaniku, "Those Massim Women," in *Papua New Guinea: A Century of Colonial Impact 1884-1984,* ed.Sione Latukefu (Port Moresby: The National Research Institute and the University of Papua New Guinea in association with the PNG Centennial Committee, 1989), 369-376.
31. Deklin, "In Search of a Home-Grown Constitution."
32. Erick Johns, *PNG History Through Stories: Book Two* (Sydney: Pearson Longman, 2006), 133-137.
33. Johns, *PNG History Through Stories.*
34. Johns, *PNG History Through Stories.*
35. Johns, *PNG History Through Storie.*
36. Carol Kidu, *A Remarkable Journey.* Port Moresby: Longman, 2002.

1. Though the term intertextuality covers a broader range of theories and applications, it is used here with variations to Kristeva's original notion as espounded in her work "Word and dialogue and novel" or "Problems de la structuration du texte. See Judith Still and Michael Worton, "Introduction,' *Intertextuality: Theory and Practices,* ed. Michael Worton and Judith Still (Manchestor and New York: Manchestor University Press, 1990),16

2. Chatterjee, "Papua New Guinean Literature," 6.

3. Norman Simms, "Towards an Assessment of Maori and Pacific Writing in New Zealand," *Pacific Writing and Publishing: A South Pacific Communication Journal,* 14: 1 (1985): 86.

4. Simms, "Towards an Assessment."

5. Subramani, *South Pacific Literature,* 2.

6. Mikail Bakhtin, *The Dialogic Imagination,* trans. Caryl Emerson and Michael Holquist, ed. Michael Holquist (Austin: Unversity of Texas Press, 1981), 262.

7. Bakhtin, *The Dialogic Imagination,* 263.

8. Bakhtin, *The Dialogic Imagination.*

9. Bakhtin, *The Dialogic Imagination.*

10. Bakhtin, *The Dialogic Imagination.*

11. Kiki, *Kiki.*

12. Goodwin, "Invective and Obliqueness ," 251.

13. Goodwin, "Invective and Obliqueness."

14. Bill Ashcroft, Gareth Griffiths, and Helen Tiffin, *The Empire Writes Back: Theory and Practice in Post-Colonial Literature* (New York: Routledge, 1989), 251.

15. Soaba's article found in the Institute of Papua New Guinean Studies archives. Unpublished manuscript written at the time when Soaba was employed with the Institue of Papua New Guinea Studies.

16. Pierre Machery, *A Theory of Literary Production* (London and New York: Routledge and Kegan Paul, 1986), 9.

17. Francoise Lionnet, *Autobiographical Voices, Race, Gender, Self-Portraiture* (Ithaca and London: Cornell University Press, 1989), 5.

18. Roy Pascal, *Design and Truth in Autobiography* (Cambridge, Mass.: Harvard University Press 1960). Heidi Stull deal specifically with the origin and development of the autobiographical tradition. See Heidi I Stull, *The Evolution of the Autobiography from 1770-1850: A Comparative Study and Analysis* (New York: Bern, Frankfurt am Main: Peter Laing, 1985).

19. Ken Hirschkop, *Bakhtin and Cultural Theory,* ed. Ken Hirschkop and David Shepherd (Manchester and New York: Manchester University Press, 1989), 7.

20. Pascal, *The Evolution of the Autobiography.*

21. Pascal, *The Evolution of the Autobiography* and Stull. *The Evolution of the Autobiography.*

22. See also Stull, *The Evolution of the Autobiography;* Elizabeth W. Bruss, *Autobiographical Acts: The Changing Situation of a Literary Genre* (Baltimore: Johns Hopkins University Press, 1976); James Olney, *Metaphor of Self: the Meaning of Autobiography* (New Jersey: Princeton University Press, 1972), and Lionnet, *Autobiographical Voices.*

23. Nigel Krauth, "Russell Soaba's Latest Work: An Investigation into Accidents Along the Road to Papua New Guinea's Indpendence,' *ACLALS Bulletin* (January 1979): 40.

24. Chatterjee, "Papua New Guinean Literature," 7.

25. Benjamin Umba, August Kituai, and Jim Baital. *Three Short Novels from Papua New Guinea*, ed., Mike Greicus (Auckland: Longman Paul Limited, 1976).

26. Michael Yake Mell and Toby Kagl Waim, *Two Highlands Novel from Papua New Guinea* (Port Moresby: Institute of Papua New Guinea Studies, 1985).

27. See Benjamin Umba, "Fires of Dawn," in *Three Short Novels from Papua New Guinea*, ed. Mike Greicus (Auckland: Longman Paul Limited, 1976), 1-36; August Kituai, "The Flight of a Villager," in *Three Short Novels from Papua New Guinea*, ed. Mike Greicus (Auckland: Longman Paul Limited, 1976), 37-86; Jim Baital, "Tali," in *Three Short Novels from Papua New Guinea*, ed. Mike Greicus (Auckland: Longman Paul Limited, 1976), 87-140; Michael Yake Mell, "Kumdi Bagre," in *Two Highlands Novels from Papua New Guinea* (Port Moresby: Institute of Papua New Guinea Studies, 1985), 3-53; Toby Waim Kagl, "Kallan," in *Two Highlands Novel* (Port Moresby: Institute of Papua New Guinea Studies, 1985), 54-119.

28. Kituai, "The Flight of a Villager."

29. Baital, "Tali."

30. Mell, "Kumdi Bagre," 3-53.

31. Kagl, "Kallan," 54-119; see also Margaret Menning, *Hagen Saga* (Port Moresby: Institute of Papua New Guinea Studies, 1982)

32. Umba, "Fires of Dawn."

33. Umba, "Fires of Dawn."

34. Umba, "Fires of Dawn."

35. Umba, "Fires of Dawn."

36. Kituai, "The Flight of a Villager."

37. Kituai, "The Flight of a Villager."

38. Mell, "Kumdi Bagre."

39. Mell, "Kumdi Bagre."

Chapter 9 Writing the Political Unconscious

1. Albert Maori Kiki, *Kiki: Ten Thousand Years in a Lifetime* (Melbourne, Chershire, 1968).

2. Kiki, *Kiki,* 6-7

3. Kiki, *Kiki, 21-34.*

4. Kiki, *Kiki, 22*

5. Kiki, *Kiki, 35.*

6. Kiki, *Kiki, 55-6.*

7. Kiki, *Kiki, 56-7.*

8. Kiki, *Kiki, 130-31.*

9. Kiki, *Kiki, 68-9.*

10. Kiki, *Kiki, 148.*

11. Kiki, *Kiki.*

12. Kiki, *Kiki, 154*

13. Kiki, *Kiki, 155-56.*

14. Kiki, *Kiki, 186.*

15. Kiki, *Kiki.*

16. Francoise, *Autobiographical Voices,"* 92.
17. Francoise, *Autobiographical Voices.*
18. Stull, *The Evolution of Autobiography,*42.
19. Stull, *The Evolution of Autobiography,* 42.
20. Ulli Beier, "Preface" in Albert Maori Kiki, *Kiki: Ten Thousand Years in a Lifetime* (Melbourne, Chershire, 1968), 1-4
21. See back cover Kiki, *Kiki: Ten Thousand Years in a Lifetime.*
22. Kiki, *Kiki,* 183.
23. Kiki, *Kiki,* 183.
24. Pascal, *Design and Truth,* 53-67.
25. Pascal, *Design and Truth,* 59.
26. Pascal, *Design and Truth.*
27. Pascal, *Design and Truth.*
28. Stull, *The Evolution of Autobiography,* 12.
29. Beier, "Preface," 3.
30. Kiki, *Kiki.*
31. Beier, *Decolonizing the Mind,* 26-27.
32. Kiki, *Kiki,* 54.
33. Michael Somare, *Sana: an Autobiography* (Port Moresby: Niugini Press, 1975).

Chapter 10 Colonialism to Cultural Fragmentation

1. Vincent Eri, *The Crocodile* (Auckland: Longman Paul, 1971).
2. Beier, *Decolonizing the Mind,* 53.
3. Beier, *Decolonizing the Mind,* 53-4.
4. Nigel Krauth, "Towards a Balanced Approach in the Study of Papua New Guinean Literature," in *Teaching Literature in Papua New Guinea,* ed., E. Brash and M. Greicus (Port Moresby: University of Papua New Guinea, 1972), 49.
5. Eri maintained in a public lecture given at the University of Papua New Guinea in 1990 that he is primarily a teacher of his people. His novel is basically about the rituals and customs of his people. It is not odd for Eri to see himself as a teacher as other writers of the colonised societies have done so. Chinua Achebe, the Nigerian author, for example, successfully taught the world about the ethos, values, and dynamic aspects of his society, one which scholars of Achebe have claimed as progressing "in a linear manner and set in an historical framework that reveals the persistence of cultural continuity despite internal and external threats to the society," in Richard K. Priebe, *Myth, Realism and the West African Writers* (New Jersey: Africa World Press, 1988), 47.
6. Eri, *The Crocodile,* 72.
7. Eri, *The Crocodile.*
8. Eri, *The Crocodile,* 75
9. Eri, *The Crocodile, 94.*
10. Eri, *The Crocodile, 31.*
11. Krauth, "Towards a Balanced Approach," 51.
12. Frances Delvin Glass, "Between Two Cultures: Interpreting V. Eri's *The Crocodile,"* in *Language and Literature in Multicultural Contexts; ACLALS Fifth Triennial Conference Proceedings,* ed. Satendra Nandan (Suva: University of South Pacific, 1983), 135.
13. Krauth, "Towards a Balanced Approach," 52.

14. Krauth, "Towards a Balanced Approach."
15. Krauth, "Towards a Balanced Approach."
16. Krauth, "Towards a Balanced Approach."
17. Krauth, "Towards a Balanced Approach."
18. Krauth, "Towards a Balanced Approach."
19. Bakhtin, *The Dialogic Imagination,* 132.
20. Eri, *The Crocodile*, 112-3.
21. Bill Ashcroft, Gareth Griffiths, and Helen Tiffin, *The Empire Writes Back*, 82.
22. Eri, *The Crocodile,* 140.
23. Ashcroft. et al., *The Empire Writes Back,* 87.
24. Ashcroft. et al., *The Empire Writes Back,* 82.
25. Ashcroft. et al., *The Empire Writes Back.*

Chapter 11 Wanpis Existentialism

1. Russell Soaba, *Wanpis* (Port Moresby: Institute of Papua New Guinea Studies, 1977).
2. Krauth, "Russell Soaba's Latest Work," 40.
3. Russell Soaba, "An Interview with Russell Soaba" Interview by Chris Tiffin, *SPAN* No. 8. (April, 1979): 15-30.
4. Krauth, "Russell Soaba's Latest Work."
5. Russell Soaba, "Albert Wendt: Pacific's Existential Writer," *Ondobondo*, 3 (1983): 37-41; See also Zak Tiamon, "Russell Soaba's *Wanpis,*" *Ondobondo*, 2, (Mid-1983): 29.
6. Donald Gutierrez, *The Dark and Light Gods: Essays on the Self in Modern Literature* (Troy, New York: The Whitson Publishing Company, 1987), 5.
7. Russell Soaba, "Scattered by the Wind," *Kovave,* 4. No. 1. (November, 1972): 30-42 and "A Portrait of the Odd Man Out," in *Lali: A Pacific Anthology*, ed. Albert Wendt, (Auckland: Longman Paul, 1980), 168-176.
8. Nigel Krauth, "Unfolding Like Petals": The Developing Definition of the Writer's Role in Modern Papua New Guinean Literature," *ACLALS Bulletin* 5, No. 1. (July, 1978): 2.
9. Krauth, "Russell Soaba's Latest Work," 40.
10. Soaba, *Wanpis*, 7.
11. Gutierrez, *The Dark and Light*, 23.
12. Soaba, *Wanpis*, 170.
13. Soaba, *Wanpis*, 104.
14. Soaba, W*anpis*, 105.
15. Soaba, "Albert Wendt," 29.
16. Soaba, *Wanpis*, 56-7.
17. Soaba, "An Interview with Russell Soaba," 22.
18. Soaba, *Wanpis*, 119.
19. Soaba, "An Interview with Russell Soaba," 21.
20. Gayatri Spivak, *Post-Colonial Critic: Interviews, Strategies and Dialogues: Gayatri Chakravorty Spivak*, ed. Sarah Harasym (London and New York: Routledge, 1991), 2.
21. Soaba, *Wanpis*, 113.

1. Paulias Matane, *Aimbe, the Pastor* (New York: Exposition Press, 1979). Later reprinted as *Ripples in the South Pacific Ocean: A Historical Novel Portraying the Dawn of Civilization in Papua New Guinea* (New Delhi: CBS Publishers and Distributors, 2003).
2. The titles in Matane's Aimbe series are *Aimbe the Challenger, Aimbe the Magician, Aimbe the School Dropout,* and *Aimbe the Pastor.*
3. From here onward I will use *Aimbe, the Pastor* or *Ripples* interchangeably to refer to the same title considered in this chapter.
4. Matane, *Aimbe, the Pastor*, 49.
5. See Peter Hempenstall from Vorstand Neuginea to deputation, 29 August 1904, RMG Conferenz Protokolle; see also Jahresbericht 1903, RMG Statinsberichte Siar; Vorstand ssitzzung 27 August 1904, RMG Conferenz Protokolle; Flierl to Mission-Inspeckto, 10 December 1904, NH Flierl Brief, see Peter Hempenstall, "The Neglected Empire: The Superstucture of Colonial State in German Melanesia," in *Papua New Guinea: a Century of Colonial Impact 1884-1984*, ed. Sione Latukefu (Port Moresby: The National Research Institute and University of Papua New Guinea, 1989), 158.
6. Hempenstall, "The Neglected Empire," 158.
7. Hempenstall, "The Neglected Empire."
8. Hempenstall, "The Neglected Empire."
9. Frantz Fanon, *Black Skin White Masks*, trans. Charles Lam Markman (New York: Grove press, 1967). See also *The Wretched of the Earth*, trans. Constance Farrington (Harmondsworth: Penguin, 1966); *A Dying Colonialism*, trans. C. Haakon Chevalier (New York: Grove Press, 1967), and Paulo Freire, *Pedagogy of the Oppressed* (Harmondsworth: Penguin Books, 1972) and wa Thiongo, *Decolonising the Mind.*
10. Matane, *Aimbe, the Pastor*, 177.
11. Malcolm Scott, *The Struggle for the Soul of the French Novel, French Catholic and Realist Novelists, 1850-1970* (Washington: The Catholic University of America Press, 1990), 27.
12. Matane, *Aimbe, the Pastor*.

Chapter 13 Fictionalizing the Contact Experience

1. Garry Trompf, "Doesn't Colonialism Make You Mad? The So Called "Mur Madness" as an Index for the Study of New Religious in Papua New Guinea During the Colonial Period," in *Papua New Guinea: A Century of Colonial Impact (1884-1984),* ed. Sione Latukefu (Port Moresby: National Research Institute and University of Papua New Guinea, 1989), 256.
2. Ignatius Kilage, *My Mother Calls Me Yaltep* (Port Moresby: Institute of Papua New Guinean Studies, 1980) later republished as Ignatius Kilage, *My Mother Calls Me Yaltep* (Melbourne: Oxford University Press, 1984). Subsequent endnotes will use this edition.
3. Kilage, *My Mother Calls Me Yaltep*, 116.
4. Kilage, *My Mother Calls Me Yaltep,* 19-20.
5. Kilage, *My Mother Calls Me Yaltep*, 62.
6. Kilage, *My Mother Calls Me Yaltep*.

7. Ronald Blaber, "This Piece of Earth: V.S. Naipaul's *A Bend in the River,"* in *A Sense of Place in the New Literatures in English,* ed. M.H. Nightingale (St. Lucia: Queensland University Press, 1986), 62.

8. Kilage, *My Mother Calls Me Yaltep,* 4.

9. Kilage, *My Mother Calls Me Yaltep,* 49.

10. Kilage, *My Mother Calls Me Yaltep.*

11. Kilage, *My Mother Calls Me Yaltep,* 64.

12. Kilage, *My Mother Calls Me Yaltep,* 49.

13. Trompt, "Doesn't Colonialism Make You Mad," 263.

14. Wolfgang Iser, "Fictionalizing: The Anthropological Dimension of Literary Fiction," *New Literary History, A Journal of Theory and Interpretation, Papers from the Commonwealth Centre for Literary and Cultural Change,* 21. No. 4. (Autumn 1990): 994.

Chapter 14 Oral History to Folk Opera

1. Kirsty Powell, "The First PNGA Playwrights and their Plays", (Ph.D dissertation, University of Papua New Guinea, 1976); Ken Goodwin, "Invective and Obliqueness," 251.

2. Kumalau Tawali, *Manki Masta* (QLD: Jacaranda Press, 1971), Arthur Jawodimbari, "The Sun," *Kovave* 2 (1) (November 1970); John Waiko, "The Unexpected Hawk,"in *Five New Guinea Plays,* ed., Ulli Beier (Milton,QLD: Jacaranda Press, 1971), 20-32; Leo Hannet, "The Ungrateful Daughter," *Kovave,* November 1970.

3. Greg Murphy, *Niugini Niugini* (Port Moresby; Education Department, 1985).

4. Peter Trist,"Living Legends, Dying Stages," *Meanjin* on PNG, ed. Drusilla Modjeska 62: 3 (2003): 115-134.

5. Murphy, *Niugini.*

6. Murphy, *Niugini.*

7. John Kasaipwalova, *Sail The Midnight Sun* (Port Moresby: Credit Melanesia, 1980).

8. Murphy, *Niugini.*

9. Regis Stella, *Tempers Unchained: The Politics and Meaning of Pre-Independence Drama,* MA Thesis (University of Wollongong, Australia, 1992).

10. William Takaku, "Living Legends, Dying Stages," *Meanjin* on PNG, ed. Drusilla Modjeska 62: 3 (2003): 119.

11. Duadua Theatre performed "Boy From the Sea" in Port Moresby. See William Ferea's review in *Ondobondo,* 5(1985): 28. The National Theatre Company performed "Ba Oro" and "Dreams of Melanesia" at the University Open air theatre in 1984 and 1987. N.T.C. performed "Eberia" for 1980 South Pacific Festival of Arts. "Ba Oro's review could also be located in *Ondobondo* 6 (1985): 27. The North Solomons Travelling Theatre performed a legend called *Matanasil* in 1986 at the University and also around the country in the same year.

12. Nora Vagi Brash, *Taurama,* (Port Moresby: Owl Books, 1985); see also Nora Vagi Brash, *Which Way, Big Man? and Five Other Plays* (Port Moresby and Melbourne: Oxford University Press, 1996).

13. See Ann Turner, "Nora Vagi Brash," in *Views from Interviews: The Changing Role of Women in Papua New Guinea* (Melbourne: Oxford University Press, 1993), 40-41.

14. Nigel Oram, "The History of the Motu-speaking and the Koita-speaking Peoples according to their own Traditions," in *Oral Tradition in Melanesia,* ed., Donald Denoon

and Roderic Lacy (Port Moresby: The University of Papua New Guinea and The Institute of Papua New Guinea Studies, 1981), 210.

15. Oram, "The History of the Motu," 211
16. Oram, "The History of the Motu."
17. Turner, "Nora Vagi Brash," 40-41.
18. Nora Brash, *Taurama.*
19. Nora Brash, *Taurama.*
20. Nora Brash, *Taurama.*
21. Nora Brash, *Taurama.*
22. Nora Vagi Brash's other plays are included in *Which Way Big Man* "The High Cost of Living Differently," "Which Way, Big Man?" "Black Market Buai," "Pick the Bone Dry," and "City Spirit," See Nora Vagi Brash. *Which Way, Big Man? And Five Other Plays* (Port Moresby and Melbourne: Oxford University Press, 1996).
23. Oram, "The History of theMotu," 227-228.
24. Benedict Anderson. *Imagined Communities* (New York: Verso, 1983), 6.
25. Anderson, *Imagined Communities,* 6.
26. Anderson, *Imagined Communities,*7.
27. Anderson, *Imagined Communities.*
28. Anderson, *Imagined Communities.*
29. Josephine Abaijah, *A Thousand Coloured Dreams: The Story of a Young Girl Growing Up in Papua* (Melbourne: Dellasta, 1991), 290.
30. Bob McKillop, "Papua Besena and Papuan Separatism," in *Micornationalist Movements in Papua New Guinea,* ed., R. J. May (Canberra: Department of Political Science, Research Schoolof PacificStudies, ANU, 1982), 300.
31. Turner, "Nora Vagi Brash," 39.
32. Bill Ashcroft, *Post-Colonial Transformations* (London and New York: Routledge, 2001), 107-108.

Chapter 15 Contemporary Undercurrents

1. Gilian Gorle, "The Second Decade: The Theme of Social Change in Papua New Guinean Literature, 1979-1989," *Pacific Studies*, 19: 1 (1996): 54.
2. Gorle, "The Second Decade."
3. Paul Silitoe, *Social Change in Melanesia* (Cambridge: Cambridge University Press, 2000), 137.
4. See Regis Stella. *Forms and Styles of Banoni Music* (Port Moresby: Institute of Papua New Guinea Studies, 1990); Regis Stella, comp. *Moments in Melanesia* (Melbourne: Oxford University Press, 1994).
5. Regis Stella. *Gutsini Posa (Rough Seas)* (Suva: Institute of Pacific Studies, 1998).
6. This part appeared as a review in *The Contemporary Pacific,* 12: 2 (Fall 2000): 35-354.
7. Stella. *Gutsini Posa,* 95.
8. Stella. *Gutsini Posa,* 94.
9. Arnold Mundua, *A Bride's Price* (New Delhi: CBS Publishers and Distributors, 2005).
10. Mundua, *A Bride's Price.*
11. Moses Maladina, *Tabu: Legacy of an Affair in Papua New Guinea* (Wellington: Steele Roberts, 2003).
12. Amirah Inglis, *"Not a White Woman Safe": Sexual Anxiety and Politics in Port Moresby 1920-1934* (Canberra: Australian National University Press, 1974).

13. Inglis, *Not a White Woman Safe.*
14. Inglis, *Not a White Woman Safe.*
15. Stephen Slemon, "Post Colonial Allegory and the Transformation of History", in *The Journal of Commonwealth Literature*, xxiii, no.1, 1988: 157-168 and William Ashcroft, "The Flesh of the Parable: Russell Soaba's *Maiba,*" *Span: Journal of the South Pacific Association for Commonwealth Literature and Language Studies,* no. 25 (Sydney; SPACLALS, 1987): 85-95.
16. Soaba, *Maiba* (Washington; Three Continental Press, 1985).
17. Ashcroft, "The Flesh of the Parable".
18. Ashcroft, "The Flesh of the Parable."
19. Ashcroft, "The Flesh of the Parable."
20. Ashcroft, "The Flesh of the Parable."
21. Ashcroft, "The Flesh of the Parable."
22. Soaba, *Maiba.*
23. Soaba, *Wanpis.*
24. Singh, "Russell Soaba: An interview," 48-56
25. Singh, "Russell Soaba: An interview," 53
26. Ashcroft, "The Flesh of the Parable," 85-95.
27. Ashcroft, "The Flesh of the Parable."
28. Ashcroft, "The Flesh of the Parable."
29. Stella, *Imagining the Other,* 192.
30. Stella, *Imagining the Other,* 192-3.
31. Stella, *Imagining the Other,* 193.
32. Stella, *Imagining the Other.*
33. Stella, *Imagining the Other,* 194.
34. Partha Chatterjee, *The Nation and Its Fragments: Colonial and Postcolonial Histories* (New Jersey: Princeton University Press, 1993), 224-225.
35. Stella, *Imagining the Other,* 67.
36. Chatterjee, *The Nation and Its Fragments* Chatterjee, *The Nation and Its Fragments*
37. Chatterjee, *The Nation and Its Fragments*
38. Joe Ketan, *The Name Must Not Go Down* (Suva: Institute of Pacific Studies, 2004), 18-20.
39. Ketan, *The Name Must Not.*
40. Chatterjee, *The Nation and Its Fragments*

Works Cited

Abaijah, Josephine. *A Thousand Coloured Dreams: The Story of a Young Girl Growing Up in Papua.* Melbourne: Dellasta, 1991.

Abaijah, Josephine. "Extract from *A Thousand Coloured Dreams*—Love Magic," in *PNG Women Writers: An Anthology*, comp. Adeola James. Sydney: Pearson Educational Australia, 1996: 205-220.

Aguang, Joseph. *The Sorcerers.* Port Moresby: Institute of Papua New Guinea Studies, 1992.

Ahai, Naihuwo and Nicholas Faraclas. "Rights and Expectation in an Age of "Debt Crisis." In *Literacy and Integral Human Development in Papua New Guinea.* Port Moresby: UPNG Press, 1991.

Ako, Lahui.*Upstream Through Endless Sands of Blessings.* New Delhi: CBS Publishers and Distributors, 2007.

Althusser, Louis. "Theory, Theoretical Practice and Theoretical Formation: Ideology and Struggle." In *Althusser: The Detour of Theory*, Gregory Elliott. London: Verso, 1987.

Anderson, Benedict. *Imagined Community.* New York: Verso, 1983.

Ashcroft, Bill, Gareth Griffiths, and Helen Tiffin. *The Empire Writes Back: Theory and Practice in Post-Colonial Literature.* New York: Routledge, 1989.

Ashcroft, William. "The Flesh of the Parable: Russell Soaba's *Maiba.*" *SPAN: Journal of the South Pacific Association for Commonwealth Literature and Language Studies,* no. 25. Sydney; SPACLALS, 1987, 85-95.

Ashcroft, William. *Post-Colonial Transformations.* London and New York: Routledge, 2001.

Bacchus, M. Kazim. *Education Policy and Development Strategy in the Third World.* Aldershot, Hants, UK: Avebury Gower Publishing Co Ltd, 1987.

Baital, Jim. "Tali." In *Three Short Novels from Papua New Guinea.* ed. Mike Greicus. Auckland: Longman Paul Limited,1985.87-140.

Bakhtin, Mikhail. *The Dialogic Imagination: Four Essays*, ed. Michael Holquist, trans. C. Emerson and Michael Holquist. Austin: University of Texas Press, 1981.

Beier, Ulli. "Preface," In Albert Maori Kiki: *Ten Thousand Years in a Lifetime.* Melbourne: Chershire, 1968, 1-4.

Beier, Ulli. *Decolonizing the Mind: The Impact of the University on Culture and Identity in Papua New Guinea, 1971-1974.* Canberra: Pandanus Books, Research School of Pacific and Asian Studies, The Australian National University, 2005.

Belshaw, C.S. "The Last Years of Ahuia Ova," *Man*, no.228-30, 131-132.

Ben Scott, Ben. *Reimagining Papua New Guinea: Culture, Democracy and Australia's Role.* Sydney: Lowy Institute for International Policy, 2005.

Blaber, Ronald. "This Piece of Earth: V.S. Naipaul's *A Bend in the River.*" In *A Sense of Place in the New Literatures in English*, ed. M.H. Nightingale. St. Lucia: Queensland University Press, 1986, 251-260.

Boman-Behram, B.K. *Education Controversies of India: The Cultural Conquest of India under British Imperialism.* Bombay: Taraporevala, 1946.

Boomer, G. ed., *Negotiating the Curriculum: A Teacher-Student Partnership.* Ashton Scholastic, 1982.

Bourdieu, Pierre. "Cultural Reproduction and Social Reproduction." In *Knowledge, Education and Cultural Change: Papers in the Sociology of Education.* London. 257-271.

Brash, Elton. "Creative Writing, Literature and Self-Expression in Papua New Guinea." In *Teaching Literature in Papua New Guinea*, ed. E. Brash and M. Greicus. Port Moresby: University of Papua New Guinea, 1974, 35-42.

Brash, Nora Vagi. *Taurama.* Port Moresby: Owl Books, 1985.

Brash, Nora Vagi.*Which Way, Big Man? And Five Other Plays.* Port Moresby and Melbourne: Oxford University Press, 1996.

Brash, Nora Vagi. "Nora Vagi Brash," in *PNG Women Writers: An Anthology*, comp. Adeola James. Sydney: Pearson Educational Australia, 1996:5-119.

Bruss, Elizabeth W. *Autobiographical Acts: The Changing Situation of a Literary Genre.* Baltimore: Johns Hopkins University Press, 1976.

Cabral, Amilal. *Revolution in Guinea: Unity and Struggle: Speeches and Writings.* London: Heineman, 1980.

Campbell, Ian C. *A History of the Pacific Islands.* Christchurch: University of Canterbury, 1989.

Carney, M. *Education and Cultural Imperialism.* New York, 1974.

Chatterjee, Kalyan. "Papua New Guinean Literature: Innocence and Self-Knowledge," *Pacific Writers: A South Pacific Communication Journal*, 14:1 (1985).1-11

Chatterjee, Partha. *The Nation and Its Fragments: Colonial and Postcolonial Histories.*New Jersey: Princeton University Press, 1993.

Christian-Smith, L. "Power, Knowledge and Curriculum: Constructing Femininity in Adolescent Romance Novels." In *Language, Authority and Criticism: Readings on the School Textbooks*, ed. S. DeCastell, A. Luke & C. Luke. Lewes, Aust., 1988.

Christie, Francis and Joan Rothery. "Literacy in the Curriculum: Planning and Assessment." In *Literacy for a Changing World*, ed. Francis Christie. Victoria, 1990.

Clifford, James *The Predicament of Culture: Twentieth-Century Ethnography, Literature, and Art* Cambridge, Mass., & London: Harvard University Press, 1988.

Crocombe, Ron "Book Distribution in the Pacific Islands," *The Written Word: Writing, Publishing and Information in the Pacific Islands.* Suva: Institute of Pacific Studies, 1985, 28-42.

Dawrs, Stu. "Naked Jazz: Re-historicizing OndoBondo Poster Poems" MA Plan B Paper, University of Hawaii, 2009.

Deklin, Tony. "In Search of a Home-Grown Constitution: The Constitutional Development in Papua New Guinea Between 1962 and 1975," in *Papua New Guinea: a Century of Colonial Impact 1884-1984*, ed. Sione Latukefu. Port Moresby: The National Research Institute and University of Papua New Guinea, 1989: 399-47.

Diringer, David. *The Alphabet: A Key to the History of Mankind*, 2nd. ed. rev. New York.

Dunar, Loujaya Kouza. "Loujaya Mojii Dunar (Kouza)," in *PNG Women Writers: An Anthology*, comp. Adeola James. Sydney: Pearson Educational Australia, 1996:221-274.

Enos, Apisai. "Niugini Literature." In *Teaching Literature in Papua New Guinea*, ed. E. Brash and M. Greicus (Port Moresby: University of Papua New Guinea, 1974), 46.

Eri, Vincent. *The Crocodile*. Auckland: Longman Paul, 1971.

Fanon, Frantz. *Black Skin, White Masks*. NewYork: Grove Press, 1967.

Fanon, Frantz. *The Wretched of the Earth*, trans. Constance Farrington. Harmondsworth: Penguin, 1967.

Fanon, Frantz. *A Dying Colonialism*, trans. C. Haakon Chevalier. New York: Grove Press, 1965.

Ferea, William 'Boy From the Sea," *Ondobondo*, 5(1985), 28.

Francoise, Lionnett. *Autobiographical Voices, Race, Gender, Self-Portraiture*. Ithaca and London: Cornell University Press, 1989.

Freire, Paulo. *Pedagogy of the Oppressed*. Harmondsworth: Penguin Books, 1972.

Freire, Paulo. *Letters to Cristina: Reflections on My Life and Work*. London and New York: Routledge, 1996.

Gelb, Ignace J. *A Study of Writing*, rev. ed. Chicago, 1957.

Gellner, Ernest. *Nations and Nationalism*. Oxford: Blackwell Publishers, 1983

Georg Lukacs. *The Theory of the Novel: A Historico-philosophical Essay on the Forms of Great Epic*. Cambridge, Massachusetts: The MIT Press, 1994.

Gilbelt, R. *The Impotent Image: Reflections of Ideology in Secondary School Curriculum*. Lewes, Aust., 1984.

Gilbert, Pam. "Authorizing Disadvantage: Authorship and Creativity in the Language Classroom." In *Literacy in the Changing World*, ed. Frances Christie. Victoria, 1990.

Glass, Frances Delvin. "Between Two Cultures: Interpreting V. Eri's *The Crocodile*,"in *Language and Literature in Multicultural Contexts; ACLALS Fifth Triennial Conference Proceedings*, ed. Satendra Nandan. Suva: University of South Pacific, 1983, 130-140.

Glifford, James. *The Predicament of Culture: Twentieth Century Ethnography, Literature, and Art*. Cambridge: Cambridge Universoty Press, 1988.

Goodwin, Ken. "Invective and Obliqueness in Political Poetry: Kasaipwalova, Brathwaite and Soyinka." In *Awakened Conscience: Studies in Commonwealth Literature*, ed. C. D. Narasimharah. New Delhi: Sterling Publishers, 1978, 251-260.

Goody, Jack. ed., *Literacy in Traditional Societies*. Cambridge: Cambridge University Press, 1968.

Gorle, Gillian. "The Second Decade: The Theme of Social Change in the Papua New Guinean Literature, 1979-1989," *Pacific Studies* 19:1 (March 1996). 53-90.

Gorle, Gillian. "The Theme of Social Change in the Literature of Papua New Guinea, 1969-1979," *Pacific Studies* 18: 2 (1995). 79-113.

Graff, Gerald. *Professing Literature: an Institutional History*. Chicago & London: Chicago University Press, 1987.

Gramsci, Antonio. *Selections from Political Writings, 1921-1926*, trans. & ed. Quintin Hoare. Minneapolis: University of Minnesota Press, 1990.

Gray, B. "Helping the Children Become Language Learner in the Classroom." In *Aboriginal Perspective on Experience and Learning: The Role of Language in Aboriginal Education*. Geelong, 1985

Greicus, M. S. "Literature in the University of Papua New Guinea." In *Teaching Literature in Papua New Guinea*, ed. E. Brash and M. Greicus. Port Moresby: University of Papua New Guinea, 1974, 43-48.

Gunn Allen, Paula. "Border Studies: The Intersection of Gender and Color." In *Introduction to Scholarship in Modern Languages and Literatures*, ed. Joseph Gibaldi. New York: Modern Language Associations, 1992. 303-319.

Gutierrez, Donald. *The Dark and Light Gods: Essays on the Self in Modern Literature*. Troy, New York: The Whitson Publishing Company, 1987.

Hannet, Leo. "The Ungrateful Daughter," *Kovave*, November 1970. 33-46.

Harvey, Bruce A. *American Geographics: U.S. National Narratives and the Representation of the Non-European World, 1830-1865*. Stanford, CA: Stanford University Press, 2001.

Hau'ofa, Epeli. *We Are the Ocean:Selected Works*. Honolulu: University of Hawaii Press, 2008.

Hau'ofa, Epeli."Our Sea of Islands." In *We Are the Ocean: Selected Works*, Epeli Hau'ofa. Honolulu: University of Hawaii Press, 2008.

Hempenstall, Peter from Vorstand Neuginea to deputation, 29 August 1904, RMG Conferenz Protokolle; see also Jahresbericht 1903, RMG Statinsberichte Siar; Vorstand ssitzzung 27 August 1904, RMG Conferenz Protokolle; Flierl to Mission-Inspeckto, 10 December 1904, NH Flierl Brief.

Hempenstall, Peter. "The Neglected Empire: The Superstucture of Colonial State in German Melanesia." In *Papua New Guinea: a Century of Colonial Impact 1884-1984*, ed. Sione Latukefu. Port Moresby: The National Research Institute and University of Papua New Guinea, 1989, 158.

Hereniko, Vilsoni and Rob Wilson (ed.). 1999. *Inside Out: Literature, Cultural Politics, and Identity in the New Pacific*. Boulder and New York: Rowman and Littlefield.

Hereniko, Vilsoni. "Representation of Cultural Identities." In *Inside Out: Literature, Cultural Politics, and Identity in the New Pacific*, ed. Vilsoni Hereniko and Rob Wilson. Lanham, Boulder, New York, Oxford: Rowman & Littlefield Publishing, Inc., 1998, 137-166.

Hirsch, Jr., E. D. *Cultural Literacy: What Every Americans Needs to Know*. New York: 1988.

Hirschkop, Ken. *Bakhtin and Cultural Theory*, ed. Ken Hirschkop and David Shepherd. Manchester and New York: Manchestor University Press, 1989.

Inglis, Amirah, *"Not a White Woman Safe": Sexual Anxiety and Politics in Port Moresby 1920-1934*. Canberra: Australian University Press, 1974.

Iser, Wolfgang. "Fictionalizing: The Anthropological Dimension of Literary Fiction," *New Literary History, A Journal of Theory and Interpretation, Papers from the Commonwealth Centre for Literary and Cultural Change*, 21. No.4 (Autumn 1990), 938-976.

James, Adeola. comp., *PNG Women Writers: An Anthology*. Sydney: Pearson Educational Australia, 1996.

Jawodimbari, Arthur. "The Sun," *Kovave* 2 (1), November 1970.

Johnson, Charles. *Being and Race: Black Writing Since 1970*. Bloomington: Indiana University Press, 1990.

Jolly, Margaret. "Ill-Natured Comparisons: Racism and Relativism in European Representations of ni-Vanuatu From Cook's Second Voyage," *History and Anthropology* 5 (3/4), (1992), 334. 331-363.

Jones, Eric. *PNG History Through Stories: Book One*. Sydney: Pearson Longman, 2004.

Kadiba, John. "Murray and Education: Some Observations on the Ambivalence of Colonial Education Policy in Papua Before World War II." In *Papua New Guinea: a Century of Colonial Impact 1884-1984*, ed. Sione Latukefu. Port Moresby: National Research Institute, 1989, 279.

Kagl, Toby Waim. "Kallan," in Waim. *Two Highlands Novels from Papua New Guinea*. Port Moresby: Institute of Papua New Guinea Studies, 1985: 54-119.

Kais, Kakah and Bernard Minol. *Pokop of Pohyomou*. Port Moresby: University of Papua New Guinea, 1995.

Kamene, Sakarepe. "Literacy With/Without Roots." In *Critical and Developmental Literacy*, ed. Otto Nekitel, Sakarepe Kamene and Steven Edmund Winduo. Port Moresby: University of Papua New Guinea Press, 1995, 79-93.

Kaniku, Anne. "Those Massim Women," in *Papua New Guinea: a Century of Colonial Impact 1884-1984*, ed. Sione Latukefu. Port Moresby: The National Research Institute and University of Papua New Guinea, 1989: 369-376.

Kasaipwalova, John. "Reluctant Flames." In *Lali: An Anthology of Pacific Writing*, ed. Albert Wendt. Auckland: Longman Books, 1980, 178-179.

Kasaipwalova, John. *Sail The Midnight Sun*. Port Moresby: Credit Melanesia, 1980.

Kazim Bacchus, M. *Education Policy and Development Strategyin the Third World.* Aldershot, Hants, UK:Avebury Gower Publishing Co Ltd, 1987.

Kelep-Malpo, Kapa Darius. *Gender Equality at the Workplace*. Goroka: Kim Printing,2009.

Keown, Michelle. *Pacific Islands Writing: The Postcolonial Literatures of Aotearoa/New Zealand.* Oxford & New York: Oxford University Press.

Ker Wilson, Barbara. *The Turtle and the Island. Legends from Papua New Guinea: Book Two* (London: Oxford University Press, 1996).

Ketan. Joe. *The Name Must Not Go Down.* Suva: Institute of Pacific Studies, 2004.

Kilage, Ignatius. *My Mother Calls Me Yaltep.* Port Moresby: Institute of Papua New Guinean Studies, 1980.

Kituai. August. "The Flight of a Villager." In *Three Short Novels from Papua New Guinea*, ed. Mike Greicus. Auckland: Longman Paul Limited, 1976, 37-86.

Knauft, Bruce. "The Melanesian Warfare: a Theoretical History," *Oceania* 60, no. 4 (1990), 250-311.

Krauth, Nigel. "Unfolding Like Petals": The Developing Definition of the Writer's Role in Modern Papua New Guinean Literature,"*ACLALS Bulletin* 5, No. 1. (July, 1978), 2.

Krauth, Nigel."Russell Soaba's Latest Work: An Investigation into Accidents Along the Road to Papua New Guinea's Indpendence,' *ACLALS Bulletin* (January 1979), 140.

Krauth, Nigel. "Towards a Balanced Approach in the Study of Papua New Guinean Literature," *Teaching Literature in Papua New Guinea*, ed. E. Brash and M. Greicus. Port Moresby: University of Papua New Guinea, 1972, 49-55.

Kumbeli, Joyce Abaneta. "Joyce Abaneta Kumbeli,' in *PNG Women Writers: An Anthology*, comp. Adeola James. Sydney: Pearson Educational Australia, 1996: 121-134.

Laclau, Ernesto and Chantal Mouffe. *Hegemony and Socialist Strategy*, trans. W. Moore and P. Commack. London: New Left Books, 1985.

Laclau, Ernesto.*New Reflections on the Revolution of Our Times.* London: Verso, 1990.

Laclau, Ernesto. "Populist Rupture and Discourse," *Screen Education* 34 (1980), 87.

Lionnet, Francoise. *Autobiographical Voices, Race, Gender, Self-Portraiture.* Ithaca and London: Cornell University Press, 1989.

Luke, A. *Literacy Textbooks and Ideology: Postwar Literacy Instruction and the Mythology of Dick and Jane.* Taylor and Francis, 1988.

Lyons, Paul. *American Pacificism: Oceania in the U.S. Imagination.* New York and London: Routledge, 2006.

Maaka, Julian. *The Confession and Other Stories* (Suva: The University of the South Pacific, 1985.

Machery, Pierre. *A Theory of Literary Production*. London and New York: Routledge and Kegan Paul, 1986.

Maladina, Moses. *Tabu; Lagacy of an Affair in Papua New Guinea*. Wellington: Steele Roberts, 2003.

Matane, Paulias. *Aimbe, the Pastor*. New York: Exposition Press, 1979.

Matane, Paulias. *Ripples in the South Pacific Ocean: A Historical Novel Portraying the Dawn of Civilization in Papua New Guinea*. New Delhi: CBS Publishers and Distributors, 2003.

McClintock, Barbara. *Imperial Leather: Race, Gender, and Sexuality in the Colonial Context*. New York and London: Routledge, 1995.

McKillop, Bob. "Papua Besena and Papuan Separatism." In *Micornationalist Movements in Papua New Guinea*, ed. R. J. May. Department of Political Science, Research School of Pacific Studies, ANU, 1982, 329-358.

Mel, Michael Yake and Toby Kagl Waim. *Two Highland Novels from Papua New Guinea*. Port Moresby: Institute of Papua New Guinea Studies, 1985.

Mel, Michael. "Kumdi Bagre," in Michael Yake Mel and Toby Kagl Waim, *Two Highland Novels from Papua New Guinea*. Port Moresby: Institute of Papua New Guinea Studies, 1985: 3-53.

Mennin, Margaret. *Hagen Saga*. Port Moresby: Institute of Papua New Guinea Studies, 1982.

Michelle. Keown. *Pacific Islands Writing: The Postcolonial Literatures of Aotearoa/New Zealand*. Oxford & New York: Oxford University Press, 2007.

Michener, James. *Return to Paradise*. New York: Random House, 1951.

Minol, Bernard S. "The Cultural and Historical Background to PNG Fiction: Mythmaking, Truth Telling and Maus Wara", Ph.D Dissertation, University of Queensland, 1987.

Minol, Bernard S. The Melanesian Way?" In *Through Melanesian Eyes: An Anthology of Papua New Guinean Writing*, comp. Ganga Powell. Melbourne: Macmillan, 1987, 164.

Mowitt, John. *Text: The Genealogy of an Antidisciplinary Object* (Durham: Duke University Press, 1992).

Murphy, Greg. *Niugini Niugini*. Port Moresby; Education Department, 1985.

Najita, Susan. *Decolonizing Cultures in the Pacific*. New York and Oxford: Routledge, 2008.

Narokobi, Bernard. "Melanesian Way." In *Through Melanesian Eyes: An Anthology of Contemporary Papua New Guinean Writing*, comp. Ganga Powell. Melbourne: Macmillan, 1987, 155-156.

Narokobi, Bernard. *The Melanesian Way*. Port Moresby, IPNGS, 1980.

Natachee. Allan. *Aia: Mekeo Songs*. Port Moresby: Papua Pocket Poets, 1965.

Nelson, H. "*The Papuan Villager*: a national newspaper," *Journal of Papua and New Guinea Society*, vol. 2. No. 1. 1968.

Nekitel, Otto. "What is Happening to Our Vernaculars?" *Bikmaus* 2: 2 (June 1984), 89-98.

Ngara, Emmanuel. *Art and Ideology in the African Novel: a Study of the Influence of Marxism on African Writing.* London: Heineman, 1985.

Ngugi wa Thiongo. *Decolonizing the Mind: the Politics of Language in African Literature.* London: James Currey, 1986.

Nicole, Robert . *The Word, the Pen, and the Pistol: Literature and Power in Tahiti.* New York: State University of New York Press, 2001.

Olney, James. *Metaphor of Self: the Meaning of Autobiography.* New Jersey: Princeton University Press, 1972.

Ong, Walter J. *Orality and Literacy: The Technologizing of the Word.* London: Routledge, Chapman, and Hall, 1982.

Oram, Nigel. "Ahuia Ova." *Australian Dictionary of Biography*, 7, 20-21.

Oram, Nigel."The Western Motu Area and the European Impact, 1872-1942." In *Papua New Guinea: A Century of Colonial Impact 1884-1984*, ed. Sione Latukefu. Port Moresby: National Research Institute, 1989, 49-74.

Oram, Nigel. "The History of the Motu-speaking and the Koita-speaking Peoples according to their own Traditions." In *Oral Tradition in Melanesia*, ed. Donald Denoon and Roderic Lacy. Port Moresby: The University of Papua New Guinea and The Institute of Papua New Guinea Studies, 1981, 207-230.

Papua Annual Report (ANR), 1927, p..21.

Papua Annual Report (ANR), 1933, 15.

Pascal, Roy. *Design and Truth in Autobiography.* Cambridge, Mass.: Harvard University Press 1960.

Paul Lyons. *American Pacificism: Oceania in the U.S. Imagination.* New York: London, 2006.

Powell, Kirsty. "The First PNGA Playwrights and their Plays", Ph.D dissertation, University of Papua New Guinea, 1976.

Priebe, Richard K. *Myth, Realism and the West African Write.* New Jersey: Africa World Press, 1988.

Slemon, Stephen, "Post Colonial Allegory and Transformation of History," The Journal of Commonwealth Literature, vol.xxiii, no.1 (1988), 157-168.

Stella, Regis. *Imagining the Other: The Representation of the Papua New Guinean Subject.* Honolulu: Center for Pacific Islands Studies, University of Hawaii, 2007.

Stella, Regis Stella, Regis. *Gutsini Posa* (Rough Seas). Suva: Institute of Pacific Studies, 2010,

Stella, Regis. *Moments in Melanesia.* Melbourne: Oxford University Press,

Stella, Regis. Forms and Styles of Banoni Music. Port Moresby: Institute of Papua New Guinea Studies, 1998.

Mundua, Arnold.*A Bride Price.* New Delhi: CBS Publishers and Distributors, 2005.

Said, Edward. *Orientalism.* New York: Vintage, 1978.

Scott, Malcolm. *The Struggle for the Soul of the French Novel, French Catholic and Realist Novelists, 1850-1970.* Washington: The Catholic University of America Press, 1990.

Seligman, C. G., *The Melanesians of British New Guinea*, Cambridge University Press, 1910.

Silva, Noenoe K. *Aloha Betrayed: Native Hawaiian Resistance to American Colonialism.*Durham and London: Duke University Press, 2004.

Simms, Norman. "Towards an Assessment of Maori and Pacific Writing in New Zealand," *Pacific Writing and Publishing: A South Pacific Communication Journal.* 14: 1 (1985), 86.

Singh, Kirpal. "Russell Soaba: An interview," *Westerly*, no.2 .Nedlands: University of Western Australia, July 1984, 48-56

Slemon, Stephen. "Post Colonial Allegory and the Transformation of History," *The Journal of Commonwealth Literature*, vol.xxiii, no.1. London: Hans Zell Publishers, 1988, 157-168.

Smith, Bernard. *European Vision and the South Pacific*, second edition. Melbourne: Oxford University Press, 1989.

Smith, Geoffrey. "Education, History and Development," in *Encycopaedia of Papua New Guinea*, vol. I., A-K, Melbourne: University of Papua New Guinea, 1972, 325.

Smith, Peter. "Education Policy in Australian New Guinea: a Classic Case." In *Papua New Guinea: A Century of Colonial Impact 1884-1984*, ed. Sione Latukefu. Port Moresby: National Research Institute and the University of Papua New Guinea, 1989, 291-315.

Smith, Vanessa. *Literary Culture and the Pacific: Nineteenth-Century Textual Encounters.* Cambridge: Cambridge University Press, 1998.

Soaba, Russell. "Scattered by the Wind," *Kovave,* 4. No. 1. (November, 1972), 30-42.

Soaba, Russell. "An Interview with Russell Soaba: Interview by Chris Tiffin," *SPAN* No. 8. (April, 1979), 15-30.

Soaba, Russell. *Maiba* Washington: Three Continents Press, 1985.

Soaba, Russell. *Wanpis.* Port Moresby: Institute of Papua New Guinea Studies, 1978.

Soaba, Russell. "A Portrait of the Odd Man Out." In *Lali: A Pacific Anthology*, ed. Albert Wendt,. Auckland: Longman Paul, 1980, 168-176.

Soaba, Russell. "Albert Wendt: Pacific's Existential Writer," *Ondobondo*, 3 (1983), 37-41.

Soaba, Russell. "The Writer's Place in a Difficult Society." In *Critical and Developmental Literacy*, ed. Otto Nekitel, Steven Edmund Winduo, and Sakarepe Kamene. Port Moresby: University of Papua New Guinean Press, 1995, 107-112.

Soaba, Russell. *Kwamra: A Season of Harvest* Port Moresby: Anuki Country Press, 2000.

Somare, Michael. *Sana: an Autobiography.* Port Moresby: Niugini Press, 1975.

Sorariba, Nash *A Medal Without Honour.* Port Moresby: University of Papua New Guinea Press, 1997.

Spivak, Gayatri Chakravorty. "Subaltern Studies: Deconstructing Historiography." In *Other Worlds: Essays in Cultural Politics.* New York: Routledge, 1988. 197-221.

Spivak, Gayatri Chakravorty. *.Post-Colonial Critic: Interviews, Strategies and Dialogues: Gayatri Chakravorty,* ed. Sarah Harasyn. London and New York: Routledge.

Spivak, Gayatri Chakravorty. "Can the Subaltern Speak?" In *Colonial Discourse and Post-colonial Theory: A Reader,* ed. Patrick Williams and Laura Chrisman. New York: Columbia University Press, 1988: 66-111.

Stella, Regis. *Tempers Unchained: The Politics and Meaning of Pre-Independence Drama.* MA Thesis. University of Wollongong, Australia, 1992.

Stella, Regis. "Reluctant Voyages into Otherness: Practice and Appraisal in Papua New Guinean Literature." In *Inside Out: Literature, Cultural Politics, and Identity in the New Pacific,* ed. Vilsoni Hereniko and Rob Wilson. Lanham, Boulder, New York, Oxford: Rowman & Littlefield Publishing, Inc., 1998, 221-230.

Stella, Regis. "Steven Edmund Winduo, Lomo'ha I am, In Spirits Voice I Call," *SPAN,* 34/35 (1992/93): 360-362.

Stella, Regis. comp. *Moments in Melanesia.* Melbourne: Oxford University Press, 1992.

Stella, Regis. *Imagining the Other: The Representation of the Papua New Guinean Subject.* Pacific Islands Monograph Series 20. Honolulu: University of Hawaii Press, 2007.

Stewart, Frank, Kareva Mateata-Allain, and Alexander Dale Mawyer (eds.). *Varua Tupu: New Writing From French Polynesia.* Honolulu: *Manoa: A Pacific Journal of International Writing* and University of Hawaii Press, 2006.

Still, Judith and Michael Worton. *Intertextuality: Theory and Practices,* ed. Michael Worton and Judith Still. Manchestor and New York: Manchestor University Press, 1990.

Stokes. Donald. *Legends from Papua New Guinea: Book Two.* Melbourne: Oxford University Press, 1996.

Stoltz, John. "The State of Literature Teaching in Papua New Guinea High Schools." In *Teaching Literature in Papua New Guinea,* ed. Elton Brash and M. Greicus. Port Moresby: UPNG, 1972,

Stull, Heidi I. *The Evolution of the Autobiography from 1770-1850: A Comparative Study and Analysis.* New York: Bern, Frankfurt am Main: Peter Laing, 1985.

Subramani. *South Pacific Literature: From Myth to Fabulation.* Suva: Insitute of Pacific Studies, USP, 1985.

Stella, Regis. "The Oceanic Imaginary," *SPAN* 48/49 (April& October 1999), 1-13.

Takaku, William and Peter Trist "Living Legends, Dying Stages," *Meanjin on PNG,* ed. Drusilla Modjeska 62: 3 (2003), 115-34.

Tawali, Kumalau. *Manki Masta.* QLD: Jacaranda Press, 1971.

Tawali, Kumalau. "Bush Kanak Speaks." In *Lali: An Anthology of Pacific Writing,* ed. Albert Wendt. Auckland: Longman Books, 1980, 183-184.

Tawali, Kumalau. *Signs in the Sky.* Port Moresby: Papua Pocket Poets, 1970.

The Papuan Villager, vol. 3. no. 1. January 1931.

Tiamon, Zak. "Russell Soaba's *Wanpis,*" *Ondobondo,* 2, (Mid-1983), 29.

Toliman, Mary."Mary Brigette Toliman," in *PNG Women Writers: An Anthology,* comp. Adeola James. Sydney: Pearson Educational Australia, 1996:275-310.

Trist, Peter and William Takaki, "Living Legends, Dying Stages," *Meanjin on PNG,* ed. Drusilla Modjeska 62: 3 (2003), 115-134.

Trompf, Garry. "Doesn't Colonialism Make You Mad? The So Called "Mur Madness" as an Index for the Study of New Religious in Papua New Guinea During the Colonial Period." In *Papua New Guinea: A Century of Colonial Impact (1884-1984),* ed. Sione Latukefu. Port Moresby: National Research Institute and University of Papua New Guinea, 1989), 256.

Turner, Ann. "Nora Vagi Brash." In *Views from Interviews: The Changing Role of Women in Papua.*Melbourne: Oxford UniversityPress, 2009: 40-41.

Turner, Ann. *Views from Interviews: The Changing Role of Women in Papua.* Melbourne: Oxford UniversityPress, 2009.

Umba, Benjamin August Kituai, and Jim Baital. *Three Short Novels from Papua New Guinea.* Ed. Mike Greicus. Auckland: Longman Paul Limited, 1976.

Umba, Benjamin. "Fires of Dawn." In *Three Short Novels from Papua New Guinea.* Ed. Mike Greicus Auckland: Longman Paul Limited, 1976, 1-36.

Visnawathan, Gauri. *Masks of Conquest: Literary Studies and British Rule in India.* New York: Columbia, 1989.

Wadega, Alice. *Listen My Country.* Sydney: Pacific Publications, 1981.

Waiko, John ."The Place of Literature in Papua New Guinea." In *Teaching Literature in Papua New Guinea,* ed. Elton Brash and M. Greicus. Port Moresby: University of Papua New Guinea, 1976, 4-6.

Waiko, John. "The Unexpected Hawk." In *Five New Guinea Plays,* ed. Ulli Beier, 20-32, Milton, QLD: Jacaranda Press, 1971, 22-35.

Waim Kagl, Toby, "Kallan," in *Two Highlands Novel.* Port Moresby: Institute of Papua New Guinea Studies, 1985, 54-119.

Waisi, Paschal. "The Laufis World View: An Attempt to locate its Metaphysical Base," BA. Honours, sub-thesis, University of Papua New Guinea, 1982.

Waisi, Paschal. *Weli Nimou,* Canberra: ANU, 1985.

Waisi, Paschal. "Lau'um Pingis (Epistemology)," *Reframing Indigenous Knowledge: Cultural Knowledge and Practices in Papua New Guinea.*ed. Steven Edmund Winduo. Port Moresby: Melanesian and Pacific Studies, 2009, 27-38.

Waisi, Paschal. *Looking Through Ancestors' Eye-holes.* Port Moresby: UPNG Press and Bookshop, 2010.

Watson, Stuart. ed. *Lost in Jungle Ways.* Melbourne: Dellasta Pasific, 1994.

Wendt, Albert. *Nuanua: Pacific Writing in English since 1980* (Auckland and Honolulu: Auckland University Press and University of Hawaii Press, 1996).

Williams, F. E. "The Blending of Cultures: an Essay on Aims of Native Education," *Anthropology Report* 16 (1935).

234

Williams, F. E. "The Reminiscence of Ahua Ova,",*Journal of the Royal Anthropological Institute*, 17 (1939), 15-36.

Williams, Raymond. *Key Words: A Vocabulary of Culture and Society.* Oxford & New York: Oxford University Press, 1976.

Williams, Raymond. *Marxism and Literature.* Oxford: Oxford University Press, 1977.

Wilson, Rob. *Reimagining the American Pacific: From South Pacific to Bamboo Ridge and Beyond.* Durham: Duke University Press, 2000.

Winduo, Steven Edmund. *Lomo'ha I am in Spirit's Voice I Call.* Suva: South Pacific Creative Arts Society, 1990.

Winduo, Steven Edmund. "Rethinking the 'Melanesian Way' as Ideology and Nationalism: A Literary Perspective," *Yagl-Ambu*, 17: 3 (1994), 50-61.

Winduo, Steven Edmund. "Classroom Culture and a Showboat,*" Times of Papua New Guinea* (26 January 1995).

Winduo, Steven Edmund. "Dancer." In *Nuanua: South Pacific Writing in English Since 1980*, ed. Albert Wendt (Auckland and Honolulu: University of Auckland and University of Hawaii, 1996), 248.

Winduo, Steven Edmund. "Papua New Guinean Writing Today: The Growth of a Literary Culture," *Manoa* 2:1 (1990), 37-41.

Winduo, Steven Edmund."Preface." In *Building a Nation in Papua New Guinea: Views of the Post-Independence Generation*, ed. David Kavanamur, Charles Yala, and Quinton Clements. Canberra: Research School of Asian and Pacific Studies, ANU, 2003, xi-xv;

Winduo, Steven Edmund. "Reconstituting Indigenous Oceanic Folktales," *Scholars Space*, Department of English, University of Hawaii online publication, 2010.

Winduo, Steven Edmund. "The Influence of Orality in Contemporary PNG Writing," BA Honors sub-thesis. University of Papua New Guinea, 1989.

Winduo, Steven Edmund."Unwriting Oceania: The Repositioning of the Pacific Writer Scholars Within a Folk Narrative Space." *New Literary History* 31: 11 (2000): 599-613.

Winduo, Steven Edmund. "Writing Our Own Books Means Reading Ourselves." In *Critical and Developmental Literacy*, ed. Otto Nekitel, Sakarepe Kamene and Steven Edmund Winduo. Port Moresby: University of Papua New Guinea Press, 1995, 102-106.

Winduo, Steven Edmund. *Cultural Invasion, Negative Knowledge, Self-Expression and the Prose Narratives of Papua New Guinea*, MA thesis, University of Canterbury, NZ, 1991.

Winduo, Steven Edmund. *Hembemba: Rivers of the Forest.* Suva and Port Moresby: Institute of Pacific Studies and Language and Literature Department, UPNG, 2000.

Winduo, Steven Edmund."Literary Culture as Intellectual Capital for Nation Building," *Savannah Flames: a Papua New Guinean Journal of Literature, Language and Culture.* 4:1 (2001), 97-109.

Winduo, Steven Edmund. "Date With Destiny," in *A Rower's Song*. Port Moresby: Manui Publishers, 2009, 41.

Winduo, Steven Edmund. ed., *Reframing Indigenous Knowledge: Cultural Knowledge and Practice in Papua New Guinea*. Port Moresby: Melanesian and Pacific Studies, University of Papua New Guinea, 2009.

Yake Mell, Michael and Toby Kagl Waim. *Two Highlands Novel from Papua New Guinea*. Port Moresby: Institute of Papua New Guinea Studies, 1985.

Yake Mell, Michael. *The Call of the Land*. Port Moresby: Institute of Papua New Guinea Studies, 1993.

Young, Michael W. and Julia Clark. *Anthropologist in Papua: The Photography of F. E. Williams, 1922-1939*. Adelaide: Crawford House Publishing in association with National Archives of Australia, 2001.

Zizek, Slavoj. "The Specter of Ideology." In *Mapping Ideology*, ed. Salvoj Zizek. New York & London: Verso, 1994.

Index

I acknowledge the intellectual influences from teachers, mentors, and academic colleagues: Bill Ashcroft, Patricia Hardy, Prithvindra Chakravarti, David Roskies, Genevieve Escure, Paula Rabinowitz, Ken Bales, John Mowitt, Charlie Sugnet, David Lipset, Kathleen Barlow, Paul Sharrad, Albert Wendt, Vilsoni Hereniko, and the late Ron Crocombe. I am honored to have been mentored by the first Papua New Guinean with a PhD in literature: Bernard Minol hosted me, as an upcoming young writer, in Queensland University and later after his doctoral studies supervised me in the BA Honours degree. I can never thank Professor Howard MacNaughton enough — the one person who put his job on the line for my sake so that I can complete my Masters degree in English at University of Canterbury in Christchurch, New Zealand. Howard believed in me and steered me into the deep ocean of scholarship in literature and cultural studies in Oceania. Half of the work in this book was written under his supervision.

It is also fitting to acknowledge those who have contributed to the emergence of this book, especially my colleagues (past and present) in the fields of literature, English, and linguistics: Russell Soaba, the late Regis Stella, Sakarepe Kamene, Aundo Aitau, and the late Otto Nekitel. My colleague, the late Regis will always be part of my life as a writer scholar, someone with whom I have shared many moments of inspiration and sharing of notes on where we were taking literature to in Papua New Guinea. We began the journey together, but I will have to finish it.

I owe special gratitude to various individuals who assisted me in having some of these chapters published or commented on over the years: Drusilla Modjeska and John Evans. Writing a book is often a journey that brings an author into contact with fellow travelers. For that I thank Evelyn Ellerman, Ted Wolfers, Caroline Sinavaianna, Robert Sullivan, Paul Lyons, Stu Dawrs, Linda Crowl, Marjorie Crocombe, Teresia Teaiawa, Katerina Teaiwa, Keith Gamachio, David Gegeo, Vincent Warakai, Terence Wesley-Smith, Tarcisius Kabutauloka, Christina Thompson, Paul Lyons, Cristina Bachilega, Richard Hamasaki, Noenoe Silva, Ku'ualoha Ho'omanawanui, Michelle Tupou, Briar Wood, and Michelle Keown.

Special *hamamas* goes to PNG writers for their enthusiasm and reactions to my, often, academic responses to their creative work: Grand Chief Sir Paulias Matane, Arnold Mundua, Nash Sorariba, Michael Yake Mell, Nora Vagi Brash, Paschal Waisi (of late), and August Kituai. Conversations and dialogic encounters with PNG writers did set the stage for my transitions and transformations as a writer scholar in Papua New Guinea. For that I acknowledge fellow writers and literary minded individuals: Andyson Bernard Kaspou (of late), Vincent Warakai, John Waiko, Jack Lahui, Robson Akis, Benjamin Nakin, Aundo Aitau, and Trevor Shearston. I thank them for their patience and graceful acceptance of my views.

Various chapters of the book were first published in journals, books, and newspapers: *Savannah Flames: A Papua New Guinean Journal of Literature, Language, and Culture* (PNG), *Yagl Ambu* (PNG), *Meanjin* (Australia), *The Contemporary Pacific: A Journal of Pacific Affairs* (Hawaii, USA), *Critical and Developmental Literacy* edited by Otto Nekitel, Steven Winduo, and Sakarepe Kamene, *A Medal Without Honor* by Nash Sorariba, *Unfolding Petals: Readings in Modern Papua New Guinean Literature* edited by Regis Tove Stella, *The National* newspaper, and the *Post-Courier* newspaper (PNG). I acknowledge the website *PNGBuai.com* for publishing the chapter "Double Consciousness Without the Instruments to Liberate."

I am also sincerely grateful to the School of Humanities and Social Sciences, University of Papua New Guinea for granting me the furlough leave and various research leaves to complete this work. I am also grateful to the students of the University of Papua New Guinea with whom I was able to discuss and refine chapters of this book. Their unfailing enthusiasm, combined with transformations in thoughts about the purpose of studying politics through literature, convinced me that the effort to decolonize is in continuum, the complete erasure of the ogre from our consciousness is far from over.

The transformation from a manuscript to a book is often from the encouraging words of a trusted reader. For that I thank Sakarepe Kamene, a senior colleague, with whom I have many rewarding experiences in scholarship and intellectual discourses generated along the gray-walled corridors of UPNG's academic environment. Not the best conditions to work in, but at least we were left alone to think, talk, and generate original discourses about our work.

Finally, but not the least, the love, understanding, respect, and patience of my family: Christine, Daphne, Cheryl, and Langston. Their strength to live without me for periods of time while I pursue the writer scholar life around islands and continents is acknowledged in this work.

Draipela hamamas na tenkiu kamap long bel blong mi na go long yupela olgeta.

STEVEN EDMUND WINDUO is a writer scholar from Papua New Guinea. He is a graduate of the University of Papua New Guinea, University of Canterbury, NZ, and the University of Minnesota, USA. He is a distinguished writer scholar of literatures and cultures of Oceania. He held the Arthur Lynn Andrews Chair in Pacific and Asian Studies, at the Center for Pacific Islands Studies, University of Hawaii (2011), Visiting Research Scholar at the East West Center, held within the Pacific Islands Development Program (2011), Visiting Professor, Department of English, University of Minnesota (2007-2008), and Research Scholar with the Macmillan Brown Centre for Pacific Islands Studies, University of Canterbury, New Zealand (2006). He was foundation director of Melanesian and Pacific Studies, University of Papua New Guinea (2002-2005). He is a senior lecturer in Literature and English Communication Studies at the University of Papua New Guinea.

www.ingramcontent.com/pod-product-compliance
Lightning Source LLC
Chambersburg PA
CBHW051148030726
47504CB00004B/1097